MARILYN BOYER & GRACE TUMAS

PORTRAITS *of* INTEGRITY

★ *A Family Treasury* ★

real people who demonstrated godly character

Portraits of Integrity • A Family Treasury •
real people who demonstrated godly character

by Marilyn Boyer & Grace Tumas

Layout & graphic design by Mary Ann Edman

First printing April, 2012
Second printing July, 2012
Third printing March, 2014

ISBN 978-0-97776858-5

Published by The Learning Parent
2430 Sunnymeade Road
Rustburg, VA 24588
www.thelearningparent.com

Proudly printed in the United States of America by Jostens

the Learning Parent

MARILYN BOYER & GRACE TUMAS

PORTRAITS *of* INTEGRITY

★ *A Family Treasury* ★

real people who demonstrated godly character

the Learning Parent

RUSTBURG, VIRGINIA

Thanks to the following people for their indispensable help in writing *Portraits of Integrity:*

Grace Tumas, for her sensitive and colorful portrayal of these heroes in writing their stories

Mary Ann Edman who, with help from her husband Ed, produced the layout and design, along with other beautiful graphic effects. Thanks, Mary Ann, for your commitment to excellence!

Judy Saunders, Krystyn Walker, and Grace Boyer for their proofreading work

Table of Contents

Introduction

Portraits of Integrity is sure to be a favorite with your family! It contains 45 stories of real people from history who, in the course of their lives, have been placed in situations where their character shone through. History is best remembered when learned through the stories of those who lived it! For many years, I have given to parents a list of 45 character qualities with Scripture verses to learn what God's Word says about each one. Principles are best learned from practical examples and that is what has given birth to this book. Through the lives of people, some of whom you have heard of and some you will be meeting for the first time, you will learn how to appreciate character in the lives of others and be inspired to become people of character yourselves. I hope you will be challenged as I have to learn of people who, often at great sacrifice, strove to fulfill their responsibilities in life and as a result left to us a legacy of character!

Psalm 25:21 says "Let integrity and uprightness preserve me, for I wait on Thee." In Psalm 101:2, the psalmist says. "I will behave myself wisely in a perfect way. I will walk within my house with a perfect heart." In verse 6, "Mine eyes shall be upon the faithful of the land, that they may dwell with me." In *Portraits of Integrity,* through stories, you will be "inviting" into your home those who will inspire your family to live a life of integrity!

Read it on your own or to your family, give as a gift, or use as a part of Character Concepts Curriculum—Kids of Character. Find out more at www.CharacterConceptsCurriculum.com.

Marilyn Boyer
April, 2012

Alertness

Definition

Being keenly aware of what is taking place around me so I can be prepared with a right response

Memory Verse

Be sober, be vigilant; because your adversary the devil, as a roaring lion, walketh about, seeking whom he may devour.

I Peter 5:8

The Virginia Giant

The Revolutionary War • the Carolinas • August, 1780

August 15, 1780. It was hot tonight, as hot as those dim, barely remembered nights on the blue island in the Azores. Sometimes, when he closed his eyes, he could see the green lawns with the mansion in the background, his sister playing, and the sound of a father's language he did not know. Now private Peter Francisco, of Colonel William Mayo's Virginia Militia Regiment, paced on guard duty as the moon gradually wore thinner, like pirates' fingers rubbing away at gold pieces of eight. At age twenty, he stood over six-foot-six and weighed 260 pounds. He had attacked Stony Point beside "Mad" Anthony Wayne, survived the Battle of Trenton, and been hospitalized at Valley Forge. Now the war was moving south. Already, Savannah and Charleston had fallen to the British. General Gates, raising a new army to fight in the Carolinas, determined to surprise the superior British forces with less than half the number of men.

The last thing Peter Francisco heard was the familiar rustling and chirping of birds as they stirred and woke to the dawn. Suddenly, Cornwallis' cavalry broke over the sleeping militiamen like water over a dike. The raw recruits scrambled to their feet, fleeing the redcoats' bayonets and trampling hooves. All but Peter. As the terrified men burst through the ragged line of Continentals, General Gates wheeled his horse and galloped from the field.

Wounded soldiers, bogged-down cannon, and thrashing horses littered the road. Peter thrust his bulk here and there, trying to stop the tide. But the men streamed past him, rolling frightened white eyes. Glancing around quickly, Peter caught sight of a small cannon abandoned between the Virginia and North Carolina Militia lines. It weighed 1,100 pounds. He couldn't leave it there, a sitting duck to aid the British. Hoisting it to his broad shoulders, he carried the field piece to a nearby position where Continental gunners wheeled it back towards the enemy. The battle was almost over, with barely a struggle. Peter slipped into a wooded area, as two of Colonel Banastre Tarleton's cavalrymen came screaming at him through the trees.

They were almost upon him now. But he kept still, holding his empty musket butt up, sideways, in a gesture of surrender. Then as the Redcoat leaned down to seize the gun, Peter swung it with all his might, cracking the man across the skull. A quick bayonet thrust at the other cavalryman sent him crashing to earth. Grabbing a sword from the ground, Peter swung onto a horse and galloped off. Just ahead, his own Colonel Mayo was trudging along, surrounded by a cordon of guards: a prisoner. Prepared to act, Peter charged. He cut down both British guards and slapped a horse towards his astonished officer. Peter later complained that his swords broke like "toothpicks" during the battle. Far away in Pennsylvania, George Washington heard stories of this Virginia private and ordered a six-foot-long broadsword forged for him.

But nothing could tie Peter down to one battle or one experience. Gripping a horse with his thighs, bearing down on an enemy, the wind in his face—the incidents at the Battle of Camden left Peter Francisco itching to join the cavalry. In 1781, he got his chance.

British resistance in the Carolinas was weakening after the battles at King's Mountain and Cowpens. Peter Francisco, recovering from a leg wound at Guilford Court House, returned to the army to act as scout against the notorious British cavalryman, Colonel Tarleton. As night drew on, he stopped at Ward's Tavern (West Creek Tavern) in the wilds of Nottoway County to rest. As he leaned on the bar inside, nine Tarleton dragoons silently encircled the inn. Peter was trapped. Tarleton's men stripped him of his weapons and dragged him outside. The moon was up, and

Peter could clearly see that they left only one man on guard. Most of the thirsty dragoons clattered into the tavern to drink in celebration. The guard leered at his silver shoe buckles.

"Take them off and hand them over," he ordered.

Peter's lips curled.

"Take them off yourselves if you want them," he dared.

Someone made a grab for them. And in that instant, Peter moved like a black panther. With a single bound, he twisted the guard's saber from his grip and struck him down. Inside, the other redcoats heard the uproar. A dragoon rushed out into the yard to see what was happening, his white doeskin breeches gleaming, crimson shell-jacket flaming like blood. He shot from the steps, a bullet hitting Peter in the side. As his body went numb, then hot, Peter sprang at the dragoon with his saber. Then the brawl began. He was whirlwind, fire, danger.

Peter Francisco

He was five years old again, playing on the lawn of a shadowy island palace, when rough hands seized him from behind. He heard his sister scream. Then she was kicking, scratching, breaking free. A cloth tied over his eyes. A gag stuffed into his mouth. His arms and legs bound. Then blackness. The slow, rolling heave of a ship. The keen smell of salt. Sometimes he listened to their voices from where he lay. The voices he had heard in the night. Were they pirates? Friends who had abducted him to keep him safe from the dark mystery that surrounded his parents? Why did he understand his mother's fluent French, but not his father's unknown tongue? Then the splash of oars. The sultry silence of a June day in 1765 broken by the sounds of a boat moving away from the pier at City Point, Virginia. Footsteps along the boards, then voices. Where am I? Strange, suntanned faces bend over him. He sees their tattered shirts, their tarry pigtails. Dockworkers? He doesn't know. He looks up at them, a sturdy little boy with an alert brown face. He chatters excitedly. Trying to tell them. They brought me here. What is this place? But the words don't come out right. They don't understand. He tries Portuguese, Spanish, French. He sees them glance at each other. He shows them his clothes, the tattered aristocratic linen coat trimmed with lace, his gleaming silver shoe buckles that form the letters "P" and "F." "Pedro Francisco," he shouts desperately as he is taken away to the poorhouse. "My name is Pedro Francisco." I belong to somebody. Maybe that is what he had been trying to do all his life. To prove that he was someone.

Peter was never quite sure how many dragoons he killed or wounded at Ward's Tavern. Three or four crawled on hands and knees or lay still. Another soldier aimed a musket at him. He heard the dry click as he lunged for the musket, knocking it out of the Redcoat's hands. The man slipped sideways to the ground, and Peter forked his legs over the horse. Shots from the lighted tavern followed him as he galloped off into the night, leading a string of eight horses.

The incident became known as "Francisco's Fight," winning him the title the "Virginia Giant." George Washington would later claim: "Without him, we would have lost two crucial battles, perhaps the war, and with it our freedom. He was truly a one-man army."

In the years following the war, Peter Francisco married three times and fathered six children. At his plantation Locust Grove in Buckingham, Virginia, he wore the bright clothes of a southern planter, hunted, fished and threw parties where he entertained guests with his fine tenor voice. In 1953, Virginia dedicated March 15 as Peter Francisco Day. Wounded six times during the

Revolutionary War, he is the only enlisted man in the Continental Army honored with a holiday. A park, a bicentennial United States postage stamp, and a fiddle tune bear his name. The dress sword given to him in appreciation by Colonel Mayo lies in storage at the Virginia Historical Society in Richmond, Virginia.

Because Peter Francisco demonstrated alertness, he overcame superior forces to save his own life and the lives of those around him during the crucial years of the Revolutionary War. While his story is rarely found in history books, his awareness of what was taking place around him enabled him to be prepared with a right response.

Questions

1. Tell what occurred on August 15 as Peter Francisco was standing guard.
2. What acts of incredible bravery did he show?
3. How did he come to be surrounded at Ward's Tavern?
4. What did he do when the dragoon tried to steal his buckles?
5. What memory did getting shot trigger in his mind?
6. How did he escape? What did he take with him?
7. What won him the title of "Virginia Giant"?
8. What did George Washington say about Fransisco?
9. How through practicing alertness did he save his own life and others as well during the Revolutionary War?
10. Think of some opportunities you have to demonstrate alertness.
11. How might alertness help you to be a better babysitter or helper to your younger siblings?

Attentiveness

Definition

Listening with the ears, eyes, and heart

Memory Verse

The ear that heareth the reproof of life abideth among the wise.

Proverbs 15:31

The Listeners

The Revolutionary War • Philadelphia • December, 1777

The winter twilight was closing in. Time to light the candles at No. 177, the tall brick house on the corner of South Second and Little Dock Streets. For Lydia Darragh, wearing a white Quaker bonnet, it seemed as if the British had occupied Philadelphia forever. In reality, they had come in September, 1777. It was now December 2nd. Just across the street loomed the big house that held General William Howe's headquarters. All at once, the parlor door opened.

"Major André." Lydia smiled warmly.

The British spy was trembling with suppressed excitement. Late tonight, he and a number of high-ranking British officers would converge on her house for an important meeting.

"And be sure, Lydia, that your family are all in bed at an early hour. When our guests are ready to leave the house, I will give you notice, that you may let us out and extinguish the fire."

He knew she would do it. As she swept the upstairs room, her mind reverted to André's words. The British were planning something full-scale. Where was Charlie tonight? Her oldest son—encamped at Whitemarsh with the 2nd Pennsylvania Regiment of the Continental Army.

It was 8:00 PM. With her children asleep, Lydia softly slipped off her shoes. The house was deadly quiet. Light glimmered under the door of the conference room as the small woman crouched in an adjoining linen closet. A murmur of voices. Then came the clipped accents of General Howe. He was reading aloud an order. On the night of December 4th, British troops were to secretly evacuate the city. According to his spies, the Americans planned to move camp. The British would then ambush them at Whitemarsh, slaughtering them in the open fields.

Oh, God. Charlie was at Whitemarsh. Pressing her ear to the wall, she listened, scarcely breathing. The voices flickered, died down like embers in the fire. Lydia crept back to bed. Almost immediately, someone hammered on the door. Lydia lay rigid. She knew André was out there. Heart pounding, she lay staring into the dark. As the blows continued, she got up and let the officers out into the night. André remarked that she must be a sound sleeper. He had had to knock three times. Back in bed, Lydia's thoughts tormented her. This was not the first time she had engaged in espionage. On her trips through British lines, she carried a sewing kit. Copying a message onto a tiny slip of paper, she sewed it into her clothing or concealed it beneath a button.

As dawn broke over the city, Lydia crossed the street to Howe's headquarters and obtained a pass go to Frankford to buy flour. Trudging the eight miles on foot and carrying an empty sack, Lydia appeared at the Rising Sun Tavern. Elias Boudinot, Commissary of Prisoners, was busy eating breakfast. Lydia came up to him with a question about flour and instead thrust a dirty needle-book into his hands. Surprised, Boudinot flipped through the pockets until he came to the last one. There, he found a slip of paper. Unrolling it, he learned that Howe was coming with 5,000 men, 13 cannon, baggage waggons and eleven boats on wheels. Boudinot (with Colonel Craig, also at the Rising Sun) galloped at once to Washington's headquarters. When the British attacked on December 4th, the Americans turned the tables on Howe's army at Edge Hill. On December 9th, Major André summoned Lydia Darragh to headquarters. His face was grim.

"Were any of your family up, Lydia, on the night when I received company in this house?"

"No," she replied. "They all retired at eight o'clock."

"It's very strange." André mused. "You, I know, Lydia, were asleep . . . Yet it is certain that we were betrayed. I am at a loss to

Lydia Darragh

conceive who could have given the information of our intended attack to General Washington! . . . We found [him] so prepared at every point to receive us, that we have been compelled to march back like a parcel of fools. The walls must have ears."

Only Lydia Darragh knew. Having learned to listen attentively and accurately, Lydia Darragh was able to prevent a British victory at a crucial time. If Washington's army had been destroyed at Whitemarsh, it is possible that the founding of America might have taken a very different turn.

Questions

1. What did Major Andre instruct Lydia and her family to do that evening?
2. Where did Lydia go to attentively listen to the British plans?
3. Why did the British think Lydia was a sound sleeper?
4. What was an extra motivation for Lydia to want to help the American cause?
5. How did Lydia deliver her message and to whom?
6. What was the outcome of the British advance on Whitemarsh?
7. How did Lydia Darragh's attentiveness contribute to the advancement of freedom?
8. How can you practice attentiveness when your parents speak to you? When you are listening to the preacher in church? When a friend is sharing his experiences or burdens with you?

Though we consider thee as a public enemy, we regard thee as a private friend. While we detest the cause thee fights for, we wish well to thy personal interest and safety.

— Lydia Darragh

Availability

Definition

Being willing to attend to a need
when I am called to help

Memory Verse

Also I heard the voice of the Lord,
saying, Whom shall I send, and who will
go for us?
Then said I, Here am I; send me.

Isaiah 6:8

Sergeant Molly

The Revolutionary War • Battle of Monmouth • June, 1778

It was so hot that the men were dropping by the roadside like flies. Twenty-four-year-old Molly Ludwig Hays craned her neck, looking for John. Where was he? He ought to be with the gunners near Wenrock Creek at Monmouth, where American Generals Stirling and Greene withstood the forces of Clinton. Sweat beaded her forehead as she scanned the smoky battlefield, sharp bayonet points glittering in the sunlight. Cannon blasts shook the ground.

Across the field, John stooped over a gun in Captain Alexander's Company of the 7th Pennsylvania Regiment. Dark hair pulled smoothly back into a queue, face browned by the sun. He worked like a demon, ramming home cannonballs, lighting the tow fuse, loading again. British grenadiers, pushing to cross the causeway, staggered back under the heavy fire. As long as the cannons kept firing, the Americans stood a chance to win. Molly shifted the pitcher to her other hand. Hitching her skirts high, she began to move towards him. As a camp follower, trailing her husband from camp to battlefield, Molly had learned lessons in availability. She also knew how to change her plans at a moment's notice and serve when needed.

A moan to her right. Behind her. To her left.

"Water. Water."

Tattered Continental soldiers lay gasping on the scorched ground. Molly hesitated, glancing towards John. The heat was killing. Grasping her pitcher, she ran to a nearby spring. Water bubbled out of the ground. Filling her pitcher to the brim, she moved back along the lines. The men could see her coming from a distance, a tall, broad-shouldered young woman in a white neckerchief, her sleeves rolled up to the elbow, stepping carefully between their dusty feet.

They began calling to her: "Molly! Pitcher!"

The name stuck. Again and again she refilled her pitcher, lifting their heads, spilling cool water down their burning throats. The temperature soared to over 100 degrees. General Stirling's cannon, barely holding the causeway, wavered between the advancing British and Washington's desperately regrouping troops. Wounded men fell, blocking the gunners' feet as the cannon rocked backwards with each explosion. Suddenly, Molly saw her husband slump to the ground. His face was pale and clammy. Molly knew the signs all too well. Heatstroke. He was alive, but unconscious. She stood up. Just then, a Colonial officer rode up to the cannon. He ordered it pushed back out of the way to make room. There was simply no man left to fire it.

Molly Pitcher

"I can do it." Molly Pitcher straightened up.

The officer stared at her, tangled hair, smudged cheeks, skirt tucked high up above her calves. This woman looked like she could do it. And she was actually offering to help. He nodded and rode away. Molly grabbed the smoking-hot ramrod—a wet rag tied to the end of the long pole—and rammed it deep into the barrel. She swabbed out the sparks and gunpowder residue. Then she packed in cannonball, powder and cotton wadding, driving home the ramrod swiftly, accurately. She blasted away into the massed Redcoats struggling on the bridge. This is for John. This is for John. Once, a British cannonball shot between her legs as she bent over the cannon, tearing away a large piece of her skirt.

Molly glanced down and laughed. "Well, that could have been worse."

The soldiers roared appreciatively; she had become one of them. Molly continued to swab and load as the hot Sunday afternoon faded into dusk. It grew darker; the firing lessened. The British troops pulled back in defeat, leaving their wounded and the exhausted Americans withdrew into the ravine. General Washington, seeing Molly Pitcher from a distance, personally commended her and gave her the rank of sergeant. Some of the men began calling her "Sergeant Molly." In 1822, ten years before her death, the House of Representatives voted to pay Molly Pitcher $40 annually for the rest of her life, "for her services in the Revolutionary War." Her name has since appeared on a postage stamp, a World War II ship was christened for her, and a stretch of US highway 11 in Pennsylvania is known as the Molly Pitcher Highway.

Molly Pitcher did not look for fame when she carried water and manned a cannon at the Battle of Monmouth on June 28, 1778. She was simply available, open to the opportunities that came her way to serve in a time of need.

Questions

1. What was Molly Hays doing at the Battle of Monmouth?
2. What job was her husband John performing?
3. How did Molly demonstrate availability to the parched soldiers?
4. What happened to John that prevented him from continuing his job?
5. How did Molly demonstrate availability when John was unable to proceed?
6. What was George Washington's response on seeing Molly engaged in battle?
7. In what ways was Molly honored for her sacrifice to the American cause?
8. How can you demonstrate availability in your home? List some ways.
9. Who in Scripture was available to meet a need when they became aware of it?

*Whatsoever thy hand findeth to do,
do it with thy might.*

— Ecclesiastes 9:10

Boldness

Definition

Facing confrontation with the assurance
that God will bless the outcome
if I'm standing firm for truth

Memory Verse

The rich man is wise in his own conceit;
but the poor that hath understanding
searcheth him out.

Proverbs 28:11

Featherbed Raid

The Civil War • Virginia • March, 1863

Midnight: Sunday, March 8, 1863. A light rain sprinkled the gum capes of the twenty-nine grey-clad men waiting on the Little River turnpike. They glanced at each other furtively. No one knew what game was afoot tonight. Sitting his horse under the canopy of trees, Captain John S. Mosby leaned forward eagerly. Cold drops bounced off the brim of his grey slouch hat. It was hard to see Mosby in the darkness. He was the color of the night, earth-tones and rain.

"Big Yankee" Ames, a deserter from the Fifth New York Cavalry, sidled close to Mosby's saddle. Ames had come to the Confederates from Union lines, and now he was leading them back again. When the Union pickets pulled back that night, they had left a gap in the line between Centerville and Chantilly. That gap was still open. Better still, General Stoughton had set up headquarters apart from his men at Fairfax Court House. It was too good a chance to miss.

Mosby felt his heart contract. If the raid didn't come off, he could kiss goodbye to his military career. The Rangers slid out onto the Little River pike. For almost an hour, there was only the pounding of hoofbeats. All at once, Mosby veered off the main road. Whippoorwills called softly; rabbits sprang from under the horses' hooves. Weaving in and out among the pines, they breached the gap in the line and plunged on the first guards like jackrabbits, capturing every man alive. Wheeling onto the Warrenton pike, they approached Fairfax from the railroad station.

It was now 2:00 AM. Most of the Rangers split off to the Provost Marshal's stables, silencing the guards and hustling out the horses. Meanwhile, Mosby and five men struck through town. It was hard to see in the slanting rain. Just west of the courthouse on Main Street, Mosby's men reached Stoughton's headquarters, a two-story brick house with white trim belonging to Dr. William P. Gunnel. A window crashed open on the second floor.

"Who's there?" an officer called.

Mosby threw back his head. "Fifth New York Cavalry with a dispatch for General Stoughton."

The Rangers rode up, surrounded the porch. Lieutenant Prentiss stood there in his nightshirt, stretching out his hand for the dispatch. Mosby seized the man by the collar.

General Edwin Stoughton

"Take me to General Stoughton's room."

Prentiss had no choice. With Mosby close behind him, he mounted the stairs. The door creaked open. In the dim, smoky light, Mosby saw Stoughton lying in bed, his face turned to the wall. Leaning over him, Mosby jerked the covers down and slapped Stoughton's bare back.

"Is this General Stoughton?" he barked.

Stoughton opened his eyes. In the glare of the lamp, three men were pointing pistols at his face. "Yes, what do you want?"

"Do you know Mosby, General?"

"Yes! Have you caught the rascal?" Stoughton grunted.

"No, but he has caught you!"

Mosby's high-pitched, powerful voice continued. "Jackson is at Centerville and Stuart is in possession of all your camps. You may have heard of Captain Mosby. I am Mosby."

Stoughton stared at him. "Oh, yes, I have heard of him, but Jackson is not at Centerville, nor could Stuart be in possession of the camps about here without my hearing of it. I think you are a raiding party and a small one, at that. Is Fitz here?"

Captain John S. Mosby

Mosby nodded. "Yes."

"Well, take me to him. We were classmates."

"Certainly, but be quick."

Stoughton began to pull on his clothes. Stooping to the fireplace, Mosby picked up a piece of charcoal and scrawled his name on the wall "Mosby." Main Street was full of Rangers herding prisoners together. Rain was still falling, the snorting horses churning the melting snow to slush underfoot. As the cavalry clattered past the courthouse, Stoughton, soaked to the skin, remarked:

"This is a bold thing you have done, but you will certainly be caught."

"Perhaps so." Mosby's voice was soft as rain.

As Mosby's Rangers melted into the woods like smoke, less than one hundred yards from the Union pickets, the main body of the Federal Army had no idea of the raid. In one bold stroke, Mosby had captured the youngest general in the Union Army, 32 men and 58 horses. It was an act that was to establish John S. Mosby's reputation for the rest of the war.

Questions

1. What act of boldness did Mosby perform in this story?
2. How did it demonstrate boldness?
3. What did he accomplish by his bold action?
4. How did Mosby's men work together to accomplish this achievement?
5. What did Mosby risk if his plan failed?
6. Are there any situations in your life that need you to demonstrate boldness?
7. Think of a situation you have encountered that boldness would help accomplish godly purposes?

The wicked flee when no man pursueth: the righteous are bold as a lion.

— Proverbs 28:1

Compassion

Definition

Being willing to expend effort to help alleviate the suffering of those in need

Memory Verse

Withhold not good from them to whom it is due, when it is in the power of thine hand to do it.
Say not to thy neighbor, Go, and come again, and tomorrow I will give; when thou hast it by thee.

Proverbs 3:27-28

Felt Boots

Nizhniy Novgorod, Russia • March, 1919

In October, the skies closed over like a grey slate, people began shutting up their houses and the roads turned to ice. Zhenya didn't need boots, then. In November, the first snow fell, and still Zhenya had no boots. Father was away on one of those trips that grew more frequent since the civil war began. She often felt like an orphan since Father married their servant girl, Mania.

They were moving house today, because it cost too much to rent the house they lived in—the place Zhenya thought of as home. At dawn, Zhenya and Mania tramped across the fields to look at the cottage. There were bedsteads to load, benches, clothes and blankets to pack. Gregory Burmistr, a local peasant, had offered to come along and help.

Strips of snow still lay in the fields. Zhenya, stepping carefully to avoid the deep puddles, scanned the countryside. Cattle with skeleton-thin ribs pawed hungrily at the yellow grass beneath the thin crust of snow. The wind tore at her sheepskin coat and her leaky boots sopped up the slushy snow, making her feel like she was barefoot. Mania, wearing heavy waterproof boots, did not seem to notice. It was too early for the buttercups to be out, though there was a sharp smell in the air as if the earth was waking up. But no sign of it yet. Not till mid-May.

Zhenya shivered. The others were far ahead of her now; black dotes on a grey landscape. It was as if she were alone in the great, wide world, with nothing but the wind blowing and a bird sailing high like a scrap of paper against the clouds.

"Have you no other shoes, Bebby?"

Gregory Burmistr had turned back. Now he crouched in

Aleksandr Ustinovich, 1994 • "A Road" • landscape • rural Russia

front of her, a big burly man in a tattered sheepskin coat. His eyes were gentle, sea-grey. She knew Burmistr slightly—a hard-working, God-fearing peasant who had built up a farmstead and mercantile business with his bare hands. But he was poor now. The same revolution that swept in like a whirlwind, promising peace and prosperity, had confiscated his house and land, and left him staring into a bleak spring.

"Don't you have any other shoes?"

"Why, no, Gregory." Zhenya felt cold water trickling against her toes. "It will be summer soon; these will last till then."

But summer was months away. If Father came home, there would be fields of yellow daisies, children playing, and barefoot days. Summer was a magical time. Everything would be all right when summer came.

But Gregory was looking at her.

"Hmm." He shut his eyes as if thinking. The wind tossed his black beard. Without another word, he caught up to Mania, telling some joke which Zhenya did not catch, its ends blown away by the wind.

The next day, Gregory brought her a pair of felt boots with elastic sides. Zhenya gasped. Though second-hand, they shone with careful polishing, and their soles were clean and whole. Only Gregory had known how she dreaded living in the village without a decent pair of shoes.

In April, Father came home. After the long winter, Zhenya no longer needed the boots. It was barefoot time. The rains came and the revolution passed over their heads and was gone, leaving a thundering silence in its wake.

But Zhenya never forgot Gregory Burmistr.

Gregory Burmistr demonstrated generosity by giving his last pair of boots to a child when he himself was in need.

Questions

1. Explain the girl's many hardships.
2. What was her need that Gregory Burmistr discovered?
3. What had caused the people to become poor?
4. Where was the girl's father?
5. How did Gregory Burmistr demonstrate compassion to the girl?
6. How did it affect the girl?
7. Sometimes acts of compassion are little things, but become milestones in the live of the receiver. Think of someone to whom you could show compassion. Work out a plan to implement it.
8. How can a simple act of compassion become a motivator in someone else's life?

---

[1]Civil War: The war (1918-1922) that followed the Communist Revolution of 1917

Contentment

Definition

Realizing that God has given me all I need
for my present happiness

Memory Verse

Not that I speak in respect of want:
for I have learned, in whatsoever state I am,
therewith to be content.
I know how to be abased, and I know how
to abound: everywhere and in all things
I am instructed both to be full
and to be hungry, both to abound
and to suffer need.

Philippians 4:11-12

Waterland

The Atlantic Ocean • November, 1873

November 22, 1873. The passenger steamer, *Ville du Havre,* sailing from the United States to Europe, cut through the frigid autumn waters and sea mists around the rocky coastline of Newfoundland at a steady clip. Within its lighted decks and third-class berths it carried 107 people. Suddenly, a heavy vessel flying the red-blue-and-white British flag loomed up out of the fog like an iron monster. Too late to turn, the *Loch Earn* struck the *Ville* with a grinding crunch. Inside, tables lurched and chairs overturned. People ran towards the lifeboats as water began gushing into the ship's hold. In twelve minutes, the deck began tilting upwards before diving straight down towards the bottom of the sea. Within twenty minutes, it disappeared completely.

Anna Spafford surfaced amid choppy waves and bits of refuse. Suddenly, a swirling vortex sucked her head underwater. Her baby was torn from her arms. Surfacing again, the waves smashed her body against a pile of debris, bruising her arms. Just then, she saw the baby's dress sinking through the water. She flailed out desperately, clutching at the soggy clothing. Her fingers closed on the seams. Then another wave knocked her away and the baby sank like a stone. Out to sea, a young man riding a chunk of wood grabbed the two girls, Annie and Maggie, and told them to hang onto his coat pockets as he searched for a larger piece of wreckage. Thirty minutes later, he seized a plank drifting by. Struggling to pull the girls aboard, he saw their eyes close and their fingers slip away. Then they were gone. Nobody saw the fourth child.

The sinking of the Ville du Havre

Gasping and shivering, her hair shimmering with salt and her dressing gown hanging in tatters from her shoulders, Anna clung with both hands to a piece of floating wreckage, bobbing like a cork alone in the pitiless water-land of an empty sea. All she could hear in her pain-numbed mind were the words, "You were saved for a purpose!"

Someday, God, I will know why this happened. But not now.

The air still smelled like fire. Sometimes it crept out of odd corners, through the sweet-smelling yellow timbers, fresh mortar and new red bricks going up all over the city. The skyline of Chicago had changed. Gone were the rickety old tenement houses, the tumbledown stables full of musty hay, the wealthy houses lining the waterfront near Lake Michigan. When the Great Fire of October, 1871, killed 300 people and left another 100,000 homeless, Horatio G. Spafford had lost almost everything to the flames. Alone in his house in the northern suburbs, he spent his final moments clearing up some urgent law business before leaving for Europe.

The house was quiet now. No sounds of girlish laughter from eleven-year-old Annie, nine-year-old Maggie, five-year-old Bessie and baby Tanetta. Together, he and Anna, his soft-faced Swedish wife, welcomed reformers and preachers into their home. But Anna's health started to crack. To help her recover, the Spaffords planned a trip to Europe in the autumn. They also wanted to assist D. L. Moody and Ira D. Sankey during their popular revivals in England. When sudden business kept him a little longer in Chicago, Spafford sent Anna ahead with the girls.

He waved the girls on board, together with their French governess, Emma Lorriaux. After a few days, he would see them again. As he cleared up the papers and prepared to leave, a telegraph messenger thrust a paper into his hand. It was from Anna. He tore it open.

Horatio and Anna Spafford

The words nearly blinded him. It was Anna screaming at him from across the sea.

"Saved alone. What shall I do?"

He had felt this way before, numb, stunned. When their four-year-old son Horatio slipped into a scarlet-fever coma three years ago, he had felt like dying, too. Now as he stood on the deck of the ship sailing across the Atlantic, he heard the captain's voice calling him up to the bridge.

"A careful reckoning has been made and I believe we are now passing the place where the *Ville du Havre* was wrecked." The captain pointed. "The water is three miles deep."

Three miles deep. He down stared at the slate-grey water. Somewhere down there his beautiful girls lay in a watery grave. Only 47 out of 300 people survived. But not one of his girls. Somehow, although he could not understand it, God had allowed this to happen. Slowly, he turned away from the railing. Sitting alone in his cabin that night, wondering what he would say to Anna when he saw her again, he began to write.

"When peace like a river attendeth my way, when sorrows like sea billows roll, whatever my lot, Thou hast taught me to say,

The American Colony in Jerusalem

'It is well, it is well with my soul.' "

Later, Philip Bliss set his words to music. In 1880, Horatio and Anna Spafford settled with their next three children at the "American Colony" in Jerusalem. He and his wife would labor for a Christian utopian community in the land of Israel for the rest of their lives.

Horatio and Anna Spafford demonstrated contentment by accepting through faith the difficult circumstances that God brought into their lives.

Questions

1. What disaster struck the *Ville du Havre?*
2. What happened to Horatio's family?
3. Tell about how the Chicago fire affected the Spafford family earlier.
4. Why did Horatio send his family on ahead to England?
5. Where was Horatio Spafford when he wrote the words to "It Is Well with My Soul?" What motivated him to write them?
6. How did the Spaffords illustrate contentment?
7. What should your response be when suffering rough circumstances?
8. Does God ever make mistakes? Is God in control of what happens to you?
9. Think of a situation you struggle with. How can you purpose to demonstrate contentment? Remember God has the big picture and He has our best interests in mind. Maybe on earth, but for sure when we get to heaven, we will understand it all, but for now we must be content to rest in God's best for us.

Courage

Definition

Standing alone for righteousness
and yielding my fears to God

Memory Verse

Have not I commanded thee? Be strong and of a good courage; be not afraid, neither be thou dismayed; for the Lord thy God is with thee whithersoever thou goest.

Joshua 1:9

Casualty

World War I • The Russian Front • Autumn, 1915

The telephone call came through at 1500 hours. Rising from the muddy ground beside the machine-gun, Colonel Aleksandr Groten loosened his collar and gripped the receiver tightly. Shrapnel burst in the trees overhead, spraying his shoulderboards with dirt.

"Groten speaking."

"What are you playing at?" Commander Menshikov's voice crackled over the wire. "I gave you orders to advance an hour ago."

Field telephones were rare and often defective. Last year, Second Army General Aleksandr Samsonov had only twenty-five telephones for his entire army. In the middle of the combat zone, buried lines snaked underground to avoid direct hits from heavy artillery shells. A second explosion burst somewhere in front of him. Groten jiggled the switch frantically and then handed it over to the army operator.

Disconnected.

In the rear, a huddle of dun-colored cavalry shifted and stamped under the hot sky. The field telephone shrilled again. Groten caught it on the next ring. "Sir, we are surrounded in a dense swamp and cannot advance without severe casualties."

He had to shout to make himself heard over the roar of the German 77 FK 96 field guns. Their own smaller 76.2 mm. guns popped in reply. "If I advance now, my entire unit will be wiped out. The *Nemetz* have posted their guns on higher ground—"

"I'm ordering you to advance at once, Colonel!" The commander's voice purpled. "Give me casualties, not topography."

Groten gritted his teeth. He would do his best. He forced himself to ease the telephone onto its hook and stood over it for several seconds, breathing heavily. Several men watched him with eyes like faded bluebells. How many children did they have?

An officer using a field telephone

He took his field glasses from the leather case at his side and trained on the still, black marsh between the scrubby pines. Then he stared up at the slope gouged by shell holes. The muzzles of the German guns, aiming over the hill, perched like black crows. Clouds of mosquitoes hung like pale gauze in the muggy air, stinging the soldiers' faces and hands. They would have to wade across 500 feet of open swamp, their rifles slung across their shoulders, the backs of their necks straight, clean-shaven, vulnerable. Groten closed his eyes. They could not creep around and flank the Germans from the rear. The swamp stretched before them for miles on either side.

When he opened his eyes, he said briefly: "Tell the *Hussars* to advance."

A metallic bugle note shimmered in the humid air. The *Hussars* in their crimson jackets with gold braid dismounted and began to pick their way across the marsh like ants. Mud sucked at their boots. Briars tore at their tight blue breeches.

The ground shook.

"Gospodi Pomeelui . . . Lord, have mercy on us."

Groten could feel the slow surge and murmur of humanity wading around him, about to be fed fodder into the war-machine by their commanders. They struggled out of sight into the dark mouth of the swamp. Death hovered over them, a double-headed eagle with black wings.

Russian army in the trenches

Drops of sweat broke out on his forehead.

Suddenly Groten shouted: "Call them back! I can't do it. If the General wants a casualty, I'll give him one."

If it's not too late.

Somewhere behind him, he heard the bugle frantically shrilling retreat. Shoulders erect, he stepped from behind his shelter and walked straight into enemy gunfire. Something slammed into him with a dull thud. He clapped a hand to his shoulder. Blood leaked hotly between his fingers. Swaying a little, he turned slowly towards his men.

"Very good. You can retire now."

He had a dim sense of bodies swirling past him, retrograding into the trees. Then his eyes hazed over. For a long time, there was nothing but the agonizing jolting of the cart, the dark tunnel of trees spiraling overhead, brilliant shafts of light. An aide rode beside him.

Groten spoke only once. "Are they safe?"

He meant his men.

"Yes, sir." The aide blinked back tears. "They pulled back an hour ago. You shouldn't have done it, Your Honor."

Groten closed his eyes. "I'm glad."

Headquarters was in an uproar. The General, fretting constantly about his tired horses, lumbered down the steps to where Groten lay in the scanty shade of the field ambulance.

"You're crazy, Colonel. You could have been killed!"

Groten opened one cold grey eye. "I'm fine." His voice was dry. "But what do you mean, decimating my men?"

By exposing himself to certain death in order to save his soldiers, Colonel Aleksandr Groten demonstrated uncommon courage and self-sacrifice.

Questions

1. How did Colonel Groten demonstrate supreme courage?
2. What did his commanding officer want him to do?
3. Why didn't he do it?
4. What did he suppose would happen if he had obeyed the order?
5. What do you suppose his men felt when he placed himself in the line of fire?
6. Why does it sometimes take more courage to obey God rather than men?
7. Think of an instance where you were afraid to do something. What should you do when faced with such a situation again?
8. Does having courage mean we are never afraid?
9. What would you do if your friends were all getting ready to do something wrong and wanted you to join them?

Then Peter and the other apostles answered and said, "We ought to obey God rather than men."

— Acts 5:29

Decisiveness

Definition

The ability to make wise, deliberate decisions based on God's standards

Memory Verse

But let him ask in faith, nothing wavering.
For he that doubts is like a wave of the sea,
driven with the wind and tossed.

James 1:6

Sea Monsters

The Revolutionary War • English Coast • September, 1779

Thursday, September 23, 1779. It was 3:00 PM when he first sighted them. A light southwest breeze scudded across the waves off Flamborough Head, forcing the two warships to drift closer. Leaning on the rail of the *Bonhomme Richard,* thirty-two-year-old John Paul Jones peered through the haze at the heavy British frigate *Serapis.* His blue coat, embroidered with gold epaulets, shone in the sunlight. His square jaw was taut, his brown hair pulled smoothly back from his brow. Behind him bunched the masts of his own four ships. He had had his eyes on the *Serapis* for hours. This was the ship he had waited so long for. At first, the sea was smooth as glass. Then as he doubled back, looking for prizes at the mouth of the Humber River, he caught sight of the British frigate running straight up the Yorkshire coastline from the Baltic Sea. A dozen ships fanned out behind the *Serapis* like a peacock's tail. They were merchant ships, en route from Scandinavia, rolling with supplies: rope, canvas, timber.

At 1:00 PM the British sighted Jones' cluster of ships drifting below the chalky cliffs of Flamborough Head. Flags began signaling: "Strange sail in sight." Jones knew it was time to act, to cut the enemy supplies off from the English coast. Among his four ships, Jones could muster 120 guns, capable of smashing over a thousand pounds of metal into the *Serapis.* But Jones' ship was old and slow, tired from cruising the seas. The *Serapis* was brand new, twice as fast and able to outmaneuver Jones' ship like a spider in a dance. A victory would not only cut the lifeline to Britain's "wooden wall"—the Royal Navy—but it would also secure him lasting fame.

Cruising towards each other, the vessels made no more than a mile or two an hour. At 5:00 PM the warships were so close that the deck of the *Bonhomme Richard* was cleared for action, chairs and tables thrust down into the hold to reduce the danger of flying splinters. Sailors sprinkled sand over the deck so it would not turn slippery with blood.

The late summer evening was soft and still light. Hazy clouds spread over the North Sea. At 6:00, Jones ran up his flags. Blue. Blue. Yellow and blue. They signalled "Line of Battle." The flags shivered in the wind. Glancing back, Jones saw his own ships, the *Vengeance* and the *Alliance,* veer away. The *Pallas* tacked off on her own course, her sails bright in the fading September sunlight. He was suddenly alone.

Now the British man-o-war was so close he could see her yellow topsides bellying up above the water. The smaller sloop huddled closely in her wake. Aboard the *Bonhomme Richard,* crews dragged chains and braced the yards, while the gun crew crouched over the 18-pounders, holding lighted matches aloft as the breeze drove the ships slowly inwards. Someone let out a joke. And the crew was roaring with laughter when the ship rocked with the first broadside from the *Serapis* a moment later. Two of Jones' guns burst, killing most of the crew nearby. Within minutes, his heaviest armament was out of action. Lieutenant Richard Dale, grimy with powder and spattered with blood and sweat, found Jones up on deck. The captain wheeled around.

"Dick, his metal is too heavy for us! He is hammering us to pieces. We must close with him. Bring your men on the spar deck and give them the small arms."

Seamen swarmed up into the rigging with pistols to take out the enemy gunners from above. The risk was great. A single spark from a flintlock weapon could blow the entire powder magazine sky high. Shells crashed into the hull, staving in the old East Indiaman's sides. But Jones instructed the men to clear the *Serapis'* rigging of British and then sweep the decks. By 6:00, the sun began to sink behind the white cliffs of Flamborough Head. The *Countess of Scarborough* ran in along Jones' port side, scalding him with gunfire. Just then, the captain of the *Pallas* realized that Jones was fighting, not surrendering. He reversed his direction and rushed back to help.

Captain John Paul Jones

Six miles away on Flamborough Head, an excited crowd watched as the ships foamed and struggled like sea monsters in the waves below. Darkness fell, and the stars came out, pricking the black sky. In the east, a harvest moon, big and orange as a cannonball, came up out of the sea. The ships' shapes were still clearly visible, but not their flags.

Suddenly the hoarse voice of Captain Pearson bellowed into the dusk: "What ship is that?"

Jones thought quickly: *"The Princess Royal."*

Both ships were East-Indiamen and roughly the same size. But Pearson was not satisfied.

"Where from?"

Jones kept silent.

"Tell me instantly whence you came and who you be, or I'll fire a broadside into you!"

Jones saw that the game was up. He scrapped his false Royal colors and ran up the Continental flag. Without warning, both ships erupted into gunfire.

A red glare spread over the sea. Many of the ships were on fire. Ropes, masts and splintered yards littered the decks. The ships were only twenty-five yards away now, blasting away with the concussion of 42 cannon. Officers, standing exposed on the deck, steeled themselves not to flinch as shot whizzed past them. At this point, Captain Pearson determined to finish off this bold American. He slid out from under the ship's lee and prepared to rake the bow with gunfire. And then, the wind died. This was Jones' chance. The *Serapis* hung just off to starboard, unable to move an inch.

"Well done, my lads," he shouted. "We have got her now!"

He leaped forward with a line to lash the two ships together. The sailors grabbed cutlasses, pikes, and pistols and prepared to board the enemy ship. They scrambled forward, clutching at the bowsprit, as the Royal Marines peppered them with musket balls. It was impossible. Slipping on the wet deck, Jones called back the attacking party. But the wind was shifting in his favor. Slowly, Jones drove the ship in closer till it lay athwart the enemy's bow. If he angled it into correct focus, he could rake the *Serapis* from stem to stern. The *Bonhomme Richard* was barely moving now. The smoke was so thick that Jones could barely see the cartridge wads from the British guns smoldering in the shattered masts. The gun room, filled with the badly burned, was abandoned. The boat began to sink below the waterline as the ship's carpenter, up to his chin in water, fought to stop the flow with canvas and wooden plugs. But the pumps were too slow.

He shouted aloft: "We're sinking!"

Two mates and an English officer on board heard it. Jones, they believed, was dead, lost to sight in the billowing smoke and darkness. They ran for the mainmast and began to lower the last American flag. Sailors panicked as the ship pitched and tilted beneath them. Suddenly, Jones heard the cry of "Quarters!" He lunged across the deck at the culprits, bringing up his pistol, just as Pearson leaned over the rail and shouted: "Have you struck? Do you call for Quarters?"

The whole world grew still. The British, almost invisible in the darkness, his own bloody and smoke-grimed men, the prisoners manning the pumps below, all waited for his reply.

Then John Paul Jones shouted: "Struck sir? I have not yet begun to fight!"

It was 10:00 PM. Four hours had passed since the *Serapis* first fired on the *Bonhomme Richard.* Then the miracle happened. A Scotsman scrambled onto the *Serapis'* platform in the darkness and began lobbing grenades across the ship's deck. Explosions rocked the British vessel. Two-ton guns blew from their carriages, somersaulting in the air. The ship was on fire in a dozen places and men began leaping into the sea. It was now 10:30 PM. Jones, hunched over a nine-pounder twenty yards away, saw Pearson's stiff figure appear on the ladder to the deck.

"Sir, I have struck!" he shouted. "I ask for quarter!"

The battle was over.

Because John Paul Jones exemplified decisiveness and made wise decisions, he was able to tie two ships together and win the battle for the American Revolution.

Questions

1. What was the mission John Paul Jones set out to do?
2. What was the name of his ship? What was the name of the British frigate?
3. What was the business of the British frigate?
4. Describe what happened during the battle.
5. What was Jones' reply when asked if he was surrendering.
6. What decision did Jones make that won the battle?
7. What is the definition of decisiveness?
8. Think of a situation when you or someone you know demonstrated decisiveness to bring about a good result.

I wish to have no connection with any ship that does not sail fast; for I intend to go in harm's way.

I have not yet begun to fight.

— John Paul Jones

DEFERENCE

DEFINITION

To hold others in esteem
and give them first choice

MEMORY VERSE

Let nothing be done through strife
or vainglory; but in lowliness of mind
let each esteem other
better than themselves

PHILIPPIANS 2:3

Sun-Swept Afternoon of Horror

*Workd War II • The Philippine Sea * August 2, 1945*

They had ordered him never to land the frail seaplane on the high seas, only on water as calm as glass. But as twenty-eight-year-old Lieutenant Adrian Marks stared down at the tiny figures barely floating on the dazzling hot sea, he could not turn his face away. No boat lay in sight. Looking around at his eight crewmen, he knew that they could all die if he touched down on those choppy waters. But he had to try.

Sailing solo through the Philippine Sea from Guam, where it delivered the first operational atomic bomb to the island of Tinian, the *USS Indianapolis* made its return trip with 1,200 men aboard. At midnight on Sunday, July 29, a Japanese submarine skipper, Lieutenant Commander Mochitsura Hashimoto, spotted the giant vessel cruising through the sea. Immediately, he sent six torpedoes hurtling through the water. Two crashed into the ship's side. Explosion after explosion rocked the *Indianapolis.* As it pitched over in the darkness, Navy signalmen frantically radioed SOS's. Rolling over on its side, the *Indianapolis* sank in twelve minutes. Over 400 men died instantly. Another 800 leapt into the water as the distress signals blinked through the night.

Due to a Navy oversight, the commanders of the Pacific Fleet did not worry when the *Indianapolis* did not show up at Leyte Gulf in the Philippines three days later. On a hot, glittering sea infested by sharks, the survivors clung to bits of wreckage throughout Monday, Tuesday, and Wednesday. Bruised, dehydrated, and burnt by the sun, the men paddled more slowly as hours stretched into days.

USS Indianapolis

Then on Thursday, August 2, at 10:00 AM, Lt. Wilbur C. Gwinn, flying a routine flight, looked down and saw them. Of the 800 men who had initially survived the Japanese torpedo attack, only 317 remained alive. Lieutenant Adrian Marks, radioed from the nearby island of Peleliu, arrived first on the scene in his PBY5A Catalina plane, nicknamed "Dumbo." On what he later called "a sun-swept afternoon of horror," he began dropping life-rafts to the men later that day. One shattered as it struck the high, cresting waves.

This was not working.

Then the lieutenant turned to his crew members. Should they disobey their strict orders and make a dangerous and possibly fatal landing on the open sea? One by one, they all agreed to try. The mass rescue began.

Dropping straight from the sky, Marks touched his plane down between crashing, twelve-foot swells. The plane bounced hard, shooting fifteen feet into the air when it hit the water. But the impact only shook and battered the little craft. It did not crack up. As "Dumbo" rode the waves towards the scattered groups of survivors, the officer and his men came to a "heartbreaking decision." They could not save everyone. Squinting at the glassy surface of the sea, the lieutenant decided that the men huddled together could stay afloat the longest. In waters filled with the darting shadows of sharks, these men could stick together and splash and shout to scare the killers away. Painfully closing his heart, Marks headed towards a single man barely treading water. The crewmen tossed him a life ring attached to a rope. Then they circled for another, bouncing on the heavy waves. After a little while, two men lay on each bunk in the seaplane. Others packed two and three deep in every compartment. Finally, when breathing room became cramped, Marks switched off the engines. Then he helped more survivors onto the bouncing wings, lashing the last of them down with strips of parachute silk. He had saved 56 men.

Lieutenant Adrian Marks

A warm tropical night pressed down on the sea. A high wind whipped up. Behind him in the bunks and compartments, Marks could hear dozens of men moaning in pain. They had run out of their last drop of water hours ago. Suddenly, a light pierced the darkness on the far horizon. The bulkhead of a destroyer, *Cecil J. Doyle,* loomed out of the sea. The first of seven rescue ships sent late to the scene, the *Doyle* spotted the little seaplane, its wings weighed down by drooping men and its engine silent, bobbing helplessly on the waves. Sailors pulled the survivors on board. Then they helped a tired Lieutenant Marks and his crewmen aboard as well. Later that night, the *Doyle* cruised around the Philippine Sea, picking up scattered survivors.

The next morning, Marks watched as the destroyer sank his seaplane, "Dumbo," too badly damaged to ever fly again. Twelve days later, Japan surrendered. World War II had ended. The survivors of the *USS Indianapolis* had weathered the worst maritime disaster in the history of the American navy. Lieutenant Adrian Marks never let himself forget what he had seen on August 2, 1945. Afterward, Admiral

PBY-5-A Catalina

Chester Nimitz, the commander of the Pacific Fleet, would pin the air medal on the young officer. Thirty years later, at a reunion of the *Indianapolis* survivors, Adrian Marks looked the men in the eye and said: "I met you on a sparkling, sun-swept afternoon of horror. I have known you through a tropical night of fear. I will never forget you."

Adrian Marks demonstrated deference by setting his own comfort and safety aside to rescue others in need.

Questions

1. What mission had the *USS Indianapolis* just completed?
2. Where was she headed now?
3. What is the name of the Japanese lieutenant who torpedoed the *Indianapolis?*
4. How long had the survivors been in the water when rescued?
5. How many men survived the ordeal?
6. What were some of the dangers being in the water so long?
7. What brave decision did Marks and his men make that was against orders? How was he later recognized for his deference?
8. How many men was his crew able to rescue? What did they do when they ran out of room?
9. What ship came to transport the men to safety?

I met you on a sparkling, sun-swept afternoon of horror. I have known you through a tropical night of fear. I will never forget you.

— Lieutenant Adrian Marks

Dependability

Definition

Honoring your word and responsibilities even if it means unexpected sacrifice

Memory Verse

He sweareth to his own hurt,
and changeth not.

Psalm 15:4b

Angels on Omaha Beach

World War II • Normandy, France • D-Day, June 6, 1944

Clouds covered the summer sky. The bullets sounded like angry hornets zooming past his head. Zip-zip-zip. In the middle of the heavily-defended German "Green Dog Sector" on Omaha Beach, Cecil Breeden, an Iowa medic, stooped over eighteen-year-old Harold Baumgarten. One of the Company A "Bedford Boys," he lay bleeding heavily on a stretcher on the beach. Wounds gaped in his mouth and face. Shrapnel had slashed his clothes and skin. Moments before, as he lay on the stretcher waiting for evacuation, a German sniper sent another bullet into his body. Soldiers from the 116th Regiment, 29th Division of the Virginia National Guards Regiment swarmed over the beachhead after the landing ramps went down at the start of the attack. Most of the "Bedford Boys" were mown down like wheat before the onslaught of German artillery and the carefully-sighted sniper fire. It took four wounds before Baumgarten fell.

As the boy opened his eyes, he could see Breeden's face hovering close above him. The medic did not flinch as German machine-gun fire thudded around him. Instead, he gently treated Baumgarten's wounds before moving off towards the next soldier groaning on the beach. Those watching never forgot the sight. Moving like an angel through a storm of shrapnel and bullets, Breeden passed untouched from man to man, giving help and comfort where he could.

Staring after him through the cloudy haze on Omaha Beach, Baumgarten knew that God had spared him for some great purpose. If he lived to get off this beach, he would dedicate his life to helping those who needed him as a doctor.

Many of the other "Bedford Boys" were not so fortunate. After a year and a half in England, most of the men looked forward to getting into action that summer. Others, with wives and children at home, admitted that they would rather stay in England than assault a beach.

Joining up during the wave of patriotic fervor that broke out in the wake of Pearl Harbor, the "Bedford Boys" vowed, like their fathers in World War I, "to whup 'em good and still be home for Christmas." During the bitter winter of 1942-43, the men trained and struggled to prove themselves, while officers and non-commissioned drill sergeants kept weeding out those who could not make it. Camping out in the driving rain on the Yorkshire fells, some of the boys found that their Captain Taylor Feller's tough exterior hid a great homesickness. Far from home, many for the first time, the "Bedford Boys" were glad to go with men that they knew. At the same time, they faced criticism from army regulars who believed that National Guardsmen could only play at soldiers. D-Day would prove them wrong.

As June opened, it brought the birth of Operation Overlord, better known as D-Day, closer. The operation's planners believed that heavy bombing would simply take out the German pillboxes. Craters blown in the sand by the bombing would provide instant foxholes for the soldiers landing on the beach. Then demolition teams would move into wipe out Erwin Rommel's hidden mines and defenses. Battleships offshore would annihilate anything left. Finally, the first wave of Landing Craft Air tanks, equipped with floating apparatuses, would grind up onto the beach and give them covering fire as the infantry charged in the first assault.

Captain Fellers, listening to the plans and role of the Virginia National Guard in them, began to doubt the success of the operation. They would need a miracle, if everything were to go according to plan. Finally, at a military meeting, he could stand it no longer. Despite his low rank as a captain, he spoke up.

"Sir, I could take one BAR [Browning Automatic Rifle] and

hold that beach."

No one answered.

As Fellers and Lieutenant Ray Nance walked out of the meeting, the captain said quietly,

"We'll all be killed, Ray."

Already, Army high command had begun referring to the 116th infantry and Company A as the "suicide wave" that would hit the French beach with the code name of Omaha. Despite his doubts, he remained committed to the operation. Then, just before D-Day, Captain Fellers went into the hospital with a severe sinus infection. Worried, his men crowded on deck, wondering what would happen now. But Fellers met them there.

American troops landing on Omaha Beach

"I've trained you and I've come to die with you if that's what it takes," he said.

Immediately, the men straightened. "It lifted our spirits to have our leader back," Roy Stevens, one of the Bedford Boys, said.

Their commander stood on the deck as the 29th Division boarded for takeoff. "Are you ready, men?" he asked.

One of them managed to say brightly: "Yes, sir, we're sure ready."

It was dark at 6:30 AM when they hit the water, slogging through it with sixty-pound packs weighing on their backs and digging into their shoulders. Unknown to them, the pilots above them could see nothing due to the blurred cloud-cover. Afraid of hitting their own troops, the planes flew too far inland, dropping the bombs on a few French farms but killing no Germans. Meanwhile, the tanks, equipped with floatation devices, got bogged down in the rear. Some of their own carriers sank, drowning the men on board. The men's hearts sank as they looked out sea. Now, their only help lay in the Battleship *Texas*, as it began shooting rockets towards the beach. Most splashed harmlessly in the water. When the "Bedford Boys" came up onto Omaha Beach, they came alone. There were no foxholes and no covering fire.

Men fell as soon as they hit the beach. Twin brothers, Roy and Ray Stevens, with dreams vbof owning a farm, stepped off onto Omaha Beach together on that June day. Only one came back. Disaster threatened all of them. Lieutenant Nance, slewing up on the beach in his Landing Craft Air tank, found that the ramps would not go down. Spattered by enemy fire and knowing that the Germans would shoot at the first head that popped up, Nance kept yelling: "GET IT DOWN!"

But the ramp was stuck. Bodies littered the beach. Men stumbling past recognized the prone figure of one of the Hoback brothers. Others saw Earl Parker fall, the man who said he would die gladly if he could only see his little girl, Danny, once more. They never found most of the bodies. Lieutenant Nance, frantically trying to lower his tank ramp, felt it thump to the ground. He lurched up and onto the beach. When he looked behind him, he could not see anyone. Most of his men had gone down within moments of landing. The officer felt sick as he stared down at the carnage. He knew these men. He had trained them personally, watched them grow from raw country boys into top-notch fighters. He felt that he should have somehow protected them. "I felt responsible for them, every last one. They were the finest soldiers I ever saw."

Crawling out of his tank, Nance headed toward a nearby cliff, the only cover visible in the rain of fire. Suddenly, a machine-gun bullet ripped into his heel. As his blood seeped away, the lieutenant stared up at the sky that had just broken into the dawn. It "had a rosy appearance," he said. "A warm feeling came over me and I knew I was going to live."

As he lay near the cliff on Omaha Beach, Nance looked up to see a spotlessly uniformed Navy Corpsman leaning over him. With tender hands, the man dressed the officer's wound. Then he stuck a shot of morphine into his arm.

Medic treating wounded soldier

"This is worse than Selerno," he commiserated. "Good luck to you." Then he disappeared.

Later, when Nance related his experience, everyone told him that he must have had a hallucination. No one could have come off a landing tank under gunfire looking spick-and-span. But Nance showed them his carefully bandaged foot to prove it. If an angel dressed like a Navy Corpsman came to him that day on Omaha Beach, he would always be grateful.

Meanwhile, medic Cecil Breeden moved around the beach on his own errand of mercy, patching up torn bodies without a thought to the ferocious enemy fire. He came through the war and entered Germany without a scratch. He would never receive a decoration for his heroism.

Later that afternoon, a sergeant picked up a weakened Lieutenant Nance and carried him over to an aid station. Lying on the ground, Nance threw out his hand and nearly put it on something that looked like a pie plate.

The sergeant bellowed: "Don't touch it!"

The officer jerked his hand back. He had nearly slammed it down on a German mine. For most of the Bedford Boys, the "Longest Day" was over.

Thousands of miles away, in Bedford, Virginia, families

crouched by their radios, listening for news of their boys. None of them knew whether the boys had gone out on D-Day or not. Captain Taylor Fellers, who told his men that he would go out to die with them, died four days later on June 10, 1944. Looking down on the body of his brother lying on the beach, one of the men muttered: "Let's get the men who did this."

In total, nineteen Bedford Boys died at D-Day on June 6, 1944. Three more would fall later. Only ten percent of Company A survived the brutal landing without being killed or wounded. A "veil of tears" hung over the quiet little town as wives and mothers mourned the men who had fallen on Omaha Beach. Bedford, Virginia, had suffered the heaviest casualties of any community in the United States during World War II.

Cecil Breeden and the other Bedford Boys had shown dependability by doing their duty even if it meant unexpected sacrifice to themselves.

Questions

1. What was Cecil Breeden's job?
2. Who were the Bedford Boys?
3. What was the Bedford Boys' mission?
4. Who was their Captain? Tell what happened to him just prior to D-Day and the choice he made that inspired the confidence of his troops.
5. What types of disaster met them as they struggled to get to the beach?
6. Tell about how Lieutenant Nance felt observing what was happening to his men.
7. Tell of Nance's injury and how the medic was like an angel of mercy to him.
8. How many of the Bedford Boys survived D-Day?
9. Tell how Cecil Breeden was an incredible example of dependability during this conflict.

Diligence

Definition

Viewing each task given to me as a special duty and putting forth the effort to do my very best.

Memory Verse

And whatsoever you do in word or deed, do all in the name of the Lord Jesus, giving thanks to God and the Father by him.

Colossians 3:17

Renaissance Man

The Revolutionary War Era • 1706–1790

Philadelphia, 1739. He listened intently to George Whitefield's clear actor's voice that boomed from the Philadelphia Courthouse steps and spread into the middle of Market Street. Pushing through the crowd, 33-year-old Benjamin Franklin, a successful businessman and printer, walked west into Second Street. Men, women and children packed the streets, listening as the man's pale, crossed eyes bored into each face. As Franklin approached Front Street and headed down to the river, he could still hear the Reverend Whitefield's voice carrying loud and clear. So he kept walking. He traced an imaginary semicircle between the streets, with his distance as the radius. He allowed each person two square feet and then checked the clarity of sound again. The results of his mathematical test astounded him. Franklin later estimated that the young preacher could easily reach a crowd of thirty thousand people with his voice alone. It would be the first of many experiments for the diligent young printer and inventor.

Tired of his apprenticeship to his older brother James with Boston newspaper, *The New-England Courant,* Franklin boarded a boat at age 17 and ran away to Philadelphia. There, he accepted a letter of introduction from Governor Sir William Keith to go to London as a typesetter and printing apprentice. The job fell through, and Franklin spent the next three years living on the edge in London. Those years taught him what he needed to know. Returning to Philadelphia, the young man worked hard as a clerk, shopkeeper and bookkeeper. But he never gave up the dream that he would someday be a prominent man.

In order to fulfill his life goals, Franklin set down and kept himself to a strict regime. When other young men spent the night

Benjamin Franklin as a printer's apprentice

on the town, he stayed home and read every book on politics, science, and logic that he could get his hands on. When his fellow printers drank beer, Franklin drank only water. He saved his pennies, kept up his health with swimming exercises and improved his mind. At age 21, he founded the Junto Club, a society of young tradesmen eager to improve themselves and their community.

Philadelphia in 1737 had no public library. Books remained, for the most part, a luxury of the rich. But these men wanted to bring a bit of culture into their club. At first, they brought in a book here and there, gleaned from their own shelves. But the result was pitifully meager. Franklin then came up with the idea of creating a subscription library. All the members would pool their funds to buy books from England. The result was the Library of Congress. Within a year, the collection grew so large that the city moved it to the second floor of the State House of Pennsylvania, now Independence Hall.

Franklin experiments with electricity

Franklin's influence grew by leaps and bounds. When the English preacher George Whitefield landed in America in 1739, the two men struck up an instant friendship. Franklin printed Whitefield's sermons, which popularized them throughout the colonies, while at the same time, the business of a world-famous preacher sent Franklin's popularity as a publisher soaring.

Meanwhile, Franklin entered into a marriage relationship with Deborah Reed, a girl he had met on his first hungry day in Philadelphia. She thriftily sold soap and fabric, while Franklin opened a bookstore. Several years earlier, he had brought out a pamphlet known as *Poor Richard's Almanac.* Offering advice to farmers on crops, growing seasons, weather, and monthly cycles of the moon, Poor Richard's Almanac also contained witty advice on daily life, such as, "A penny saved is two-pence dear," often misquoted as, "A penny saved is a penny earned." The almanac sold ten thousand copies per year—the equal of three million copies today.

Interested in improving life for his fellow Philadelphians, Franklin organized a fire fighting team: Philadelphia's Union Fire Company. "An ounce of prevention is worth a pound of cure," he claimed. In order to help families who had lost their homes through devastating fires, Franklin organized the "Philadelphia Contribution for Insurance Against Loss by Fire." Citizens who took out a policy found aid waiting for them when a fire came. He also launched projects to clean up streets swimming in muck and water, dig a drainage system, and install streetlamps.

The plight of the sick worried Franklin. With health in mind, he spoke to several wealthy Quakers in the city and channeled their money and resources towards building the Pennsylvania Hospital.

With his publishing and philanthropic business well underway, Franklin turned to the field of invention. He noticed how his friends suffered from the cold Philadelphia winters. The open fireplaces they used sucked what little heat they generated straight up the chimney. Such fireplaces, he reasoned, only warmed the edges of the room.

The Franklin Stove

Benjamin Franklin

Puzzling over this problem, he set to work. By 1743, he had developed the Franklin Stove: an iron box standing on four crude legs. Filled with coals, the furnace efficiently heated homes across the city. During the next few years, Franklin invented bifocals, glasses with a split lens that allowed him both to read a book in his hand and scan the horizon far off. He also invented swim fins, the lightening rod, and the glass armonica. As postmaster, Franklin mapped out the routes for delivering mail. During his long carriage rides, he found that he needed some way to measure the roads and keep track of the distance. In answer to this need, he invented an odometer, fixed it to his carriage and set off.

In the 1750s, he experimented with the unknown force of electricity with a kite in a lightning storm. He developed the wave theory of light as well as ideas on electrical conductivity, meteorology, and economics. Franklin refused to take out patents on any of his inventions, since he created them with the intent to help society.

Franklin also found himself drawn into politics. In 1763, when a gang of local toughs known as the Paxton Boys massacred a number of peaceful Susquehannock Indians and then marched on Philadelphia. Franklin rushed to the local militia to defend the city. Then he went out to talk to the Paxton Boys and persuaded them to turn back. During this conflict about colonial security known as Pontiac's Rebellion, Franklin lashed out against racial prejudice, demanding: "If an Indian injures me, does it follow that I may revenge that Injury on all Indians?"

By 1775, he actively engaged in the meetings of the Continental Congress, making several slight changes to Thomas Jefferson's draft of the *Declaration of Independence.* From 1776 to 1785, he served as the American ambassador to France, where he charmed men and women alike with his shabby fur hat and down-to-earth common sense. He later put his signature to the Treaty of Paris, ending the war with Britain. Toward the end of his life, Franklin freed his slaves and became a leading abolitionist. His desire to understand, master, and invent aspects of science, math, chess, language, philosophy, and music make him a unique figure in 18th-century America: a man who had all the qualities of a Renaissance man in the age of education and discovery.

Throughout his life, Benjamin Franklin demonstrated diligence in his business. By hard work and industry, he helped better society and establish a more perfect form of government.

Questions

1 How many people did Franklin estimate could be reached by George Whitefield's voice?
2. What jobs did Franklin hold as a young man?
3 What type of schedule did Franklin set for himself?
4. How did he apply himself to learn character?
5. Tell of some of Franklin's ideas he implemented to make life better for all?
6. What was Poor Richard's Almanac? How many copies sold per year?
7. List some of the things Franklin invented.
8. What was Franklin's involvement in civic affairs?
9. Would you say Benjamin Franklin was a diligent man? What are some evidences of that?
10. What are some ways you could improve in diligence?

Discernment

Definition

The ability to identify
subtle untruths or motives

Memory Verse

For the word of God is quick, powerful,
and sharper than any two-edged sword,
piercing even to the dividing asunder of
soul and spirit, and of the joints and
marrow, and is a discerner of
the thoughts and intents of the heart.

Hebrews 4:12

The Sub that Sank a Train

World War II • Japanese Coast • June, 1945

Patience Bay: June 18, 1945. It was 4 AM. The submarine *USS Barb* hovered in the dark waters off Karafuto, Japan, like a glowing green spaceship. Bending over the table, Thirty-two-year-old Commander Eugene Fluckey studied the railway line on the map spread out before him. It was Fluckey's fifth patrol in Asian waters, scoring eight direct hits on six enemy ships. Now the Navy wanted to make it his last. Four patrols was the limit before turning over command to a new captain. But Fluckey wasn't about to give up on his men. He was like a father to them. He asked for one last mission, a "graduation patrol," if his fourth proved a success. Admiral Lockwood had agreed. For almost six weeks the *Barb* cruised the seas, annihilating Japanese coastal defenses and supplies with the first American submarine-launched ballistic missiles of the war. They called him "Lucky" Fluckey. He had another name, too: "The Galloping Ghost of the China Coast," for his speed and daring vanishing acts. By July 18, Fluckey had worked up his finale. They were going to bag a train.

If they could blow up the main railway line running inland from the coast, the damage might halt the enemy advance in that region for days or even a week. Smiling, he rubbed tired, creased eyes. In the next compartment he heard excited chatter, the high tenor of boys and the deeper tones of the older men sitting around in their undershirts. The men knew about the upcoming strategy, but only that they planned to destroy the rails.

Straightening up, Fluckey walked through the sub to the control room, something he did several times a day. He liked to talk to the men, to gauge their mood and gain their perspective at the

Commander Eugene Fluckey

height of a mission. He knew each of the eighty men aboard by name. He asked them about their wives and families; which baseball team they liked best or where they went to school.

You had to get used to living in a sub. The cramped space and lack of sunlight created inevitable tension among men new to the business. But these men were seasoned veterans. If a submarine had to dive to avoid *akikazes,* fast, low-lying Japanese minesweepers, the world suddenly became a closed torpedo, floating in lightless subterranean depths. There were nerve-wracking minutes when the *Barb* had to surface during a chase due to shallow water. Unable to dive, the submarine would skim along the surface of the coastline, heading out to sea with Japanese gunboats in full pursuit. If the *Barb* were hit by a Japanese sub, the crew wouldn't stand much of a chance swimming out of the wreckage alive.

But Fluckey wouldn't trade this life for a comfortable desk job behind the lines. Other submarine commanders lost their subs or their lives in the China seas, but Fluckey, with a curious blend of discretion and daring, had kept intact and afloat through five missions. Now as he faced a cluster of officers and men, he dropped the bombshell. Not only were they going to blow up the rails, but they had to time the detonation for the instant that one of the Japanese supply trains passed, without blowing their own shore patrol sky high. The men nodded at each other. This sounded more like "Lucky" Fluckey, the tough submarine commander and recent recipient of the Medal of Honor. Fluckey warned them of the risks involved. It was a comparatively easy task to dynamite a railway line and a harder one to hit a train in motion without killing the men sent ashore. But by avoiding reckless actions, they could do it. "We don't have problems," he stated calmly, "only solutions."

1147 AM. "Battle Stations!"

Too late now to discuss ways and means. A Japanese freighter appeared on the horizon, accompanied by a pack of frigate escorts. It drew closer, its steel prow looming up out of the water, big and menacing. On the upper deck, Commander Fluckey peered at it through his binoculars. Little black figures swarmed the ship's bridge.

1200: "Hitting time."

The bowshot technique—setting off a bomb underwater straight into a vessel's bow—was a last-ditch effort. The freighter exploded, the Rising Sun flag blowing into the air. By noon, the frigate lay in pieces on the ocean floor. When the Japanese learned of the wreckage by radar, the *Barb* would become a hunted ship. A Soviet ship trailed them for a time before turning aside.

Then 1807: "Dive! Dive! Plane closing fast, nine miles."

Enemy planes circled overhead. Cruising slowly beneath the surface, the *Barb* spent an hour unable to come up for air. Fourteen hours had passed since the first decision to blow up the supply train and they still hadn't figured out the logistics.

Bill Hatfield, an electrician from West Virginia, spoke up. "I've one idea."

Fluckey nodded. "Let's have it."

According to Hatfield, they had to bury a 55-pound high-explosive charge under the track to catch both track and train. The bomb was big, over a foot long and wide, so they had to dig a hole and sandwich it between two ties. Then they could bury the batteries wired to it in a nearby hole and activate the charge. Then to complete the circuit, the engineers would hook in a microswitch. Placed on the surface between the next two ties, the switch would do the job.

The Commander listened intently. "Sounds simple enough,

but please explain to us simpletons just how do we set off the microswitch?"

"You don't, sir. The train does."

"Okay. How?"

Bill grinned. "The rail sags underneath the weight of the engine. So we mount the switch on two wedges, slip it under the rail, the engine comes along, the rail sags, closing the switch, and she blows!"

Fluckey clapped Hatfield so hard on the back that he staggered. The idea was perfect, discreet and did not pose such a threat to the lives of his men. But they still had to figure out how much the rail sagged. It depended, Bill said, on the size of the engine. Japanese engines were about one-third the size of American ones, so it would take less impact to explode the charge.

"When I was a kid," Hatfield said excitedly, "we used to crack nuts that way. Oh, I'd say the rail sags enough to crack a good-sized black walnut laid on a hunk of wood."

"How much is that?"

Hatfield pinched together his thumb and forefinger. "About yea big."

Fluckey decided "yea big" was about an inch. It would work.

One of the crewmen appeared. "Captain, we're still submerged and twilight is ending."

Fluckey nodded. "Take her up."

They would use rubber boats. But enemy frigates still hovered near the coast and the *Barb* sensed radar interference from all of them. The Commander stalked back and forth.

"Jim, we can't get ahead of them unless they leave that coast. Nor can we surface in this bright moonlight without being gunned."

He stared through the night periscope as the frigates sailed out to sea. Then he turned the sub around and headed back for Patience Bay. The train was now top priority. Still, Fluckey worried about the crucial amount of give in the railroad ties. An overestimate could cause the risky operation to fail. As for an underestimate, he did not even consider the possibility. Though his eyes pricked with sleep, Fluckey went to his cabin, hauled out a thick book of engineering and started scribbling equations. It was a long night. When the lieutenant came to the door of Fluckey's cabin, he found the commander sound asleep, his head resting on his arms. The engines throbbed quietly as the *Barb* drifted through nighttime seas.

2337: "Captain, contact. Showing Soviet lights."

"Keep clear, Bill."

Morning came. As they cut across Patience Bay towards the western shore, Fluckey shut his cabin door and drew the curtains to draw up the list of men for the sabotage party. Lieutenant Bill Walker, the biggest and strongest officer on board, would lead the mission. All types, from electricians, motor machinists and torpedo-men to the lead cook had a fair chance to serve. Only married men could not go. If the party had to flee and survive under critical conditions, it would be through the mountains of northern Karafuto to the Russian part of Sakhalin Island.

Satisfied, Fluckey left his cabin to tell the men. They watched as he singled out the marine commandos. Detailed to land as a shore patrol, these men would carry out the operation while the *Barb* covered them from a distance. Fluckey refused to unnecessarily risk his men's lives, but he did want to blow up that train. As the names rang out, men stepped out by twos and threes and stood aside. Faces clouded with disappointment as reality sank in: only eight could go ashore. The selected party beamed when informed they were to go.

Quietly, the commander finished: "I'll lead the saboteurs. This isn't a combat situation, yet it's too risky to turn over to someone else. I'm sure I could pull it off."

One of his officers stopped him. "Sir, I swear I'll send a message to ComSubPac if you attempt this. It's not in the best interests of the men."

Reluctantly, Fluckey agreed. "I suppose you're right, but I hate to miss this once-in-a-lifetime opportunity."

For the next few days, the men trained and gathered equipment. Seamen strapped on combat gear and inflated lifejackets. Weapons lay in rows for test runs. They even had a waterproof firing system for wet weather. In his cabin, the Captain double-checked his equations for mistakes. The rail sag was 1/10 inch. Every few hours, he took a quick walk through the boat to check the pulse of the sub. Everyone was calm, peaceful. Those who didn't get to go gave helpful suggestions. Suddenly, someone mentioned the danger of attack dogs.

Fluckey sent for a Japanese prisoner nicknamed "Kamikaze." Rolling his expressive black eyes, Kamikaze said that Japanese guards patrolled the cliffs, rocks, beaches and villages. On foot, they passed at a regular interval of two hours, night and day. Sometimes they had two guards, usually one. Carrying pistol and rifle, they always kept a dog close by their side. The patrols' purpose was to keep Soviet spies off the island. The captain told the men to carry a few steaks apiece to throw to the dogs. That was better than trying to fight them.

Fluckey spoke again to the crew. Only one man must approach the rails to make the final live connection. While he stooped to do that, all the others must lie down flat on the ground at least twenty yards away. Keep exposed body parts turned away and eyes closed. He didn't want anyone killed or blinded by the flash if there was a mistake. For four days, they scanned the sky. They needed a moonless night. Or a night with drifting clouds that threatened to cover the moon. As soon as the cloud blotted out the white disk, the commandos could move in. In the meantime, the submarine lay still. The sea must lie perfectly quiet, lulled into a false sense of security, before the attack.

During that time, the engineers built the microswitch the train would trigger as it passed over. A team went down to the boiler room and cut up steel plates. Heating the sheets to white-hot temperatures, they bent and shaped the metal into picks and shovels. The work done, the men waited anxiously. Only five days of their patrol remained. They had to act now or never.

1837: They dove and observed the island. When they surfaced, it was bright moonlight. Cloudless. They cruised softly around, looking for a lone sampan—a native boat—that they could capture to help the men in landing. On the submarine deck, the commander watched the sky. But days passed, and still their chance did not come.

U.S.S. Barb

July 21: Dawn spread over the twin peaks of the green mountains visible further inland. This would be their guide for paddling in. Crewmen brought the *Barb* in to less than 1000 yards from the beach by radar before the commandos disembarked. Meanwhile, the engineers built a test circuit to iron out any kinks. The men's spines tingled with anticipation.

July 22: Commander Fluckey, standing on lookout in the early twilight, scanned the two green peaks. White cirrus clouds capped the mountains, wreathing their heads in dense white fog. Slowly, a luminous cloud bank drifted across the sky, piling up behind a three-quarters moon. Fluckey turned to the men. Tonight was the night.

The party could return no later than 0230 and twilight commenced at 0245. A sampan, looking like an ancient basket, floated along the beach while the *Barb* hooted at the moon. Softly, the men communicated with each other as they launched the rubber boats. When one group approached the other, it let out a low, clear whistle: "Bob white!"

Fluckey listened to the signal for assembly, the liquid cry of the American whippoorwill.

"Ti-la-ti."

He prayed that the Japanese wouldn't know their bird calls and suspect foul play. The men practiced communication in the final moments. A blast on whistle meant an emergency dash for the boats. Two stars from a Very rocket sprinkling the sky signaled "We are in trouble."

Fluckey had some final words with Lt. Bill Walker. If the spot isn't good or the odds poor, don't risk it. Bring the men back immediately. Move with discretion. Make sure every man has meat to throw to the dogs. Booby trap the train. Slip in and out again. Do not be detected. He looked into Bill's eyes. Most importantly, bring the men out alive.

Flooded by moonlight, the *Barb's* silhouette looked like a Spanish galleon floating on a golden sea. In the dark of the moon, the Japanese would not see the boats from shore. No one would dream that a submarine could swim so close in such shallow water. The men clambered down, noiselessly inflating the rubber boats. There was a quiet jostling, the tinkle of equipment.

Nighttime raids suited him best. He loved slipping through the water under cover of darkness. Sleek, torpedo-grey sharks cut through the cove, driving silvery swirls of fish before them. Sharks were the original torpedoes, built for speed and silence, their dorsal fins jutting at a ninety-degree angle. They could lurk underwater, surfacing in a flash to grab a fish or a man's leg. In this nautical underworld, the *Barb* glided through Karafuto Bay like a giant beast of prey.

2230: Radar detected. Small boats came down the coast, zigzagging towards them. They passed safely.

July 23, 0000 hours: "Launch the boats." The commandos went in, silently dipping their oars. Fluckey, heart beating, listened for the sound of shouting, shots, the spurt of a flare. Nothing reached his ears. There was only thick darkness. The boats scraped up on the beach. No lights glimmered anywhere. It was a primitive feeling, like the dawn of time. His thoughts went to the men hiding in the bulrushes, to Bill. Bulrushes crackled and snapped at every move. The men of one party, moving forward, ran into each other. Someone reached for a throat, nearly strangling the man before he saw it was a friend. Whispers raw with anger and relief, hissed among the bulrushes. "Why didn't you give the signal?"

"My throat got dry."

They were digging feverishly on the railroad ties when a man came running up to Bill. "Captain, a train is coming up the track!" No!

There was no light except a faint red glimmer from the firebox. White smoke swirled out behind like a magician's cape. No wonder they had not seen the train coming until it was almost on top of them. The Japanese were masters at blacking out trains, concealing every crack of light. The boys must be smack in the middle of digging the battery hole.

Bill sweated copiously. "I hope the holes in the track don't send the train careening off the rails. This could ruin everything."

A glow like a red eyeball went by on the track. As it passed in a rush of hot wind, the men pressed their ears to the rail, listening. No sound. The crew scurried back to work. No sooner had they begun again, the breeze from north to south roaring in their ears, than they heard a train bearing down on them less than eighty yards away.

The men panicked. Bill jumped clear of the tracks and into a brier patch. They lay flat on the ground as the train roared by, the engineer leaning out of the cab and staring at them. But nothing happened. No alarm bells went off. When the second scare had passed, the men raced to finish the holes in twenty minutes. Soft whippoorwill calls floated across the night air. If something happened to a commando, the next man knew how to take over the job.

Now the moment came. Nobody wanted to hide in the bushes. They all wanted to see Bill complete the final step. With seven men breathing down his neck, Bill Hatfield began connecting the

Crew of the U.S.S. Barb

live switch. Somebody said, It won't work. Another reached down and patted it till Bill rasped, "Stop it, before you blow us all to kingdom come!"

The switch connected. Leaving the tracks, the commandos headed for the beach through the swaying clumps of bulrushes. The group softly whistled "Bob white" twenty yards away from the boats where the others crouched.

1045: Train coming. The men leaped into the boats and paddled fast. White smoke enveloped the tracks.

1047: Boom! Wham! The charge blew the engine into the air. Boilers exploded, creating flying wreckage, cars cracking and writhing. Orange and blue flames lit the horizon. Silence for several seconds. Then came the snapping and grinding sound of tortured steel. Commander Fluckey, standing on the deck of the submarine, heard it. He swept the area with his binoculars as the *Barb* swung out to sea. They were alone.

The men pulled the rubber boats close for boarding as their fellow crewmen pulled them up. Hatches sprang open. There were shouts, cheers. They had done it. A large Japanese supply train had gone up in smoke.

Safe on board the mother ship, the men began singing "Down the Valley." And as the submarine purred out towards the open sea, Fluckey could hear them shout again and again: "Hear the *Barb* blow!" It was a night neither he nor the United States

Navy would ever forget. In total, Commander "Lucky" Fluckey destroyed more gross tonnage than any other submarine commander in the Pacific theatre. More importantly, the expedition at Karafuto Bay was the only instance that American troops set foot on Japanese soil during World War II.

Eugene Fluckey demonstrated discernment by carefully choosing trustworthy and knowledgeable men to use for the job in order to not endanger their lives and to assure the accomplishment of their mission.

Questions

1. What was the purpose of this mission Commander Fluckey was leading?
2. How did he feel about his men? How did he treat them?
3. What idea did Bill Hatfield come up with to accomplish the mission?
4. Why was this mission especially dangerous to his men?
5. What type of weather were they waiting for before attempting the mission?
6. What type of signal did they use to communicate with each other?
7. Was their mission a success?
8. For what was it distinquished?
9. How did Commander Fluckey demonstrate discretion?
10. How can you best avoid any actions or words that would give the appearance of evil in your life?

Discretion

Definition

Avoiding any words, actions, or attitudes that could give the appearance of evil

Memory Verse

The proverbs of Solomon the son of
David, king of Israel …
to give subtlety to the simple, to the
young man knowledge and discretion.

Proverbs 1:1, 4

Race to the Dan River

The Revolutionary War • Virginia • February, 1781

February 13, 1781. They moved under cover of darkness, horses, wagons and men. Thirty-eight-year-old Major General Nathanael Greene, his large figure looming in the saddle, watched from the bank at Boyd's Ferry as Continental soldiers streamed past, torchlight gleaming on their straggling hair, exhausted faces and torn, bloody uniforms. Greene moved with a heavy limp. He cocked his ear, listening intently. On winter nights like these, sound traveled for miles. The clink of a saber or the rattle of military accoutrements would sound like a gunshot in the darkness. Melting snow and rain splashed underfoot, creaked under the wheels of the gun caissons, fell with a soft plop into the Dan's frigid waters. It seemed as if the whole world was hushed in wet snow.

Just two months before on December 2, Congress had chosen Greene, Quartermaster General of the Continental Army, to replace the ineffective Horatio Gates in command in North Carolina. The war for the South hung in the balance. Robert Howe lost Savannah. Benjamin Lincoln surrendered Charleston without a fight. And in August 1780, Horatio Gates' army ran in wild confusion from the Camden battlefield. In despair, Washington wrote to Greene of his decision to select a new general for the southern theatre. He ended: "It is my wish to appoint You." Known as the "Fighting Quaker," Greene would win a reputation as a savior of the army.

Facing Cornwallis' well-armed and superior forces, Greene decided to divide his troops. According to military books, this was the wrong thing to do. Dividing troops into two wings weak-

General Nathanael Greene

ened an army's central core and lessened its punch effect. But Greene did it anyway. By splitting up his own troops, he forced the British to split as well. The gamble paid off with the American victory at King's Mountain. All at once, the war shifted in favor of the Revolution.

The race started the day after Cowpens, when Greene sent General Daniel Morgan into South Carolina with one wing of the army. The day Cornwallis forgot to look behind him and found Morgan crashing into his rear. After luring British cavalry under Colonel Banastre Tarleton away from any hope of reinforcements, Morgan closed in, decimating nine-tenths of the British troopers and capturing over 800 men. Cornwallis spun like a tiger. His one goal: to free the redcoat prisoners and destroy the rebel army before it could reach safety in Virginia. Greene knew what was going on in Cornwallis' mind. The British commander hoped that Morgan, retreating towards Salisbury with a clutch of booty, would not be able to link up with the brilliant and discerning Nathanael Greene. The rag-tag army began their run before dawn. Cornwallis, camped near Ramseur's Mill, burned his wagon train and started after them.

If the Continentals could reach Virginia and the main body of the army, they would be safe. Greene, receiving urgent messages from Morgan, swiftly swung his wing north to join him. Greene set off in the grey dawn with three dragoons and a guide. The damp, cold air pressed in on them. Stealthily, they glided through the bleak countryside of Anson County, zigzagging to avoid detection by British foraging parties until they came upon Morgan's hidden position. The next day, a rainy Thursday, Greene, Morgan, General William Davidson of the Salisbury District Brigade of North Carolina Militia, along with Colonel William and Captain Joseph Graham sat huddled on a log in the raw weather a few hundred yards from camp to trace their next moves. Greene shrewdly calculated their resources. He had only Morgan's flying army and Davidson's 600 militiamen to face Cornwallis' pursuit. He spoke seriously.

Morgan would hold the upper ford, Sherrald's Ford. Davidson would move farther down to guard the lower fords at Beattie's Ford, Cowan's Ford, and Toole's Ford. When he could hold it no longer, he would fall back to Salisbury for shelter and supplies. Greene knew that they could not stay there long. Cornwallis, only a few hours behind them, scouted out the fords at the Catawba. He saw that Morgan held Sherrald's Ford in force, while Davidson strongly defended Beattie's. Cornwallis sent a feinting attack towards Beattie's Ford, while he shifted downriver to capture Cowan's Ford. Davidson guessed what had happened. In the ambush and skirmish that followed, Davidson fell mortally wounded. When several discouraged patriots withdrew to Tarrant's Tavern, cavalrymen under Tarleton followed them there and cut down ten of them.

Cowan's Ford

On Thursday evening, his troops wet and tired, their powder soaked from the rain, Greene slipped by Tarrant's Tavern several hours before Tarleton arrived. While his men loaded wagons with food, ammunition and weapons, Greene dashed off letters to General Huger and "Light-Horse Harry" Lee, asking them to come to his aid. He had already written Patrick Henry for more troops, adding, "In all probability, you will find me on the North side of Dan River . . . I [will] in turn race Lord Cornwallis as he has done me." Early Saturday morning, in driving rain, Greene watched from horseback as his men slogged through the rapidly rising Yadkin River.

The race began. Pushing their prisoners in front of them, they avoided the few roads that existed. They waded through deep creek-beds and struck out across muddy fields under torrential skies. Cornwallis, paddling across the Catawba, regrouped on the other side and rested all day. Meanwhile, the Continentals kept marching. Greene kept the British frustrated and guessing which direction he had gone. He formed a special operations group under Colonel Otho Williams to spy out British movements and cover the main army's retreat. On February 6, Morgan reached Guilford Courthouse in a steady downpour of rain and sleet, while Cornwallis kept up the hunt for him within a radius of twenty-five miles. Greene arrived the next day, and the two wings of the army joined again. The result numbered a paltry 2,036 exhausted and hungry men.

Now they approached the Dan River. They had been on the march for almost three weeks now, a deadly race that brought them out of the rolling hills of North Carolina to this broad, menacing stretch of icy water. Beyond them lay the flat lowlands of Virginia—and safety. Colonel Williams, ordered to stall or distract the British at any cost in order to facilitate the crossing, galloped with his cavalry just ahead of the van of the British army.

As they neared the end of their run, Greene sent out urgent messages to every ferryman in Halifax and Pittsylvania Country: Bring every boat you can find. A flotilla of rafts and little fishing boats appeared out of nowhere. On Tuesday, February 13, they began crossing in the darkness at Boyd's and Irvine's Ferry, dragging animals and equipment through the bone-chilling water. Mass after mass passed on the boats, faces streaked in the torchlight, the cannons bobbing and the horses swimming. Other soldiers hunkered behind hastily constructed earthworks ready to fight the British off if they came pouring down the bank. The "light" troops skittered along behind, fighting off skirmishes on the slippery, muddy roads, destroying bridges and interrupting British intelligence. The last of Greene's men clambered up the opposite side.

General Greene crossing the Dan River

The British outriders, close behind them, could hear the sound of voices and see the flickering torches. But they could not reach them in time. Cornwallis arrived on the banks of the Dan at 8 o'clock on Thursday morning. It was Valentine's Day, the river was running high and all of the boats had gone. Balked, Cornwallis could not cross. The three-week race over 250 miles of rainy and sleet-covered roads, fighting off attacks and crossing major rivers had ended. Safe on the other side, General Greene slept for a few hours before pushing deeper into Virginia. By avoiding a pitched battle with his men in a weakened condition, Greene conducted one of the greatest strategic retreats in history. Collecting fresh troops, he turned back into North Carolina to face Cornwallis again at Guilford Courthouse.

General Nathanael Greene demonstrated discretion by carefully weighing his situation and deciding on the wisest course of action, first by dividing up his troops and then by choosing to retreat rather than plunge into a fight.

Questions

1. What position in the Continental Army did Nathanael Greene hold?
2. Why was the south in such bad straits?
3. What decision did Nathanael Greene make that defied military advice?
4. What was Greene's strategy?
5. How did he end up executing his plan?
6. How did the retreat turn out?
7. In what way did Greene demonstrate discretion?
8. Think of a situation where you acted without first weighing the situation and making a wise decision. How did it turn out? If given a second chance, what would you do differently?
9. Think of someone in Scripture who acted with discretion and tell how God's purposes were accomplished as a result.

America must raise an empire of permanent duration, supported upon the grand pillars of Truth, Freedom, and Religion, encouraged by the smiles of Justice and defended by her own patriotic sons.

— Nathanael Greene

Endurance

Definition

The inward struggle to endure tribulation with determination

Memory Verse

For what glory is it, if, when ye be buffeted
for your faults, ye shall take it patiently?
But if, when ye do well, and suffer for it,
ye take it patiently,
this is acceptable with God.

1 Peter 2:20

The Catacomb Church

Post World War I • Russia • August 1936

Alma Ata, August, 1936. He glanced over his shoulder. Had the secret police followed him here? Metropolitan[1] Joseph Petrovykh stopped and peered into the narrow street, just fading into grey dawn. The pungent smell of dust filled his nostrils, mingled with the odor of sheep dung from the great Kazakh herds grazing out on the steppe. Looking up, he saw the curtains tightly drawn across the apartment windows. Not a crack of light escaped. He tapped on the drainpipe near the window.

"Glory to God!" Arsenii's wife pulled him into the passageway. "They're all here."

He couldn't see a thing. But he could hear her hands scraping at the floor, peeling back the carpet that covered the trap door. He gripped the rungs of the ladder, oblivious as his long black cloak caught on the protruding nails. Then a cool gust of air. The smell of earth. They were in the vault, now. Groping in a corner of the cellar, he began pulling out one stone after another. Within seconds, a hole appeared. Stooping, he crawled forward on hands and knees, squeezing his shoulder against the tight wall. His breath came heavily. And then he was standing in their midst, his hand raised in blessing. The place was small, jewel-like, candlelight flickering on the glass lamps, the faces of Christ and the apostles. Faint singing died away as he entered. Very tall, he seemed to fill the room, aging, and yet ageless, his snow-white hair covered with a dark hood.

But all Metropolitan Joseph saw was their faces. His sheep. His own face was thin, deeply-lined; his kind eyes shone like quicksilver, bearing their joys, their pain. He looked at the circle of faces in the yellow lamplight-Arsenii, the sub-pastor, men with straggling beards, old women with tattered kerchiefs and swollen, blue-veined hands. He opened the Bible, smoothing the pages covered in Cyrillic script with his palms. His voice like St. Paul's pierced the darkness.

"Invoking God's blessing upon the shepherds and all the faithful, I beg you to continue the work of prayer, of salvation and divine service, humbly submitting to the civil authority."

Ten years ago, Metropolitan Sergius, the head of the church in Moscow, issued a "Declaration" announcing the church's loyalty to the Communist government. In a series of firm letters, Joseph denounced the heretical new church, an act that led to his arrest. What was the purpose of the church? Was it to serve Christ or the Communist state? To live in Christ was far better than to preserve external traditions. On his release, Joseph took the faith underground, for he knew that the Soviets intended to destroy all religion under a guise of tolerance. Then in 1930, he was arrested again and sentenced to five years in a labor camp in the desert of Kazakhstan.

Now he spoke urgently. "Beware, lest little by little we lose the freedom which our Lord Jesus Christ, the Liberator of all men, has given us as a free gift by His own blood."

He could see it in their faces. The love. And the endurance, too. The lamplight blurred.

In Kazakhstan, they forced him to live in a sty with pigs, surrounded by a stake fence. He slept on bare boards in bitter cold and suffocating heat. Once a poisonous snake, clinging to the rafters, crawled right onto his head. And in his dreams, Metropolitan Sergius came to him three times, as he had come to the prison cell, his glossy black and white robes sweeping the floor.

"Give in, Joseph. We are the true church. It would be so much easier to give in."

A dog chained outside, barked loudly. Everyone turned startled eyes towards the entrance. Someone blew out the lamp. They waited tensely, in utter darkness. Across Russia, "Josephite" churches crouched in caves under threat of death. This is what it must have been like for the early church. Waiting in the darkness, listening for footsteps, the bark of a dog. Not knowing if their bishop was still alive. Clinging to him, they sang a hymn. It was a psalm he had set to music using the battered organ given to him, knowing that he might never see them again.

Chemkent: November 10, 1938

Metropolitan Joseph Petrovykh

"Joseph Petrovykh?"

"Yes." He raised himself from the cross-cut saw, its jagged teeth biting into the fir log, and faced the GPU guards, tall, fragile, his beard as white as snow. "What do you want?"

After fifteen months of harsh interrogation, the authorities delivered a verdict: "You are guilty of encouraging the enemies of the Soviet state as head of an illegal religious organization."

He smiled faintly. "Even here, I have served the Lord and taken delight in Him."

They pushed Metropolitan Joseph out into the courtyard. Before him, he saw a blank grey wall rising sheer towards the sky. His lips moved: "Love your enemies. It is the supreme triumph of love that filled the first martyr Stephen when he, his face shining like an angel, prayed for his murderers: *Lord, lay not this sin to their charge.* Before him were the opened heavens, the Son of God at right hand of the Father. And so, even if all should leave us, may the Heavenly Pastor not leave us, according to His unfailing promise to remain in His Church to the end of the age."

He closed his eyes, opened them again, seeing nothing in that last moment—only the white breast of a dove flying above the prison roofs, straight into the blinding glory of the sun.

Through Metropolitan Joseph's endurance in persecution and imprisonment, the catacomb church that he led, as well as a widening circle of believers, continued to grow for years to come.

[1]Metropolitan: A pastoral leader or elder in some Christian churches.

Questions

1. Where was Joseph Petrovych headed when he went into the narrow passageway?
2. What was his position?
3. Why had he been imprisoned? For how long?
4. What had he endured while in prison?
5. What was his message to the believers?
6. What was the dog barking at?
7. What was Joseph's conviction?
8. How did his endurance serve as a beacon for those to whom he ministered?
9. Are there any rough circumstances in your life right now that you could better face by learning endurance?
10. Who in Scripture demonstrated endurance?

Enthusiasm

Definition

Expressing joy in each job I am given to do

Memory Verse

And whatsoever you do, do it heartily
as to the Lord, and not unto men.

Colossians 3:23

The Black Robe

The Revolutionary War • Virginia • January, 1776

Woodstock, Virginia: January 21, 1776. The cold, cracked logs hummed with warmth and a babble of German and English voices. Outside, blue ridges rose over the Shenandoah Valley cloaked in snow. Stepping into his pulpit in the Lutheran meeting house, Thirty-year-old Pastor John Peter Gabriel Muhlenberg adjusted his heavy, long black robe. It fit him smoothly from his wrists to his ankles. Framed by a soft white wig, his thin-lipped face gazed over the congregation. Men in homespun breeches and women in caps and shawls, with children clinging to their hands, waited in silence.

His eyes moved over their faces, studying each one. The war hadn't touched this valley yet. But drums beat in Massachusetts to the north. Soldiers marched in red waves. It was only a matter of time till the clash came. Last year in the crowded St. John's Church in Richmond, he saw a red-haired man leap to his feet. Gripping the pew in front of him, Patrick Henry shouted: "I know not what course others may take; but as for me, give me liberty or give me death!"

He thought of George Washington's face as he asked him to rally more men to fight. Today, he would leave this valley, and he would take with him the sturdy log walls, the bite of snow in his face, the grip of the tough valley men. But he would not leave them behind. They had not called him "Devil Pete" for nothing when he fought with the dragoons in Germany twelve years before.

Now Muhlenberg raised his head. His voice rang out, strong and clear:

Pastor Muhlenberg rallying his congregation

"There is a time for all things: a time to preach and a time to pray, but those times have passed away. There is a time to fight—and that time has come!"

Suddenly, Pastor Muhlenberg threw back his robes. Underneath, he wore the blue-and-buff uniform of a colonel in the Revolutionary Army. His eyes pierced the congregation. Stepping down from the pulpit, Muhlenberg waved his hand. Drums outside the door began to beat. One by one, men stooped to kiss their wives and children. Muhlenberg watched as they streamed into the roughhewn aisles. His enthusiastic demonstration had worked a miracle. In half an hour, 162 men from three congregations had joined the Continental Army. When Muhlenberg led the 8th Virginia Militia out from Woodstock the next day, the ranks had swelled to 300.

Some historians now argue that mention of Muhlenberg's spectacular disrobing that Sunday in January, 1776, is conspicuously absent from all contemporary accounts. While it is not known how much of this story is fact or myth it is certain that Peter Muhlenberg preached a stirring sermon and then marched at the head of his regiment to join the Continental Army.

Next, Muhlenberg headed south to defend the coasts and swamps of Georgia and South Carolina. In 1777, he raced north to support Washington's troops during the bitter winter at Valley Forge. Serving through the bloody battles of Brandywine and Monmouth, Muhlenberg earned the rank of brigadier general just as Washington and French forces under Rochambeau laid siege to Cornwallis at Yorktown. Joining the attack, the enthusi-

General John Peter Muhlenberg

astic preacher-turned-soldier and his men stubbornly held the right flank as Washington's army closed in for the kill. While Lafayette's Light Division trundled cannon through the darkness, Muhlenberg crouched with his men in the trenches, waiting for the signal to attack. On the night of October 14, 1781, Muhlenberg's infantry charged the slopes of Redoubt No. 10 with fixed bayonets. The British lines caved in. Soon, a white flag fluttered over the embankments. Cornwallis had surrendered.

Muhlenberg's famous robe is still in existence. It resides in the historical collection of the Lutheran Theological Seminary in Philadelphia.

Peter Muhlenberg demonstrated enthusiasm both through his words and actions. As a result, he influenced hundreds of men to fight in one of the first Virginia militias of the war.

Questions

1. In what part of the country did John Peter Gabriel Muhlenberg preach?
2. What speech had inspired Pastor Muhlenberg about a year earlier?
3. What section of Scripture did he preach on that day?
4. What did he do that suprised his congregation?
5. How many men from his congregation joined him that day?
6. How many men joined him to become the 8th Virginia Regiment?
7. Tell of some of the exploits in which he and his men were involved.
8. How did Muhlenberg's enthusiasm influence the men in his congregation?
9. How can enthusiasm for the right things be used to accomplish much good?
10. Think of a way you could be enthusiastic to inspire others to do good for the Lord.
11. How could enthusiasm to be used in your home to help others to cheerfully manage everyday tasks?

There is a time for all things, a time to preach and a time to pray, but those times have passed away. There is a time to fight, and that time has now come.

— General John Peter Muhlenberg

Flexibility

Definition

Cheerfully being willing to change
my plans when circumstances
beyond my control require it

Memory Verse

Be anxious for nothing; but in everything
by prayer and supplication with thanksgiving,
let your requests be made known unto God.
And the peace of God,
which passeth all understanding,
shall guard your hearts and minds
through Christ Jesus.

Philippians 4:6-7

Caesar Rodney's Ride

The Revolutionary War • Delaware • July, 1776

July was a time for storms. For uprisings. For revolts. Caesar Rodney, Brigadier General of the Delaware Militia tore open the note. His eyes quickly scanned the message. It was from the Continental Congress in Philadelphia. His friend, Delaware delegate Thomas McKean, was deadlocked with George Read on the vote for independence. As Delaware delegate, only the absent Caesar Rodney could break the tie. Would Delaware go to war against Britain or not? The general hesitated.

It was late afternoon. He was tired after a long day spent crushing a Loyalist revolt in Sussex Country. The countryside was a nest of Loyalist vipers crawling under his feet. After the hunt, the Loyalists scattered into the swamps. Some boarded British ships and sailed away. Others lay low, masking their hostility. So far, nine colonies had voted for independence, two against, while New York had abstained. Delaware was stuck with a split ballot. And his vote alone could alter the future of the state and the coming war. That decided it. He was a delegate and it was his duty to vote. But the voting began early tomorrow morning in Philadelphia, eighty miles away. Without stopping to eat or change his clothes, he saddled up his horse.

It began to rain. Caesar Rodney pulled on boots and spurs. He knotted a cape over his shoulders. He looked like a crane, hunched over the horse's neck, slender as a reed, a head no bigger than a large apple swaying gently on his thin neck. Even Molly Vining, the woman he loved many years ago, had never called him handsome. But his face had fire, sense, humor. He galloped out onto the Delaware road. The rain came harder, spattering his shoulders like bullets and churning the dusty summer road to a lake of mud. If this kept up, it would be a challenge to get to Philadelphia in time.

Rodney could not remember a time when he had not been in some public office. Was it twenty-eight years? Twenty-nine? At forty-eight, the years tended to pile in on him, mingling his roles and functions. Registrar of wills, recorder of deeds, clerk of the orphan's court, High Sheriff of Kent County, representative in the colonial legislature at Newcastle, member of the Stamp Act Congress, brigadier general of the Delaware militia and Speaker for the state assembly. He had never married. After Molly Vining rejected him and ran off with a vicar, he had never found anybody else to care for him. He buried himself in his work. His country became wife, family and child to him. Perhaps it had always been that way.

General Caesar Rodney

Forty miles. The rain lashed his face, slanting off the brim of his hat. Lightning split the sky. Thunder crashed against the trees overhead. He could hardly see the road in front of him, swirling with mud and water. July was the time for storms. For war. He planned his speech to the Virginia delegates. They always looked down their noses at the smaller states as if to say, "We'll take care of you. We are the rock on which Independence rests."

Despite the rain running down his neck, Rodney tingled all over. "Let Virginia be of good cheer. . . Yes, that was the way to put it. She has a friend in need. Delaware will take her under its protection and insure her safety."

Seventy miles. His thighs ached from the saddle. He was a good horseman, but he had never ridden eighty miles in a storm. The horse staggered; he stopped to change it for another. He could feel the night spinning, turning over into the next day. July 2, 1776. Through the rain he could see the sparse, flickering lights of Philadelphia. Almost all the city lay in grey darkness, waiting for what the morning might bring. Peace or war. In the hall of the Continental Congress, only the delegates were awake. Sitting over candles burned down to nubs, they hotly argued the issue of independence. New York still refused to cast a ballot. Thomas McKean stared down George Read. Neither would budge an inch. The real voting was due to begin any moment now.

Suddenly, there was a clatter of spurs in the hall. Heads swiveled towards the entrance. Tall, soaking wet, and bringing with him the smell of the rain, Caesar Rodney stood in the doorway. He was ready to vote. The ballot he cast that day thrust Delaware decisively into the war and gave Congress the unanimous vote it had been waiting for. He was tired. But not too tired to puncture the egos of the Virginia delegates. Turning towards them, General Rodney said loudly: "Let Virginia be of good cheer . . . Delaware will take her under its protection."

Because Caesar Rodney showed flexibility, he was able to cheerfully change his plans at a moment's notice and ride eighty miles out of his way to cast his vote for independence.

Questions

1. Caesar Rodney himself was suffering from skin cancer and feeling rather ill when he returned home that night. How did he demonstrate flexibility when he received the message upon returning home?
2. Why was his vote so important?
3. How did his vote cast that day affect you today?
4. What hardships did Caesar Rodney endure to get there on time?
5. What other character qualities did he demonstrate besides flexibility?
6. Again, we have a demonstration of the sacrifice of one person affecting an entire world! Why is is so important for you to develop the disciplines of godly character into your life? How can your diligence to learn flexibility now make you a more profitable servant for God?
7. Think of an instance where you didn't want to show flexibility recently. Commit to memory the verses Philippians 4:6-7 and bring them to mind the next time you are tempted to be selfish instead of flexible.

*That these United Colonies are,
and of right ought to be, free and
independent States, that they are
absolved from all allegiance to the
British Crown, and that all political
connection between them and the
State of Great Britain is, and ought
to be, totally dissolved.*

— *Declaration of Independence*

Forgiveness

Definition

Picturing how Jesus died on the cross
for my sins so that God's love can flow
through me to others who have wronged me

Memory Verse

Forbearing one another,
and forgiving one another,
if any man have a quarrel against any:
even as Christ forgave you, so also do ye.

Colossians 3:13

Angel's Wings

World War II • Japan • 1941–1945

He heard the sound of planes before he saw them. At 7:49 on the morning of Sunday, December 7, 1941, Japanese planes led by 39-year-old flying ace **Mitsuo Fuchida,** honed in on Pearl Harbor, Hawaii, through the mists. Fuchida, sporting a small black mustache, felt his heart squeeze with pride. He was not a *kamikaze*—Japanese pilots who chose to go down with their planes. Selected by the government to fly this special mission and with 49 bombers under his command, Fuchida knew little of the men he had been sent to destroy. Only that they were enemies. Glancing out of the pilot's window to his left, he saw 51 dive bombers cruising at an altitude of 200 meters above him. Slightly below him to his right, droned 40 torpedo planes in shark formation. At his back, covering the attack, hovered an additional 43 bombers. Visibility cleared over Honolulu.

In the port waters, heavy with the dark silhouettes of battleships and cruisers, the shark goddess Kaahupahau lurked, slashing her tail in the shallow green depths. As he gave the signal to attack, bombs dropped on Ford Island, Hickam Field, and Wheeler Field, blowing heavy bombers stationed on the ground into the air. Peering through binoculars, Fuchida ordered all ten of his squadrons to fall into a single line of attack. Just then, the anti-aircraft aboard the nearer ships burst into orange flame. They were shooting back. Fuchida's plane shook with the impact. Without hesitation, he dropped his bombs. Far below, the ships *Utah, The West Virginia* and *Nevada* bunched like sitting ducks. The bombs looked like seeds falling. Then there came a white flash and a jolting explosion. Waterspouts from the bay shot into the air. Red-

Japanese planes attach Pearl Harbor

black smoke ballooned like mushroom clouds 1,000 feet into the air, darkening the sky. Four or five ships were on fire. Others listed, huge gashes torn in their sides as water poured in and wounded seaman thrashed, trying to keep from drowning in holds rapidly filling with water. Some of the American pilots tried desperately to get their planes off the ground. Fuchida watched in admiration as they flew in, trying to get a hit at the Japanese aircraft. An hour after the first attack, the second wave of planes swooped in. The entire seaplane base was a mass of flames. Fuchida, noting the damage, turned his bomber back towards Admiral Nagumo's fleet, where he urged a second attack. The Admiral, ignoring his suggestion, hoisted the flag of the Rising Sun and sailed out to sea, leaving Fuchida to face the Emperor's questions as to the attack on Pearl Harbor.

Sergeant Jacob DeShazer, stationed on KP duty at the US Air Force base in Oregon, idly listened as hip-wriggling jazz tunes and snatches of news about the War in Europe filled the kitchen while he peeled potatoes. Suddenly, he stiffened. Japanese planes had attacked the American Pacific Fleet at Pearl Harbor.

His light eyes blazing and his mouth compressed into a thin line, he listened, stunned, as the casualty list mounted. Eight battleships and ten vessels out of 92 ships had been crippled or sunk; 170 planes went up in flames and roiling black smoke, and 3,700 US officers, soldiers and military personal had died in the three-hour attack. DeShazer threw a potato against the wall, shouting: "The Japs are going to have to pay for this!" Rage swelled

Sergeant Jacob DeShazer

in his chest, making it hard to breathe. He had to personally kill as many Japanese as possible. Coming on the heels of the Bataan Death March—where 10,000 American troops captured by Japanese troops at Corregidor died of starvation and physical abuse—this was the limit. Men, women and children—nothing was sacred to him anymore since the Japanese bombed Pearl Harbor.

In the days and weeks that followed, all he could think of, all he could talk about was a "payback." Reassigned to an air base in South Carolina, he along with fellow members of the 17th Bomb Group, volunteered for active duty with a newly-formed unit called "Doolittle's Raiders." Commanded by Lieutenant Colonel Jimmy Doolittle, the Raiders practiced carrier-deck takeoffs, low-level night flying, bombing at low altitude and over water navigation. At the close of these extensive flying exercises, sixteen crews, including Jacob DeShazer, boarded the carrier *Hornet* for Japan. No one knew exactly the nature of their mission when Colonel Doolittle gathered the crew together in the empty mess hall. The plan, as he put it simply, was "to bomb Japan."

Launched off the deck of naval carriers, 13 bombers would drop their four bombs apiece on Tokyo. The rest of them would hit Nagoya, Osaka, and Kobe. Because of internal security measures, no bomber had ever gotten within 500 miles of Tokyo. Since their orders required them to ditch their planes in small fields in China after using up all their fuel for the flight over Japan, the carrier-launched bombers would not be able to return to their carrier once they landed. It was a one-way trip.

Doolittle's famous raid began on April 18, 1942. Japanese intelligence was unable to locate them by radar until two days before they hit. While the American bomber formation headed westward, the Japanese were confident that Tokyo was safe. The Japanese people basked in the golden spring sunshine and the scent of cherry blossoms. No one worried.

Meanwhile, aboard the planes en route to Tokyo, crewmen chalked up slogans like "I don't want to set the world on fire, just Tokyo," or "You'll get a BANG out of this!" Others tied imperial Japanese medals to the bombs ready to blast off. The fun ended when Doolittle announced that Task Force 16 had arrived a day ahead of schedule. They were going in. Doolittle was prepared to take the ultimate risk, but he didn't want to end up a prisoner: "I'm going to bail my crew out and then dive it, full throttle into any target I can find where the crash will do the most good. I'm forty-six years old and have lived a full life."

B25 lifts off from USS Hornet on Doolittle Raid

Detecting two enemy ships by radar while still 700 miles from their goal, the men spent anxious minutes till the "All Clear" signal sounded. The sky was grey with clouds. At dawn, Doolittle climbed aboard the bomber, roaring the engines till they threatened to catch fire. Jacob DeShazer was the bombardier of B-25#16, lovingly called the "Bat." Commanded by Lieutenant William G. Farrow, it was the last of the sixteen B-25s to launch from the *USS Hornet.* At first, it seemed as if they would never get off the ground. Those out still on deck watched tensely, knowing that if Doolittle couldn't make it, even with the help of a stiff wind, they wouldn't make it either. DeShazer's plane struggled to get off the deck, skimmed the water and then angled up towards the sky, following the bomber formation.

It was 7:20 AM, just twenty-nine minutes short of the time that Mitsuo Fuchida bombed Pearl Harbor. They approached the green coast of Japan. As they flew inland, they scanned the ground close to see the flash of officers' swords at military bases and people scuttling about like ants. The Japanese Prime Minister, troubled by vague rumors of an enemy force on the island, decided to visit the Mito Aviation School by plane anyway. Just as they taxied onto the runway, a "weird-looking," two-engine craft came into sight. It zoomed past them without firing a shot. As it winged out of sight, the Prime Minister's secretary realized that there had been something strange about the face looking out the pilot's window. It was American.

At 12: 30 PM, Doolittle's Raiders were directly over their target. The Japanese below, out all day for an air-raid drill, thought that this was a sequel to the drilling festivities. Black-haired schoolchildren, mistaking the circular red, white and blue markings for the spot of the Japanese Rising Sun, waved back cheerfully. No on fired at them. Then the bombs came, falling on the streets in explosions of fire, dust and brickwork. Circling the Emperor's palace and the hospital grounds, the Raiders dove aside and roared off.

Fuel gauges began to run dangerously low. Straining to reach the Asian mainland, Jacob DeShazer and his B-25 flew straight into the black heart of a storm. They floated in darkness, unable to see either the horizon or the ground below. The rushing 125-mile tail-wind buoyed up the plane, extending the gas' lifetime for a few hours. At midnight, as fuel ran out and a thick fog closed in, preventing any hope of landing, Doolittle's Raiders began to bail out. Parachutes opened with a snap. Deep in the Chinese interior,

DeShazer's plane kept going longer than anyone else's. As it faltered, a broad yellow band slipped into sight in the swirling dusk. It was a bend of the Yangtze River—held by the Japanese. Fastening his parachute straps, DeShazer jumped into darkness. The pilot died when he reached the ground. But DeShazer floated for miles in his parachute and crashed.

Doolittle Raiders in China after crash-landing

The force of the impact stunned him. He lay in a tangle of parachute ropes and silk, too numb to feel the sharp twinge of his fractured ribs. When he opened his eyes, he didn't know where he was. Glancing around him in the darkness, he saw it was a Japanese graveyard. Warm April rain poured down, soaking his uniform. Slashing the parachute into bits, he held a piece of silk over his head to keep the rain off. Then he began to walk.

There was nothing here but muddy rice fields, slipping in troughs of water, catching at crumbly stalks of rice that came away under his grasp. He stumbled and fell. As he opened his eyes, he knew he had to get back to his crew. Staggering blindly along the mud-covered road, he walked straight into a Japanese patrol. The next thing he knew, guards crammed him into a tiny cell surrounded by wooden bars, along with other hapless members of Doolittle's mission. He hadn't eaten all day. Blindfolded and stripped of personal items, he was forced to use a wooden box as a latrine.

The Japanese interrogated him for hours, taunting him with stories about how the Japanese had bombed and taken possession of American territory. They laughed in his face. But he refused to talk. Within the next few hours, he was blindfolded, handcuffed and deprived of blankets. Cameramen took snapshots as the guards herded them like animals into trucks.

Arriving in Shanghai, blindfolded, handcuffed, and under death sentence, the captives shambled towards the notorious "Bridge House." After sixty days of punishment and deprivation, the men could hardly move. Their shoulder-blades and ribs stuck out painfully. Crammed into a 12 by 15-foot cell with fifteen Chinese prisoners, each man received a small cup of boiled rice for breakfast, four ounces of bread for lunch and four ounces for dinner. The guards gave the Americans only two quarts of water per day. Bedbugs, rats, and lice swarmed over their bodies in the roasting heat. An additional torture the guards invented was to force them to sit up straight all day. If they even leaned back on their elbows, the guards hit them sharply with bamboo sticks.

One day during this punishment, one of the officers passed out. Some of the men had dysentery, forcing their comrades to carry them to the bathroom every fifteen minutes. When three of the eight Doolittle men had already succumbed to the firing squad, news came that the Emperor had pardoned the rest of the Raiders who bombed Tokyo—including DeShazer.

Back in his cell, DeShazer's body thrilled with strange joy. He had fully expected death. Instead, he was alive. Even if the war went on for years, he might yet survive. But winter came upon them. The prison was cold as ice, without heat. Some of the enlisted men managed to stay well in spite of it.

Kept on a starvation diet and subjected to brutal beatings, one of the officers, kind and good-humored Lieutenant Robert Meder, became very ill. Soon he was too weak to sit up. Jacob DeShazer could not forget the dying officer's calm face. "He seemed to understand the Bible well. He told me that Jesus Christ is the Lord and coming King; that Jesus is God's Son and that God expects the nations and people to recognize Jesus as Lord and Savior. He said that the war would last until Jesus Christ caused it to stop."

Crouching beside him as he grew weaker, Jacob DeShazer could not understand what he meant. Looking up at DeShazer, Lieutenant Meder pressed his hand against his chest. His heart hurt, he muttered. Then on December 1, 1943, after almost 20 months of captivity, the man Jacob had learned so much from died of starvation. DeShazer knew nothing until heard the sound of hammering next morning. Crawling to look out into the prison yard, he saw the Japanese guards knocking together a coffin. On December 2, Jacob went alone to see Lieutenant Meder's body. He lay in a handmade box with a wreath of flowers, his hands clasping a Bible.

When someone reported the officer's death to the authorities, policy towards the prisoners began to change. The Japanese captain of the prison, knowing Lieutenant Meder had starved to death, asked the prisoners if they wanted anything. Jacob DeShazer surprised himself by asking for a Bible. Finally, in May 1944, he received one. He could only have it, the guard insisted, for three weeks.

As he flipped through its leaves, DeShazer thought of gentle Lieutenant Meder. Meder never hated anyone, even when he lay dying. How was that possible? He knew something of this mysterious Christian love. Across Europe, Africa, and Asia, men killed each other. Civilians died. Americans hated Japanese and Japanese hated Americans. DeShazer's hands trembled with eagerness to find the answer. Chapter after chapter, the words gripped his heart, swallowed him. He read about man's fall from grace and how a Redeemer came to save mankind and restore him to fellowship with God.

By June 8, 1944, he had plunged into the depths of 1 John, and read: "If we confess our sins, He is faithful and just to forgive us our sins and cleanse us from all unrighteousness." Something woke in Jacob DeShazer. Light flooded his soul. Reading the passages about the crucifixion, he saw how Christ suffered. He, too, was beaten, mocked, and tortured, yet he prayed "Father, forgive them." Bowing his head, Jacob asked God to forgive his enemies as well. He asked for grace to love the men who had killed Lieutenant Meder and locked him in solitary confinement for thirty-four months. Standing at the bars of his cell as water blew in from a tropical rainstorm, Jacob received the rain as his baptism into the faith.

A year passed. Still starved and treated harshly, DeShazer found himself changing despite the fact that his circumstances remained the same. He learned a few words of Japanese. He spoke gently to his guards whenever possible. Soon the men started to treat him with the same kindness. Another hot summer passed into bitter cold autumn. Snow covered the ground, increasing the frailty of the men who had undergone these conditions for almost 40 months.

Suddenly, Spring, 1945, blossomed and American paratroopers dropped from the sky into the Peiping prison compound. Grey and haggard, the men staggered out of prison into blinding sunlight. The war was over—just as Lieutenant Meder had said it would be. As soon as Jacob's plane landed in Washington, D.C., he telephoned his parents on the farm in Oregon. For almost three years, they had no idea if he was alive or dead, only that he was a prisoner. With a cropped prison haircut, sunken cheeks and too-bright eyes, he was a walking ghost of the young man who left them to fly the Doolittle Raid in 1942. Now he told his mother, who had

DeShazer (left) being released from Peiping prison compound, 1945

Jacob DeShazer preaching in Japan

prayed daily for his salvation, he wanted to go back as a missionary to Japan.

In 1945, the United States government awarded DeShazer both the Distinguished Flying Cross and the Purple Heart for his participation in the Doolittle Raid. Three years later, with his wife Florence and a degree from the Christian Seattle Pacific College, Jacob DeShazer set foot on the land he had once come to destroy.

On the Yokohama docks, reporters clamored for interviews. How could a man tortured by the Japanese possibly love his captors? Over the next few months, DeShazer spoke in over 200 different places. People wrote to him, thanking him for sharing the gospel. They cried as he spoke of his months as a POW, unable to comprehend the love God had given him in spite of his circumstances. One girl, whose lover had died in DeShazer's raid on Nagoya, learned he had come to town and determined to kill him. She slipped into the service where DeShazer was speaking, waiting for her opportunity. But forgiveness pervaded DeShazer's messages. The forgiveness of God to man and the forgiveness of men to each other. As she listened, the spirit of God overpowered her, and she broke down and gave her life to Christ.

At a service held in the a theatre in Osaka, Japan, where bombs had fallen in 1942, two of DeShazer's former prison guards pushed forward and asked to receive Christ. Over the next few years, Jacob DeShazer had an opportunity to share the gospel with the Emperor's brother, Prince Takamatsu, and thank the Japanese Emperor for sparing his life. With tears in his eyes, he even led Captain Kato, the man who gave him his first Bible in Nanking Prison, to the Lord.

Then in 1950, the incredible happened. The worlds of Jacob DeShazer and Commander Mitsuo Fuchida collided. Following the attack on Pearl Harbor, Fuchida's life was spared in miraculous ways. The day before the bomb fell on Hiroshima, Fuchida received an unexpected long-distance call from Navy Headquarters, demanding his return to Tokyo. Twenty-four hours later, the A-Bomb obliterated Hiroshima.

Commander Mitsuo Fuchida

When the war ended, it took with it Fuchida's entire military career. Discouraged, he went back to his home village near bombed-out Osaka to take up rice farming. As the years passed, he grew older and sadder. Then the war trials came. Summoned to testify before General Douglas MacArthur in Tokyo, he found that no one accused him of war crimes. But the trials investigating Japanese atrocities against POWs, reminded him of his lost life, Japan's disgrace in international eyes and his current reduced status. One day, as the former officer slowly got off the train in Shibuya Station, he saw an American standing on the corner, passing out free literature. As the captain passed by, Jacob DeShazer handed him a pamphlet titled *I Was a Prisoner of Japan.* Great.

Another American who capitalized on the war trials. Just what he needed, when he was harassed with inquiries dealing with these very issues. With nothing else to do, he politely took a leaflet and stuffed it in his pocket. Maybe he'd read it later. At home, he took it out and glanced through it. In it, he read an amazing story, the kind of story he hadn't even dreamed about. The story spoke of forgiveness, peace, and love. Fuchida's heart yearned to taste that kind of love. As a child, he had honored his parents according to tradition. In the imperial service of Japan, he did his duty unflinchingly. But no one had ever spoken of love like this.

He looked the tract over carefully. So, the American had found this love and peace in the Bible. As a devout Shintoist and military man, Fuchida had never read the Bible. He went out and bought one. Alone, he devoured the scriptures for weeks as DeShazer had done years before. The man who had bombed Pearl Harbor without flinching now found himself gripped unspeakably by the story of the Crucifixion. At that moment, he seemed to see Jesus for the first time. He saw not only his crimes against humanity, but his sins against God.

Mitsuo Fuchida and Jacob DeShazer preached the gospel together throughout Japan after World War II.

"I was impressed that I was certainly one of those for whom Jesus had prayed. The many men I had killed had been slaughtered in the name of patriotism, for I did not understand the love which Christ wishes to implant within every heart."

On April 12, 1950, Commander Fuchida gave his life over to Christ. His old comrades could not believe their eyes. Again and again, they tried to dissuade him from this "crazy idea," his new-found faith. They mocked him, called him a puppet trying to impress the Americans. Newspaper headlines screamed: "Pearl Harbor Hero Converts to Christianity!" But Fuchida did not care. He had found something worth more than medals and heroism.

Shortly afterwards, Captain Fuchida met Jacob DeShazer. The boy determined to "make the Japs pay" now embraced the lead pilot who dropped bombs on Pearl Harbor. Together, the American

POW and the Japanese captain, stiff from war wounds, toured the country preaching the gospel. Following World War II, the Emperor Hirohito announced to the world that he was not God, for the first time in a thousand years of Japanese history. This admission helped open the way for the gospel to spread in the country of Japan. For Jacob DeShazer and Captain Fuchida, they had come home on angel's wings from the winds of war.

Jacob DeShazer showed forgiveness to his enemies. By returning to the place of his imprisonment with a new heart, he was able to show the people he once hated, the love of Christ.

Questions

1. What was Jake DeShazer's attitude to the Japanese on hearing of the bombing of Pearl Harbor?
2. Why was Jake DeShazer so eager to enter the service?
3. What part did Jake play in the bombing of Japan?
4. Describe DeShazer's treatment by the Japanese after his capture.
5. How long was DeShazer held and mistreated by the Japanese?
6. Tell how another prisoner's reliance on Jesus Christ impacted Jake's life.
7. Explain how Jake came to give his life to Christ.
8. How did his new conversion affect the way he lived while in prison?
9. What did Jake do when released from prison?
10. What amazing evidence do you see in Jake DeShazer's life that he internalized the true meaning of forgiveness?
11. How was God specifically able to use Jake's testimony of forgiveness in the lives of others? Tell of others who then received Christ's forgiveness as a result.
12. How do you see the hand of God in the events that occurred concerning Mitsuo Fuchida?
13. Think of anyone in your life that you have struggled to forgive. Remember God is still working and wants to bring about miraculous situations in your life as well. List anyone you have trouble forgiving and make a plan to correct the situa-

tion. Ask God for the grace you need to experience true forgiveness toward others in your life and ask God to use you for His greater purposes as he used Jake DeShazer in this amazing story of forgiveness.

NOTE: As an elderly man, Jake DeShazer developed Altzheimer's disease. As his memory began to fail him, he remembered preaching to the lost in Japan, but forgot he was ever tortured by them.

Generosity

Definition

Giving unselfishly to the needs of others

Memory Verse

Give, and it shall be given unto you;
good measure, pressed down, and shaken
together, and running over, shall men give into
your bosom. For with the same measure that ye
mete withal it shall be measured to you again.

Luke 6:38

Dead Money

The Revolutionary War • Philadelphia • December, 1776

"The Hessians are coming!" On an icy December day in 1776, a rider burst into the calm session of the First Continental Congress. General Howe, massing 30,000 troops, had attacked Cooper's Ferry opposite Philadelphia with an army of kilted Highlanders and fierce, pig-tailed German dragoons.

Forty-two-year-old Robert Morris, head of a rich merchant firm and signer of the Declaration of Independence, was on his feet, his massive and dominating body squeezed into a dark silk suit. His square face, with its powdered grey hair tied loosely behind, looked grim. While the members rushed home to pack for Congress' retreat to Baltimore, John Hancock, with a price on his head, turned to three delegates and gave them last words of advice. Robert Morris, with Clymer and Walton, would remain in the blighted city to carry on the work of Congress.

Now one day later, Morris was alone. Standing in the empty Congress hall, Morris watched the two men leave and hurriedly cross the street. Moving to a table covered with papers, inkwells and feather pens, he picked up an authorized bill. With it, he must borrow $10,000 for the defense of the Marine Committee. His wide, sensitive mouth tightened. Now to see to the barricades across the Delaware.

From where he stood, he could not see the broad grey expanse of water, perfect for shunting a fleet of warships across to fire on Philadelphia. With a dark cape thrown over his shoulders, Morris emerged into the street. Beds, furniture, and trunks teetered on the sidewalks as panic escalated in the city. Only the Quakers were staying—and Robert Morris.

Robert Morris

For three months, Robert Morris was to become Congress. He served as chairman of the Finance Committee. He sent daily reports to the President of Congress. As head executive, he authorized loans, signed documents, served as intelligence officer, warden of the port of Philadelphia and directed the construction of the first Continental Navy. His grey hair blowing in the wind, he strode through the shipyards urging men to work faster, shoring up defenses and inspecting fire-rafts along the Delaware, forcing the pace on shipbuilding and repair. Day and night he knocked on doors, borrowing money for the cause. Inflation rose sharply, creating dead money by the bushel, while housewives fed fires and papered their walls with Continental currency.

As new demands rained down on him, Morris put the dying money to work. "There are no carpenters." "The crews will desert unless they are paid." Again, he dug into his own pocket to shell out wrinkled Continental bills. George Washington needed 150 pounds to pay his spies; the Marine Committee was deep in debt. Morris borrowed in silver, repaying in gold.

Then at sundown on December 31, 1776, a messenger galloped up to Morris' door. He brought an urgent letter from General Washington at Trenton. He needed $50,000 immediately. Howe intended to cross the Delaware and capture Philadelphia as soon as the river froze over. Without pay and with their enlistment time up, Washington's ragged troops were on the brink of desertion. By sheer willpower and the promise of $10.00 bonuses, Washington had managed to keep his men from deserting for another six weeks. But he was not sure he could hold them that long.

Could Morris get the money? Morris tossed all night, his mind racing. This was the biggest demand yet. The treasury was empty. He had already given all of his own money to Congress. But he never dreamed of refusing Washington. Early morning sunlight filtered through the windows. Robert Morris dressed quickly. As New Year's Day broke over the city, Morris set off towards the Quaker residential section. He rang the doorbell at his friend Abel James' house. "What news so early, Robert?" The Quaker looked startled.

"The news is this, my friend." Morris' cheeks looked ruddy with cold. "Washington needs a sum of money and I must send it to him immediately. I would like you to lend me $50,000."

Abel James hesitated. "But what is thy security, Robert, for this large sum?"

Morris stared straight into his friend's eyes. "My word is my honor."

"Thee shall have it," the Quaker replied quietly.

Pen in hand, Morris wrote to Washington: "Sir, I am up very early this morning to dispatch a supply of $50,000 to your Excellency." The troops reenlisted. On the night of January 3, 1777, Washington's troops crossed the Delaware and defeated the British at Princeton, saving Philadelphia.

Robert Morris continued to serve till the end of the war. His generosity and skill in finance enabled him to rescue his country at a crucial time in history, earning him the title "Financier of the American Revolution."

Questions

1. What caused people to flee the Philadelphia? Why did Robert Morris stay?
2. What earned Robert Morris the title of Financier of the Revolution?
3. What functions did Robert Morris perform while in Philadelphia?
4. Who depended upon him to raise money to supply the army?
5. What was the special need that arose on December 31, 1776?
6. How much money did Gen. Washington need?
7. How did Robert Morris obtain the money?
8. For what purpose was the money used?
9. What campaign was won with the use of that money? What effect did this have on freedom you now enjoy?
10. How did Robert Morris exemplify generosity?
11. What opportunities do you have to practice generosity in your home? in your church? in your community?

In accepting the office bestowed on me (Superintendent of Finance), I sacrifice much of my interest, my ease, my domestic enjoyments, and internal tranquility. If I know my own heart, I make these sacrifices with a disinterested view to the service of my country. I am ready to go still further; and the United States may command every thing I have, except my integrity, and the loss of that would effectually disable me from serving them more.

— *Robert Morris*

Gentleness

Definition

Responding to others in a kind,
understanding manner

Memory Verse

And the servant of the Lord
must not strive;
but be gentle unto all men,
apt to teach, patient.

2 Timothy 2:24

After the Battle

The Civil War • Washington, D.C. • September, 1862

Washington: September, 1862. His steps slowed as he entered the Navy yard. The sinking sun glinted off the iron hulks of ships lying belly-deep in the Anacostia River, on the yellow curls of wood shavings under his feet. Near the Eastern Market on Pennsylvania Avenue and 9th Street, the grim, dirty windows of the naval hospital loomed up before him like a brick prison. Leaves were beginning to fall somewhere in the city—crimson, golden, brown. How many hospitals had he visited today? Thirty? Forty? After walking the halls of Georgetown University Hospital at dawn, he had lost count. There were hospitals in homes, hotels, schools and churches, on Capitol Hill, in the Patent Office, the Armory Square building and Camp Alexander, even in wooden shacks. A city of 75,000 civilians found 50,000 wounded crowding their doors. Moving from east to west, he had tried to visit every hospital in the city.

They were waiting for him as he walked up the broad steps.

"This way, Mr. President."

He never let them announce his name. He appeared in the high-ceilinged ward, moving slowly, his long black frock coat swaying against his knees. They lay in rows, without words, their eyes turned towards him. He grasped their hands, his tenor voice a blend of Indiana and Kentucky bluegrass. They are children. Some of them almost babies. Their shirts were open at the throat, their eyes fixed on him.

"My brave boys. Some had old eyes, eyes that had seen Union victories and defeats at Shiloh, Bull Run, Antietam. God, this war. What are we doing? How can we love and hate at the same time? Why are we fighting? For what?"

He knew the answer. So that thousands of men, women and children could live free. So that the freedom they died for would not be in vain. But looking at their faces, he forgot them—forgot that the boys lying here in their grey coats were enemies.

"Do they know that I don't hate them? That I never wanted this war? But they will say I did, that I pushed the country into this."

He moved along, touching their bedclothes, saying a few words, trying to infuse his strength into them as he passed. "I can't stay, boys," he said. "I hope you are all comfortable and getting along nicely here."

The face stared up at him from the cot. A thin, white face. Almost a child. He could see bandaged limbs, the loose grey Confederate coat, the body making barely a ripple under the blanket. "What are you doing here? Why did they let you go?" The eyes looked up at him without fear. Trusting. He paused by the cot for a moment, closed his eyes in prayer. "What more can I do?"

His carriage was waiting in the yard, black as a funeral hearse. Nearby came the sound of lapping water. He put his square-toed boot on the step, reached to pull himself in. Suddenly, a woman's voice called out. He looked back. A nurse came running towards him.

"Please, Mr. Lincoln. The dying Confederate boy wants to see you again."

It was time to go home, now. Home to Mary's dark face, stacks of papers from the War Office, critical newsmen and gloomy cabinet ministers, then dinner, lying on the carpet while the children hauled a goat and cart through the library. Weariness sucked at his bones, weighing him down. But he was in the race. He could not give up when so many depended on him. A smile creased his tired face, lighting up the dark hollows of his eyes. It shone softly through the gaunt cheeks like a light through an alabaster vase.

"I'll go."

They were lighting the lamps as he entered the ward. The face was a little greyer now, the shadows bluish.

"What can I do for you?"

He saw the pleading in the boy's eyes.

"I am so lonely and friendless, Mr. Lincoln"—the voice came in a whisper—"and I am hoping that you can tell me what my mother would want me to say and do now."

Old Naval Hospital, Washington, D.C.

If only those big, gnarled hands, scarred from years of chopping forests, could reach out and envelop all these boys. His boys. "My concern is not whether God is on our side," he once said. "My greatest concern is to be on God's side, for God is always right."

He knelt in the yellow lamplight. "Yes, my boy. I know exactly what your mother would want you to say and do. And I am glad that you sent for me to come back to you. I can pray, now. I have learned to pray since this war, since my boy Willie died.

"Now, as I kneel here, please repeat the words after me." The sun dropped lower in the western sky, gilding the high windowpanes and falling on the young face. He cradled the boy's head on his arm, easing those last moments with his own strength as he whispered the words.

Now I lay me down to sleep:
I pray the Lord my soul to keep.
If I should die before I wake,
I pray the Lord my soul to take.
And this I ask for Jesus' sake.

President Abraham Lincoln

It was a simple prayer, one that his mother had taught him. A prayer spoken between friends. A nighttime prayer to end the day.

Abraham Lincoln showed gentleness towards the captured Confederate soldier. Rather than seeing just another prisoner, Lincoln saw a lonely boy who needed prayer and assurance as he prepared for his final journey.

Questions

1. What was President Lincoln doing?
2. How many wounded were the townspeople caring for?
3. Why did he go back into the hospital after leaving?
4. How did he show gentleness to the young Confederate boy?
5. What did the boy request?
6. How did Lincoln answer him?
7. To whom do you have the opportunity to show gentleness?

Gratefulness

Definition

Realizing God has given me all I need
and being appreciative to God and others

Memory Verse

Giving thanks always for all things unto
God and the Father in the name of
our Lord Jesus Christ.

Ephesians 5:20

Brown Eyes

India • March, 1901–January 1951

County Down, Northern Ireland: 1872. She closed her eyes with a wish. God lived somewhere in the star-sprinkled sky above the green fields in the little village of Millisle. She dreamed of her mother's china blue eyes. All of her brothers and sisters had eyes the color of the sky over Ireland on a clear day. But Amy Carmichael's eyes were a dark, muddy brown. Her mother had told her that God could do anything. Maybe he could even change the color of her eyes. As light streamed through the window, Amy jumped out of bed and ran across to the mirror. She lugged a footstool against the dresser and climbed up. Then she peered into the mirror. Disappointment almost choked her.

Her eyes were still brown.

At that moment, she knew that she had to accept with gratitude the fact that God had made her different.

March, 1901: A slim, dark-eyed woman dressed in a loose, flowing *sari,* her skin dyed brown by coffee, padded through the dusty streets of southern India. Above Amy's head loomed a temple of the Hindu goddess Kali. She stared into its ageless, carved eyes. The thin, cruel lips narrowed. Kali danced towards the twisting, pyramid rooftop covered with hundreds of unnamed gods and goddesses. Her eight dancing arms and legs looked black in the hot sunlight.

But inside it was dark and cool. Priests, with sacred red dots painted on their foreheads, moved about the interior like cats. Their white kilts swished with each step. They were feeding the huge black idol that stood in a niche in the far wall. Small, brown-

Amy Carmichael

skinned girls also tended the idol, black with filth and slim from thousands of worshipers' kisses. The girls belonged to the priests. As soon as they reached the age of seven or eight, they would be "married" to one of the temple gods. Sold into slavery by their starving parents, they faced a bleak and terrifying future.

Amy had just finished her day's work in the village when she heard a cry. A five-year-old girl came running towards her. Screaming temple priests and women with jangling earrings and painted foreheads rushed at her, trying to seize the girl. Amy wrapped her arms around the girl. She did not back down. After a few minutes, the muttering crowd retreated. That night, the girl named Preena, or "Pearl Eyes," told her rescuer things about her life in the temple that made Amy's blood run cold.

Suddenly, Amy's mission to India took on a new focus. She began to steal into Hindu temples after dark. Shaking a girl awake from her pallet, she led her out into the safety of the night. Sometimes the children escaped to her house in the city's suburbs. Girls began to disappear from the temples in such large numbers that her enemies called her the "child-snatcher Amy." Often Hindu priests dragged Amy into court, accusing her as a kidnapper.

Hindu temple

She knew that someone who looked like an Englishwoman could never do the job that God had called her to do. Such a person could stain her skin, but she could never change

Amy with Dalit *girl*

her blue eyes to brown. As a child, she could not understand why God had deprived her of something she wanted so much. But now she knew. In 1887, when she heard Hudson Taylor pour out his heart for China at the Keswick Convention, she felt that God, too, had called her to the East.

Breaking through the caste system was almost impossible. Part of India's culture for thousands of years, the caste system uplifted a few and trampled others in the dust. The *Brahmins,* the priestly caste, stood at the top. Beneath the workers and artisans huddled a group known as the *Dalits,* or the Untouchables. Destined to live and die in poverty, ignorance, and filth because of the caste they were born into, the Untouchables could not find work. They were accused of poisoning wells with their touch. They could not attend school or mix with higher castes. *Dalit* girls faced the worst future of all as forced slaves. Gathering these despised girls around her, Amy taught them that Christ had died for all, not just for a privileged few.

As the number of children grew, Amy, with a few Christian Indian women, began building a haven for these girls. Located in the Tamil Nadu region just 30 miles from the sunny tip of southern India, Dohnavur Fellowship's first mud-walled, thatched buildings swelled into a great missionary compound. Whenever Amy learned of a mistreated girl, she set out along the dusty roads, walking miles on foot to save just one child. She kept a pile of *rupees* on hand, knowing that sometimes she would have to buy a child from its owners. Soon, parents began giving her their unwanted baby girls instead of leaving them to die or selling them for profit.

Dohnavur Fellowship

During the Sepoy Wars of the 1850s, India came under the control of the British Empire. Unlike other British missionaries who wanted to bring the native children up like little English girls, Amy respected the Indian culture. As a result, all of Dohnavur Fellowship's workers wore loose, light Indian dress. They spoke in the Tamil language and gave the children Indian names. Gradually, over a thousand children lived and played and learned at Dohnavur Fellowship. Amy loved all her children, but some became her own special babies. One girl, whose father sold her to the local temple at two months old, she named Jewel. The children, in turn, called Amy "Amma," which meant "mother" in Tamil. For many of them, Amy Carmichael was the only mother they had ever known. In 1918, the first baby boy appeared at Dohnavur. Over the next few years, hundreds of unwanted boys would fill the small village built next to the girls."One can give without loving," Amy declared, "but one cannot love without giving."

"Amma" Amy

Amy Carmichael spent fifty-six years working for the underprivileged children of India. Despite a bad fall that crippled her and kept her bedridden for the last twenty years of her life, Amy wrote thirty-five books and cared for her "Precious Gems" who regarded her as a kind of great, universal mother. She never married, but she had more children than any wife and mother could ever have. When she died at Dohnavur Fellowship at age eighty-three, her children placed a stone bird-bath over her grave. It had only one inscription on it: "Amma."

To an eager young girl who had written her to ask, "What is missionary life like?" Amy Carmichael replied simply: "Missionary life is a chance to die." Her example would later spur Jim and Elisabeth Elliot to Christian service overseas. The girl who prayed for God to change her eyes demonstrated gratefulness by accepting herself as the person God had made.

Questions

1. Why did Amy want blue eyes?
2. What happened once Amy was in India to change her focus on her ministry.?
3. How did Amy come to realize that God had planned for Amy to have brown eyes as part of his master plan for her life?
4. What did Amy focus on teaching her girls she rescued?
5. Tell of the special relationships Amy developed with some of her children.
6. What did Amy say missionary life was like?
7. Who were inspired to become missionaries by Amy's life?
8. How did Amy demonstrate gratefulness in the way God madc her?
9. Do you believe God has wonderful plans for your life? If so, let this inspire you to be grateful to Him for the way he has made you. Think of some things in your life for which you struggle to be grateful. Purpose to begin thanking God whenever you are tempted to be unhappy about it.
10. List people for whom you are grateful. Write them a letter expressing your gratefulness.

Honesty

Definition

Speaking the truth in all situations

Memory Verse

Lie not one to another,
seeing that ye have put off
the old man with his deeds.
Colossians 3:9

One Life to Give

The Revolutionary War • New York • September, 1776

September 21, 1776. He had arrived late at the meeting. Now, Captain Nathan Hale felt Colonel Knowlton's eyes piercing each face in the room, raking his athletic, almost six-foot body, his fair hair and blue eyes. By the end of June, the British had invaded Long Island. General George Washington, driven towards Harlem River, could barely hold his position. He desperately needed a volunteer officer to slip behind the British lines, obtain accurate information and come back again. "We have not been able to obtain the least information as to the enemy's plans," Washington had declared. But today his officers in their blue-and-buff coats kept silent. Captain Hale saw Colonel Knowlton turned to an experienced French non-commissioned officer.

"Will you go?" he asked.

The Frenchman's lilting voice was grim. "I am willing to be shot, but not to be hung."

No one else moved. Captain Hale saw the disappointment in Knowlton's face as he knew that he would have to report his failure to Washington. Suddenly, Hale stepped forward.

"I will undertake it." His face still looked white from his recent sickness.

William Hull, his friend and classmate, tried to talk Hale out of the notion that evening. Don't go, he warned. This is not in your line of duty. Besides, you are too frank and open a person to be a spy and face its dangers. "It will probably lead to a disgraceful death."

But Hale would not go back on his word. "I want to be useful," he said quietly, "and every kind of service necessary to the public good becomes honorable by being necessary. If the exigencies of my country demand a peculiar service, its claims to perform that service are imperious."

Nathan Hale

Those were the last words he spoke before he plunged into the unknown. Hull never saw him again. On September 12, Hale left Sergeant Stephen Hampstead and his servant Asher Wright at camp to take care of his uniform and a few belongings. Then he changed into civilian clothes and rowed across the Hudson to Huntington, or Oyster Bay, not far from Long Island. He carried with him his college diploma, certifying him as a Connecticut schoolmaster visiting New York to look over the schools. By crossing over into British-held territory, he had committed an act of spying punishable by immediate death. At Oyster Bay, he told the boatman to come back for him on October 20. Avoiding detection, he at last reached New York.

Suspicion ran high in the city. The great fire raged through New York City, consuming a quarter of the lower part of Manhattan. British troops, wading through smoke-blackened debris, suspected that American saboteurs had set the fire as Washington retreated towards the northern tip of the island known as Harlem Heights. Others believed that the British themselves set torches to homes and buildings in an attempt to frighten the few patriots still left in the city. The Provincial Council had taken down all the bells used to ring the alarm from the churches. The fire engines refused to work. Sir William Howe, stationed at his headquarters in the Beekman Mansion, began rounding up and jailing more than 200 Americans as suspects.

In Manhattan and Long Island, Hale passed straight through the British army. He made detailed sketches of the fortifications and made notes on their number and various positions.

As Captain Hale sat in a New York tavern one day, his Loyalist cousin Samuel Hale and Major Robert Rogers of the Queen's Rangers glanced across at him. They saw straight through the disguise and recognized him as one of Washington's officers. Introducing himself to Hale, Major Rogers lured him into a friendly chat. He claimed to be a secret patriot himself.

On October 20, Hale returned to the secluded spot at Flushing Bay near Queen's, New York, where he had left the boatman a week before. He gave the signal and the boat swung towards him. Too late, he saw that it came from a British frigate lying offshore and screened by a thick fringe of trees. Rogers and his Rangers caught up with Hale before he could run.

Nathan Hale signaling his boatman

They took him to Beekman Mansion, standing on a rise at the head of Turtle Bay, where Howe waited for them. Inside the house, the British searched Hale thoroughly. They found the maps, sketches, and incriminating notes—written in Latin—hidden in the soles of his shoes.Hale did not try to dodge. He admitted his name and rank. According to eighteenth-century protocol, the military leaders of both sides considered spies as illegal combatants worthy of death. There was no trial. Howe gave orders to hang him next morning.

Hale spent the night of October 21 in a glass-sided greenhouse on the property, in the hands of the brutal Provost-Major, William Cunningham. As night wore away towards dawn, Hale begged Cunningham for a Bible. The request was denied. A little later, the captain asked to speak to a clergyman. Again, Cunningham turned him down. Early the next morning, Captain Montresor, an English officer stationed nearby, asked permission to let the American captain sit with him in his tent while making his final preparations. On entering, Hale asked for paper, quills and ink.

Montresor gave them gladly. Captain Hale sat down and wrote two letters, one to his mother and one to a brother officer. But the letters never arrived. Cunningham, seizing them from the prisoner, destroyed them on the spot. He didn't want the rebels to know that one of their men could die with "such firmness."

The execution of Captain Hale

The final march began. Hale walked under guard along the Post Road till they came to the Artillery Park between Rutger's orchard and the Dove Tavern. Bill Richmond, a 13-year-old slave freed by the British, threw the rope over the branch of an apple tree and tightened the knot. With the noose fastened and dangling behind him, Nathan Hale lifted his head.

"I only regret that I have but one life to give for my country."

Several of the British officers watching later noted that the captain had a gentle dignity about him. His face was calm, his voice firm as he spoke. He was twenty-one years old.

117 years later, Edward Everett Hale, Nathan Hale's great-nephew, declared: "And because that boy said those words, and because he died, thousands of other young men have given their lives to his country."

Nathan Hale demonstrated honesty by owning up to his identity as a spy. As a result of his refusal to lie, the entire Continental Army was inspired by his example.

Questions

1. What job did Colonel Knowlton need a volunteer to do?
2. Why was Nathan Hale willing to volunteer?
3. How did he go about his mission? Did he acquire the information?
4. How was he discovered?
5. What were the conditions of his capture?
6. What did Nathan Hale request of his captors? Did he get his request granted?
7. What words did Nathan say just before his death?
8. How did he demonstrate honesty, knowing what his fate would be?
9. How was Nathan Hale's honesty used to inspire others?
10. How can you demonstrate honesty every day? List some examples of times you've been honest/dishonest. What were the consequences of both?
11. What verse can you learn to bring to memory when tempted to be dishonest?

Honor

Definition

Viewing and treating others as
a special creation of God

Memory Verse

Honor all men. Love the brotherhood.
Fear God. Honor the king.

I Peter 2:17

The Black Baron

The Russian Civil War • Crimea • October, 1920

October 16, 1920. An east wind came in the night, steadily blowing the salt water from the Sivash Marsh. Ordinarily too deep to cross on foot, the marshes formed the last line of defense. But not tonight. And in the darkness, Pharaoh's army, wearing red stars on their caps, crossed over onto dry land. Now they were marching, and nothing could stop them.

Thick fog crept up from the sea, blotting out objects close at hand and bringing with it a chill of loneliness. On the hills above Perekop, a handful of worn-out defenders battled the cold. They had been fighting and retreating for three days without food or sleep. White Army men lay huddled in shell holes crisscrossed with twisted jumbles of barbed wire. Officers wore shabby grey greatcoats with the insignia drawn on in black ink. Some of them stuffed straw into their shirts to keep warm. As the sun spread slowly across the horizon, they could see the landscape dusted with silver hoarfrost. In the grey dawn, the Communists came over the earthworks like an avalanche. 60,000 strong and outnumbering the Whites three to one, the Reds scrambled up the ravine. The Whites responded with the crack-crack of rifle fire. Shrapnel burst with white puffs left and right, spitting bits of snow like millions of pine-needles into their faces. Then they struggled back through the barbed wire to the second, unfinished row of trenches.

Forty-two-year-old General Pyotr Wrangel listened grimly to the radio reports at army headquarters. His tall slender figure, in a tight-fitting black cherkeska coat with cartridge-pockets sewn on the chest, grew rigid as he sent out a message for help.

Baron General Pyotr Wrangel

The Black Baron in his cherkeska

His fine face with its clipped mustache contorted for a brief moment in anguish. He had no troops left under his command.

When Vladimir Lenin's Communist Party seized control of the government in 1917, the fate of the country remained undecided. Who would win: a ruthless, left-wing party determined to subordinate all to its atheistic control, or groups of men dedicated to the right of the people to choose their own representative democracy?

The White Army fought through blinding blizzards and suffocating heat. They had starved and survived. Last year, a year of miracles and victories, they came within 100 miles of taking the Communist capital, Moscow. Then the American and British forces pulled out. Without aid, the little army began backing southward towards the Crimea, pursued by hungry wolves. With resistance crumbling across the country, Baron General Pyotr Wrangel's White Army stood as the last threat to Communism.

They called him "The Black Baron" because of the black cherkeska that he wore. They wrote songs about him. They feared his courage, charisma and honor.

He stared out the window as darkness closed in again. The temperature stood at twenty degrees below zero. Water froze in the pumps in the street. All through the night, he kept sending desperate messages to General Kutepov, ordering him to rush to the aid of the defenders at the Sivash March. By October 20, whole divisions were surrendering. The Reds gleefully rode trains piled high with booty, prisoners and ammunition. The whole front had collapsed. Reflecting on that time he later said:

"The dead weight of failure was crushing my heart. Again and again I asked myself if it had not been my fault. Had I foreseen everything? Had all my calculations been accurate?"

When he took over the army in March, it seemed a lost cause. Abandoned by its commander-in-chief, it had become a rapidly degenerating army swelled by thousands of refugee women and children. During weeks of incredible hard work, he had organized them into a new army, fed them with words of honor and courage, giving them the hope that they could win again. During the past eight months, they beat back superior forces and took back ground they thought they would never walk on again. But in sweeping cavalry moves, the enemy had gobbled up all of Northern Caucasia, won with such blood and sweat that last summer. Now, boxed into a narrow strip of beach, they would be cut to pieces. Their only hope lay in escape. General Abramov's Cossacks threw themselves on the enemy's flank, breaking open a way to the Crimea and the sea. Fighting every step through the Perekop Pass, the Whites managed to slip through.

On October 22, General Wrangel held a meeting of the local government in Sevastopol. He concealed the worst of the situation, in order to prevent panic behind the lines. Putting on a cheerful face, he forced himself to attend a musical party that evening. His chest tight and throbbing with pain, his mind remained with his men at the Sivash Marsh.

General Wrangel praying with his troops.

"The storm was approaching; our fate was hanging by a thread; we had to strain every moral and intellectual force. The slightest irresolution, the most insignificant mistake, and all would be lost."

Meanwhile, he organized every hospital, train, and dozens of ships capable of carrying 20,000 men. He had to evacuate the able men and the wounded, as well as old men and women carting luggage, pianos, lap dogs, and children. Seeing the end in sight, he planned each detail to avoid chaos. As his calm and desperate plans went forth, reports still bled through from the front. Several units had rallied on their own and taken back their positions from the enemy. But they were too weak to hold them for long. Throughout that last long night, men frantically shoveled coal into the furnaces of the transport-boats as the Red Army drew nearer.

November 2:

They could hear him pacing the floor upstairs in the empty palace on the shores of the Black Sea. He looked haggard, deep lines circling his eyes. He was making his last preparations. A staff officer waiting below heard his long, regular strides in the ballroom and then a terrible crashing sound. He rushed upstairs. In the twilight, Wrangel had laid the topographical maps, raised bumps showing their units and positions, on the floor and walked the length of them, trampling them flat. When the Bolsheviks arrived, they would find nothing but crumpled scraps of paper. Staring down with tired grey eyes, he could see lights bobbing like Japanese lanterns in the harbor. Almost 100,000 men, women and children milled in the darkened town like sheep, waiting to board the boats. And there were not enough boats. I will bring you out alive, he had promised. And he would keep that promise if he died.

Russian exiles leaving Crimea, 1920

November 3:

The massive operation went into action. The cold spell had broken. Gulls wheeled above them in the blue sky with shrieking cries. Wrangel felt sweat trickle down his face as he watched the shore in a pink haze. The embarkation went on through the early morning hours. No one pushed or shoved. They boarded quietly, in an orderly fashion. French, Turkish, and Greek fishing smacks floated out of the sea, pulling refugees aboard. Wrangel's voice rang across the quay: "We are going into exile; we are not going as beggars with outstretched hands, but with our heads held high, conscious of having done our duty to the end." People crowded around him, kissing his hands and weeping. At two o'clock, he received a radio message from the chief of the fleet: "Embarkation finished. Everyone on board to the last soldier."

His shoulders lifted and fell with relief. In a brilliant piece of organization, the vast flotilla set sail across the Bay to freedom, like Moses and his people. They had outrun the Reds, who remained a day behind. "I felt an immense weight fall from my mind. God had helped me to do my duty. He would bless our journey into the unknown." He was the last man to board the ship.

The post-war years remained ones of constant struggles for Wrangel. Detained in wretched camps by the French on the isle of Lemnos, he not only kept up the men's fighting spirit and skills, but he fought to gain rights, recognition and jobs for thousands of his people. He answered hundreds of letters personally and helped poor refugees out of his own dwindling pocket. He even took in a legless Cossack without any relatives who lived under the staircase in his crowded house. He organized an aid society that still exists today. During 1920–1926, he kept the army knit together, intending to return and take up the fight again. Having won their love, respect and admiration, General Wrangel gained the status of a Christian knight among his men.

The Communists still feared him. They knew that he would return and fight if possible. They now took ruthless steps to eliminate the man they viewed as a threat. In April, 1928, a Soviet sailor, brother of Wrangel's butler, appeared at the family's three-story brick home in Belgium. He spent all day in the kitchen and then left abruptly. All at once, the General fell violently ill as if poisoned. Doctors could not find what caused the high fever and hallucinations.

His brain played the last battle scenes in the Crimea over and over, unwinding like shaky old movie reels. He kept solving mathematical problems, drawing up charts and commands. He struggled to stand up, to give orders, to lead again. Raw dawn flowed over the steppe, cold and clear as chloroform. In the distance, he could see the flat roofs and chimneys of Sevastopol. Shadows of war raced like wild horses through his dreams.

Saying goodbye to the sharp, sweet taste of Russian air and winter hurrying from the mountains, he boards the Waldek Rousseau, his tall grey figure with its high sheepskin hat casting a long shadow on the water. "Night is falling. The stars are gleaming in the darkening sky; the sea is all a-twinkle. The lonely lights on my native shore grow fainter, and then vanish altogether, one after the other. And now the last one fades from my sight." Today he would leave forever, and the city that he had loved and hated would go away into the misty places of memory, the haunt of seagulls and wild horses, from which there is no going and no return.

For thirty-eight days he suffered. Then at 9:00 AM on April 25, 1928, General Wrangel died in his sleep. He was forty-nine years old. His last thought was for the welfare of his people.

He had lived up to the spirit of his memoirs: *Always with Honor.* He had made a promise to the people under his protection to lead them to safety and freedom and he had kept it.

Questions

1. Against what were Gen. Wrangel's men fighting?
2. Why did Wrangel's men call him the "Black Baron"?
3. How was the war going at this time?
4. What was the only hope for his men?
5. What kind of preparations did he have to make for successful evacuation?
6. What promise had Gen. Wrangel made to the people?
7. What did he say to encourage them?
8. Was his plan successful?
9. How did his army feel about him? How did the Communists feel about him?
10. What led to his death?
11. How had he succeeded in treating his people with honor?
12. Name some people to whom you could show honor.
13. Find a veteran you can walk up to, shake his or her hand, and thank them for their service to our country.

Hospitality

Definition

Making those who visit our home
feel comfortable

Memory Verse

. . . Given to hospitality.

Romans 12:13b

The Gift

Fort Abraham Lincoln • the Dakotas • Christmas, 1875

Christmas Eve brought bright sunshine and six feet of sand-dry snow. Beyond the stockade, the Dakota plains swept east and west to the low, unbroken chain of hills bounding the right bank of the Missouri River outside Fort Rice. Officers of the 7th Cavalry, back from hard-riding patrols, moved about the snow blanketed parade ground, their lean cheeks covered with unshaven stubble. The harsh temperatures, soaring to 110 degrees in the summer months—aggravated by razor-sharp buffalo grass, black flies, and stinging alkali dust—dropped to well below zero in December. Then an area of 864 feet by 544 feet surrounded by a ten-foot-high log stockade became a prison, penning 235 men within the stifling confines of barracks, post kitchen, stables, trade store, and guardhouse.

Ice frosted the windows of the low clapboard headquarters building. Kate Gibson turned to survey the room, her blonde hair shining in the light from the window. It was hard to keep this place warm. Homemade adobe bricks, stacked between the rickety wall studs, helped insulate from drafts. But the cold still did its best to penetrate the sawn cottonwood walls.

The door blew open. Lt. Frank Gibson stumbled in, pushing two soldiers with armfuls of squatty sage and cedar brush. He grinned at her, teeth flashing under his dark mustache.

Dear Frank. This was their first Christmas.

Helplessly, she inspected the prickly scrub. She thought of the big, soft green pines glowing with wax candles she had known in the South. There were no trees out here. Only the occasional lonely cottonwood, its bark grey and shaggy as an elephant hide,

Fort Abraham Lincoln, North Dakota

its silver leaves gone. She looked into Frank's eager face. Well, this would have to do. They must have a tree for Christmas.

Bunching and tying them together, she propped the branches into a kind of tree. Annie Yates and Mrs. Moylan climbed up on benches to hang greenery in rows from the ceiling. Feathery brushes of cedar almost swept the floor. Kate pushed a washtub covered with brightly painted paper underneath, poured sand into the tub and crammed it with simple gifts brought in on horseback from the town of Bismarck. She thought of them all—little Benny Hodgson, who had met her first, Lieutenant Van Riley's gentle teasing, the half-French scout Mitch Boyer, Tom Custer, who taught her how to ride. By opening her home to them, she wanted to do something to make this Christmas a happy one. To blot out for a few hours burning villages, raids into the Black Hills and scalping parties of the Comanche and Sioux.

The hours before dark went quickly. Yards and yards of paper cut into strips festooned the ceiling. Paper twisted into cornucopias burst with homemade candy. Nuts appeared out of nowhere. Kate tore the silver wrappings off carefully-hoarded cigars. Her slim fingers wrapped and pinched and covered the nuts with foil. Officers, ducking shyly into the room at rare intervals, offered ancient Christmas cards, bits of home life they had lovingly treasured, some from as far back as 1868. Bow-tied with faded scraps of ribbon, they swung on the scraggly branches like stars. Firelight winked on the beads of silver nuts.

Shadows began to fall, lengthening across the parade ground. It was warm inside the Gibsons' headquarters. Stoves crackled with smoking cedar and cottonwood branches, green sap hissing as it dripped onto the flames. Soon guests began to arrive,

Fort Abraham Lincoln officers 1875

crowding the room with their tight-fitting, dark-blue uniform coats, boots and rattling sabers. The tree glowed like a friendly spirit, while crimson candles perched jauntily on the branches. Sandwiches, cake, candy, and ersatz lemonade disappeared under laughing mustaches. Some ducked under the big red paper bell floating overhead, its edges pasted with cut-out pictures of Santa Claus.

It was impossible to keep her eyes off her husband. He moved easily among the men, tasting the ice-cream frugally whipped up with condensed milk, whisked gelatin, and precious egg-whites smuggled in beneath the mail courier's buckskin shirt. Frank's saber knocked against his long, blue pants legs as he moved. He had removed the chinstrap of his tall campaign hat with the sleek brown horsetail dangling behind, and his thick dark hair swept his forehead. Thank God, she whispered. Thank God. She hadn't lost him to frostbite or typhoid fever. He hadn't fallen somewhere among the dusty buffalo grass with an arrow in his chest. He was here. He was safe. For another day.

Someone struck up the "Virginia Reel." Stamping their feet, swinging their partners, the officers plunged in, sashaying across the room to the plink-plunk of an ancient banjo, the rhythmic strumming of a guitar, the metallic wheeze of a jew's-harp. Clasped hands and sweating faces swayed in the light of the red Christmas candles.

Midnight struck.

Kate saw Frank wish everyone goodnight before slipping out into the cold entry. As Officer of the Day, he had to make his rounds of the stockade that night, checking up on security, questioning the guards who watched the plains for a puff of smoke, the

silent flight of an arrow, the distant thundering hooves of a war party raiding cattle and killing traders. She helped him throw the cape over his shoulders, tugging the strap under his chin and pulling on his gloves. His gold epaulettes gleamed faintly as she opened the door for him.

Up on the outposts, the sentries braced their backs against the wind so as not to be blown off. The temperature had dropped again, and the wind brought with it a few big flakes of snow.

The party was almost over. Officers clustered around the table, drinking up the last of the lemonade before putting on their coats and going off to their bachelor quarters.

Goodnight, Merry Christmas.

They were gone at last. Giving one last glance around the room, at the paper garlands and the candles melting down, puddling, Kate moved towards the kitchen. She held the candle high, yellow flickers chasing the shadows down the walls. She opened the door, shivering at the cold blast of air. Where was Frank? She pictured him striding through the silent stockade, footsteps crunching in the snow. The candle flame stabbed the darkness. And she gasped.

Huddled in the side shanty were four or five little figures.

Indians.

One was barely tall enough to peek in the window. What did they want? Then she saw the tree gleaming dazzlingly through the window, like something out of a magical fairyland. She wondered how they had managed to slip into Fort Rice past the sentries. Then she remembered a slight gap in the stockade wall, just big enough to let a child slip through. It was bitterly cold. I don't want to frighten them. They're just children. Softly, she opened the door and stood aside.

"Come in."

The tall boy stared at her, supple and straight as a willow wand. She could see fear struggle with yearning in his eyes. Then he stepped forward, grasping the hand of a brown-faced, four-year-old girl. The others followed in single file. She wondered how they had known about the Christmas party going on in the white officer's headquarters.

The tree sparkled through the open living room door. "Someone tell Indian boy about it?" She spoke slowly, carefully, so that he could grasp the words.

He nodded jerkily.

"Who tell Indian boy?"

The answer was quick. "Horn Toad."

"Oh." So that was it. The friendly, good-natured Indian scout loved children, red or white, inside the stockade or without.

The little group pressed up against the hot stove, thawing out and staring at her. Nobody moved. Nobody said anything else. She bent down to the little squaw.

"And who is she?"

"Sister." The boy spoke abruptly.

Kate stared down into big black eyes. A chubby little brown hand clung tightly to the boy's. She shivered, clutching an old piece of gunny sack over the shoulders of her thin calico dress. She wore little buckskin leggings and tiny beaded moccasins. A rawhide strip kept back her tangled dark hair. Kate shook herself. This was a terrible hour for these children to be up. She thought of their mothers. They must go back at once.

Then she looked at their shy, eager faces. They must have spent hours out in the cold night, pressing their faces to the window for a glimpse of this glittering paradise. Never mind the time. Their mothers could worry an hour longer. Closing the door, she shoed them into the living room. There stood the Christmas pie—the washtub that had held the officers' gifts. Digging into the sand, she came up with a Jack-in-the-box. She wrapped the little girl's hands around it. Her black eyes jumped with joy. Hands trembling, she clutched the toy to her chest. Now all the children crowded round the tub, digging busily in the sand.

Kate got up and ran into the kitchen. There was still some hot cocoa left. She was heating it up on the cook-stove when she noticed the sentry was leaving. Suddenly, she pictured Indian women in tattered calico and gunnysack headbands standing forlornly outside the fort, waiting for their children. Perhaps an Indian brave with warm buffalo robes and a copper armband. It was best to avoid worry and trouble.

"Oh, Alkorn," she called out, "go to the nearest bastion and tell the sentinel to relay to other sentinels that, in the event of any Indians hanging around and looking for children, they are at Lieutenant Gibson's quarters and will be along soon."

Carrying a pot of steaming hot cocoa, she went back to the living room. The children were pawing through the tub, shyness forgotten. There were shrieks of joy as rag dolls and toy pistols came to light. At first, they would not look at the food. Even cocoa held no such magic as these toys. But at last they came to the table. Cradling the cups in their hands, they drank eagerly. Soon color flooded their pinched cheeks and the chilled little fingers grew warm. The children should go home now. But somehow she couldn't send them away. While they sat at the table, she heaped their laps with goodies, candy, popcorn and nuts. There was some ice cream left, too. She couldn't let them go without feeding them. The children stared at the whipped pink-and-white stuff. It was cold. Fluffy. Then the little squaw dipped her finger in and licked it. A soft smile spread over her face. All at once, the boys attacked it, stuffing themselves till they ached.

Smacking sounds followed her as she ran upstairs. There must be some old clothes around here somewhere. Blankets, stockings, socks. It was unbearable to think of the little ones going out, facing the cold again with uncovered faces and blue fingers. There—one of her short coats, a couple pairs of mittens, some warm mufflers. Suddenly, she stopped on the stairs, alert, listening. There was a clapping of hands and a weird chanting, soft and first, then louder, more insistent. Then came the shuffle of moccasins. Whoops pierced the air. Sinking down on the steps, she peered through the lower banisters. Her eyes froze.

The oldest boy was the chief. One brave and the little girl stood off to one side, clapping loudly. She swayed her hips and body in time to the music, imitating the older women in a dance of sunflower seeds and deer. Their lips moved in a monotonous chant. There was no tune. Behind them came the young braves, circling the red-hot stove, stamping, shuffling. Their dance was the trampling of buffaloes in the tall grass, it was the fierce lightness of the wildcat, it was the grass itself, swaying, bending, flowing effortlessly. She sat frozen, watching them. Their brown necks tipped back; eerie whoops burst forth. The candles trembled. Sand was ground into the carpet. But she saw only the graceful young bodies swaying like reeds in the wind. It was a peace dance, a dance of greatness and thanksgiving.

The dance changed. Now it was fast, choppy. The clapping and chanting grew faster. The children whirled, leaping, whooping. The floor shook with their thunder. Then suddenly it all was all over. The young chief held up his hand. The children dropped down, exhausted, on the carpet. Catching up the bunch of winter clothes, Kate hurried downstairs. In the entryway, she bundled the little girl up tight, tied the too-big mittens onto her hands. The scarves, blankets and boots she handed out to the boys and helped them struggle into them. Then she went to the tree, stripped off all the colored gifts and silver nuts, slipped the rest of the cake and candy into a bag, and gave it to the tall boy.

Indian child

It was hard to let them go. She felt as if they belonged to her. Yet they were part of a way of life she knew little about. The evening spun before her, the officers' boyish faces, their shining eyes, their jokes; and these shabby little strangers, thanking her in the only way they knew how. Tomorrow, these same officers might ride out to face a storm of arrows and carbine bullets from the children's fathers and brothers. Snow crunched crisply as the little group marched single-file across the parade ground. Stars winked above the log palisades. As she stood watching, one by one, the children, clutching their toys, turned for one last look. A last smile. Then the boy bringing up the rear patted his mouth with a slim brown hand, sending the farewell call of his people into the night. In the hall, the clock struck one.

Kate Gibson wearily closed the door. Blowing out the kerosene lamp, she trudged upstairs to bed. Frank would be home at dawn. Outside, the snow drifted down and the sentinels' hollow cry passed from post to post: "One o'clock and all's well." It was Christmas Day, 1875.

By welcoming the strange children into her home, Kate Gibson demonstrated that hospitality should not only be shown to friends and people we want to invite, but to strangers needing food, comfort or love.

Questions

1. How did Kate use the quality of hospitality to extend warmth and kindness to others?
2. Whom did she invite for a Christmas celebration?
3. What did she use for a "tree"?
4. How did Kate improvise to make a memorable celebration for the men?
5. Who were the surprise visitors?
6. How did Kate extend hospitality to the children? What was their response?
7. To whom might you extend hospitality? Think of someone who would be blessed by your effort and plan to surprise them.
8. Remember, being hospitable to others is not always convenient for us, but God will bless our efforts. How did Kate feel as she wearily made her way to bed?

Humility

Definition

Acknowledging that any good I have achieved is a gift from God, and my life is to be used as an instrument in His hand.

Memory Verse

He hath shown thee, O man, what is good;
and what doth the Lord require of thee,
but to do justly, and to love mercy,
and to walk humbly with thy God?

Micah 6:8

"Operation Auca"

Shandia Mission Station, Ecuador, South America • January, 1956

The small yellow airplane circled above the village just visible through the dark green jungle foliage. Peering through the window, 27-year-old Jim Elliot saw the dark-skinned Auca Indians staring up at the plane. The other men in the plane, Ed McCully, Peter Fleming, and Roger Youderian, watched breathlessly. This was the first time that a white person had seen had any of this tribe. Suddenly, a friendly greeting in the Auca language boomed out of the plane's loudspeakers. The pilot, Nate Saint, made another turn. Then he lowered a plastic bucket stuffed with beads, cloth, machetes, and a photograph of each man. After a few minutes, the Aucas sent up a parrot and a riot of feathered headdresses. Soon, the Indians let them land on a strip of sand that they named Palm Beach. "Operation Auca" had begun.

Graduating from Wheaton College, Jim Elliot answered the call go to the Quechua Indians in Ecuador. In October, 1953, he married Elisabeth, who also felt called to go. The mission outpost, medical station, a cluster of houses, and a small airstrip stood in the middle of nowhere. To reach it, Jim and Elisabeth had to fly in by plane, piloted by their friend, Nate Saint. Then, it took a strenuous two-hour hike through the rainy jungle and swamplands to reach Shandia.

During his linguistic classes, he had heard of a tribe called the Aucas. They had never had any contact with the outside world. For three or four months, the men continued to fly over the village and drop gifts. Then they decided to establish a base on a strip of beach near the Curray River. Soon, four Auca warriors emerged from the jungle. Cautiously, the two groups approached each other. The missionaries gave food and presents to show

Betty & Nate Saint & the yellow airplane

their friendship. As the men set up camp, they would step to the edge of the beach every now and then and shout Auca phrases into the jungle. They did carry guns, but agreed not to use them unless they had to.

They waited for four days before the Aucas showed themselves again. Suddenly, two Indian women and a man appeared on the opposite side of the river. They stood motionless within the dark canopy of the jungle. The missionaries jumped to their feet, shouting wildly in Auca to attract their attention. The Auca man called back. He pointed to one of the women, saying something over and over. Without hesitation, Jim Elliot plunged into the river and swam across. Startled, the Indians began to melt back into the jungle. Showing them a knife that winked in the sunlight, Jim persuaded them to cross over to camp. After a moment, they agreed.

Coming up on dry land, the girl started waving towards the plane. The man, whom the missionaries dubbed "George," moved closer to her and stared at it, too. They called the girl "Delilah." Thinking the Indians would like a ride in the plane, Nate offered to fly them over their village. Swooping over the trees, he saw the Indians staring up at the great bird. "George" hung excitedly out the plane window, yelling in Auca to the villagers below.

During the rest of the day, they showed the Indians around their campsite. They played with rubber bands, balloons, and balls. Then they cooked up a lunch of hamburgers smeared with mustard. They also snapped photos of "George" crouching beside the plane and of Delilah standing on the strip of beach. They showed these photographs to the Indians after they had quickly developed them. As night came on, the Indians still lingered. Setting up a hut, the men offered to let the Aucas sleep there. Sudden-

Nate Saint with "George"

ly, Delilah gave a sharp cry. Spinning on her bare brown heels, she took off into the jungle. "George" followed her at a run. A moment later, the older woman also melted into the evening shadows.

Ecstatic from the visit, Jim Elliot and the others decided to put "Operation Auca" into full action. They spent the morning of January 8 singing songs and praying on the beach. Then they spoke to their wives by radio, saying that they were going into the village. They would send them a message about 4:30 PM. The next day, Nate and Ed McCully skimmed along the river towards Shell Mera in the plane. All at once, they saw a crowd of ten Aucas moving steadily towards Palm Beach where the other three men had stayed. Excitement bubbled up in them.

They shouted into the radio: "Guys, the Aucas are coming!"

The others quickly began tidying up the camp. Turning the plane around, Jim and Nate headed back toward the beach. Jim radioed Elisabeth, saying, "We'll call you back in three hours." Around noon on January 8, Nate called his wife Marj and told her he would call at 4:30.

The women back at the Shandia Mission base huddled together in prayer as their husbands went to meet the Aucas. At 4:30 PM., they listened to the radio. When no message came through, the women set up an alarm. Within an hour, Ecuadorian Air Force, U.S. Army Air Force and Navy helicopters hummed over the jungle, scanning the Curray River area for any sign of the missing men. At last, one of the pilots spoke into his radio. He had spotted five bodies on the beach. Jim Elliot's body, along with three others, was found downstream. Spears and machetes protruded from their bodies. Nate Saint's watch had stopped at 3:12 PM, the time of the attack. Nearby, the little plane stood stripped of all its fabric. The Indians had tried to kill it.

Back at the mission station, the wives listened calmly to the news. "The Lord has closed our hearts to grief and hysteria, and filled in with His perfect peace," they said. They remembered what Jim Elliot once said, "He is no fool who gives what he cannot keep to gain what he cannot lose." Nate Saint said, "People who do not know the Lord ask why in the world we waste our lives as missionaries. They forget that they too are expending their lives . . . and when the bubble has burst, they will have nothing of eternal significance to show for the years they have wasted."

Rachel Saint, Nate's sister, continued the work her brother began and gave her life to the work of translating the Bible into the Auca language. Years later she learned that one of the natives had told a lie about the missionaries which precipitated the fatal attack. She personally demonstrated forgiveness to her brother's killers and saw many in the village come to Christ, including seven of the nine killers. Nate demonstrated humility in allowing his life to be used as an instrument in God's hand, and as a result many of the Auca people gave their lives to the Lord Jesus Christ.

Questions

1. What were the missionary friends trying to accomplish through Operation Auca?
2. What types of things did the men do to try to communicate their friendship for the tribe?
3. Why do you think the men chose not to use their guns to protect themselves?
4. How did the men's sacrifice help to bring about the salvation of many of the Auca people?
5. How did Nate Saint portray a sincere attitude of humility?

Initiative

Definition

Seeing a need and taking responsibility
to meet it without being asked

Memory Verse

Whatsoever thy hand findeth to do,
do it with thy might.

Ecclesiastes 9:10a

General in Disguise

The Civil War • Lebanon, Kentucky • Spring, 1862

Lebanon, Kentucky: Spring, 1862. "Click-click! Click-click!" In the little telegraph office, the Union operator crouched over his desk, his fingers racing as he typed the dispatch from Louisville to Nashville. Soldiers in blue coats patrolled the town, waiting for something to happen. A few minutes ago, a telegram had come in, ordering Don Carlos Buell's Federal Army of the Ohio to transfer the recently captured Confederate prisoners from Colonel John Hunt Morgan's regiment to Nashville for safety. The Union Army at Louisville expected trouble. Determined to get his men back, Morgan might attack at any time. A chill ran down the civilian operator's spine.

He muttered: "Who knows, but that guerilla may pounce like a hawk on me, too. If I only had him here, wouldn't I put an end to his villainy!"

Horses' hooves clopped in the road outside. The operator rushed to the window to look out. A tall, broad-shouldered man wearing a butternut suit had just dismounted from his horse. He wore a clustering auburn beard and mustache. Soft auburn hair curled from beneath the torn brim of a shabby slouch hat. He deftly tied his horse's bridle to a fence near the door. A moment later, his shadow darkened the office floor. Chocolate-colored Kentucky mud spattered his coat and boots. Walking slowly over to an empty chair, he sat down.

"What news?" he asked, casually.

"No news." The operator's voice was curt. He smothered a yawn and turned back to his instrument.

Grasping his riding whip in one hand, the stranger picked up the Louisville morning journal lying on the desk. Opening it,

Civil War telegraph operator and telegraph

he glanced down the first column and lifted his eyebrows.

"John Morgan at work again!" he murmured. "A pity that man can't be caught."

The telegraph operator could not keep quiet. The indignation that had been seething inside of him all morning since he read the telegram boiled over. He leapt to his feet. Pacing back and forth across the room, he burst out:

"Yes, the scoundrel, the villain! If I had him here, I would soon put a ball through his cursed body. No more pranks from him, the mighty John Morgan, I tell you!"

The stranger looked up at him with large, clear grey eyes. "Why, you wouldn't kill him, would you?" he asked quietly.

The operator clenched and swung his fist.

"Kill him? Aye, that I would, sooner than I'd shoot a mad dog. I just dare him, at any time, to cross that door, and if he isn't a dead man in five minutes, there's no truth in me!"

The man slid the folded paper across the desk. Then he rose, swept off his hat and stepped up to the operator. Slipping his hand into his hip pocket, he held out a pistol in front of him.

His soft, musical voice was gentle. "I am John Morgan, sir. Now execute your threat. Here is a pistol; you entirely welcome to use it."

The gun lying on the outstretched palm did not falter.

The operator turned as white as cheese. But Colonel Morgan stared at him with intense grey eyes. Trembling from head to foot, the operator began backing away.

Colonel John Hunt Morgan

"I, I—didn't know—I hadn't any idea—that you were Colonel Morgan, Sir—indeed, Sir, I didn't—I beg pardon, Sir, ten thousand times, Sir."

His voice shook. He kept edging away, holding out his hands, until his back struck against the wall. All the time, he kept babbling incoherently.

"You have my pardon, sir." Morgan's voice was firm now. "Another time, I would advise you to be less boastful of your courage and veracity."

Then his voice changed. It turned sharp like a winter wind whistling through Cumberland Gap. "Be quick. Seat yourself and send the messages that I shall dictate to Louisville."

Morgan stood behind the operator with a pistol as he quickly slid into his chair. "Make no mistake," Morgan warned him. "If you do, your life is the forfeit. I understand the operation, sir; therefore, don't attempt to give any information but what I instruct you."

The messages winged on their way under the operator's fingers. As he finished, Morgan demanded, "Now, show me all the dispatches that have passed through his office in the last 24 hours."

Lebanon was full of Union troops. But the operator could not alert them or cry out for help without risking a shot in the back of the head. Slowly, he pushed the stack of messages towards Morgan. The Colonel scanned them carefully, his eyes flashing up and down the pages. At last, he laid them down. Pushing his slouched hat back on his head, he walked to the door.

"That will do, sir," he called over his shoulder. "Good morning." Striding to his horse, he sprang into the saddle and galloped away.

During Union General Edward McCook's occupation of Nashville, Morgan struck on a plan to lure a large number of Union troops into an ambush. Dressed in a homespun coat and trousers, he climbed into a farmer's wagon and drove into Nashville. Bags of meal bought from a local miller bounced behind him. Morgan stopped in front of the hotel where General McCook always ate his meals. Leaving his assistant to watch the horse, Morgan sauntered into the hotel. He sniffed the air and stared at the menu, but all the time, his eyes darted around the room.

General Edward McCook

Suddenly, he spotted General McCook, with long mustaches and thinning dark hair, sitting at a table across the room. The farmer shambled up to the table and fell into a chair.

"Is this heah Gineral McCook?" he drawled.

The General smiled pleasantly up from his meal. "That's my name."

"Wal, Gineral," the lazy tones droned, "if thar's no Secesh 'bout, I've got sum'pen ter tell you right heah." He dropped his voice. "I live up close by Burk's Mills in the middle of a nest of red hot Seceshers and they swar' yer sojers shant hev a speck o' meal if they starve for it." A grin spread across his face. "But Gineral, I got a wagon load of meal ground, and I hev' brung it down heah ter day, and it's now out thar in the street and you kin hev it if you want it."

General McCook, touched by the man's loyalty and generosity, smiled his thanks warmly. But he could not take a farmer's hard-earned flour without any payment."Take the meal, my friend, to the Commissary," he offered kindly. "He will pay you for it in gold and silver."

Morgan tucked into his dinner with an appetite. When he had cleaned his plate, he lurched out of his chair, bumped the table and gave a clumsy little bow. Dragging his feet, he left the room. Half an hour later, he went down to Federal Headquarters. A staff officer assured the farmer that McCook was in. Morgan shambled up to the General with sleeve-plucking eagerness.

"Gineral—" His voice was anxious—"Can't yer send 150 men up thar to the neberhood of Burk's Mills? I'll guide 'em into that nest er traitors and secheshers; and they kin capture too a mighty big sight er meal."

General McCook could not thank this patriot enough. "The men, my friend, shall certainly be sent. Which day shall we choose? Let the appointment be as early as possible." He paused impressively. "I suppose this is a busy time with you farmers, but when one's country calls, the plough itself must stop in the furrow."

Morgan agreed. He protested loudly that his farm could fall to pieces before he would allow one Secessionist to escape. Then he set the date and time for the meeting.

A few days later, 150 Union cavalrymen trotted out to the lonely place to meet up with the Kentucky farmer. Instead, they came face to face with Morgan surrounded by more than a company of Confederate raiders. The astonished soldiers surrendered on the spot.

The brother-in-law of Robert E. Lee's General Ambrose Powell Hill, John Hunt Morgan continued his raiding expeditions through Kentucky and Tennessee. In spite of his success as the "Marion of the West," there is evidence that the Confederate authorities began to investigate Morgan's activities as a bandit.

In April 1863, he crossed the Ohio River into southern Indiana and Ohio on an expedition known as "Morgan's Raid." Mor-

Morgan's Raiders, prisoners-of-war in Ohio State Penitentiary

gan intended to relieve pressure on Bragg's forces currently besieged by General Rosecrans' troops.

Pushing north towards Cincinnati, Morgan escaped the pursuing Union cavalry for almost a week. After a final clash with 450 Home Guard troops while trying to cross into West Virginia at Buffington Island, Morgan found himself imprisoned in the Ohio State Penitentiary.

But Morgan did not give up. Using handmade tools, Morgan and six of his officers chipped away at a wall for twenty-three days. Then they broke through to the soft, dark earth and began digging a 100-foot tunnel. At midnight, they stuffed their flannel shirts with bed-sheets to make dummies. Then they slipped into the tunnel. Breaking out into the yard, they descended to the ground below using a rope made out of blankets and the aid of a bent iron poker. Breathing the cool night air again, the Confederates faded past the guards into the darkness. Morgan made his way home alternately by foot, wagon and train.

General John Hunt Morgan demonstrated initiative by inventing ways out of difficult situations and employing methods of disguise to achieve victory over enemy forces.

Questions

1. Why were the Union soldiers on edge?
2. What threats toward John Morgan did the telegraph operator make?
3. What happened to shock him?
4. What did John Morgan command him to do?
5. How did Morgan lure Union troops into an ambush in Nashville?
6. Tell how Morgan and his men made their escape from prison.
7. Give several examples of initiative in John Morgan's life.

Joyfulness

Definition

Choosing to have a good attitude even when circumstances are tough to bear

Memory Verse

Rejoice in the Lord always;
and again I say, Rejoice.
Philippians 4:4

Fortress Escape

World War I • Germany • February, 1915

He was the eighth highest-scoring French fighting ace, with twenty-seven "kills" under his belt. The first man to drop an espionage agent behind German lines. He could not know that the story of his escape and his attitude under adversity would inspire the greatest anti-war film of all time.

February 8, 1915. As his plane crashed to the ground, riddled with bullets, Lieutenant Armand Pinsard saw pale-blue trench coats and spiked German helmets running across the field towards him. Then pain engulfed his body, searing it like flames as he spun into oblivion.

Armand Pinsard, staring down the window in his prison quarters, watched German soldiers goose-stepping in the courtyard below. His straight nose and elegant, mustached profile made the French fighting ace look older than his twenty-eight years. Single-handedly, Pinsard would shoot down eighteen German bombers and nine observation balloons filled with lethal gas; strafe trains loaded with enemy troops and halt a deadly German counterattack from the air.

Again he felt his squadron N26 plane forced down behind German lines. The grinding crash. The black weeks of pain. After a month, the pain began to subside. He could get out of bed, walk to the window and back. Now he could think of escape. Behind him, the other officers crouched on their beds, playing cards and chaffing at their imprisonment. Technically, the Germans could not force officers to do hard labor. Compared to the soldiers who slogged it out in muddy camps at Soldau or Oberhofen, this was paradise. But it was also an illusion. While treated with greater dignity, he knew it was easier for soldiers to escape while on work detail into the nearby woods or fields. Camp regulations forbade officers to wear or receive civilian clothes. This made the chance of escaping and blending in with the German countryside virtually impossible.

From where he stood, Pinsard could see, like succeeding rings of frost, the solid barracks wall, the motionless statues of the guards, and beyond that the outer circle of closely-meshed barbed wire. The way to survive was to keep his spirits up. The war might be over before he could get out, and then it might not. In the days since he had been here, he had heard disturbing rumors of "prisoner's syndrome," men who could not cope, who threw themselves against the barbed wire in a hopeless fury of despair. He must not do that. He must keep cheerful. And sane.

Pinsard did not wait long to rejoin the French Air Service. Between March, 1915, and the spring of 1916, he attempted multiple escapes: through a heating duct, in a garbage bin, via the sewers, in a laundry basket. Each time he was frustrated. For punishment, he and several other officers who attempted to escape found themselves confined in the medieval fortress at Ingolstadt. Security was heavy here. Shut up in a tower and allowed out only for roll-call, Pinsard had little hope of escape. If caught, he would be shot. But he refused to grow discouraged. A golf course is for golf. A tennis court is for tennis. A prison camp is for escaping.

It was that simple.

Absolutely without self-pity, he threw himself into his work. Taking another officer into his confidence, he plotted afresh. This time, they would tunnel beneath the twelve-foot-thick wall separating them from the world outside. They could only dig at night, after the guards had checked the room and called their names. Crawling on hands and knees, sometimes on his belly, Pinsard scraped out the earth with the aid of a soup tin and his bare hands. Finally, on March 26 1916, they broke through to the rocky slope far enough beyond Ingolstadt to escape the sentries' gunfire. For two weeks, he worked his way through the dangerous countryside till at last

Captain Armand Pinsard

he slipped over the border into Switzerland. After 13 months of imprisonment, Pinsard was free. It was his first escape from prison, but it would not be his last.

In the months that followed, Pinsard received the rank of captain and flew solo for the foremost French fighter squadron. Once, he crashed with massive injuries. When he got out of the hospital, he painted his fighting plane black and renamed it "Revenge IV." Then in 1916, fact became fantasy. On an early November afternoon, the future film director Jean Renoir flew over Lechelle, snapping aerial photographs of the enemy position. Suddenly, a German Fokker swooped down on him. Before he could respond to the attack, a French pilot, invisible in the cockpit of a Spad VII roared in and shot the German down in flames, saving Renoir's life. Twenty years later, the director and the pilot Armand Pinsard met again.

So impressed was Renoir with Pinsard's attitude towards his imprisonment that he based his great anti-war film, *Grand Illusion,* on the French pilot's story. Most people would have given up on life after more than a year in a German prison. But Armand Pinsard was unstoppable. By maintaining a good attitude in impossible circumstances, he was able to stay sane after thirteen months in captivity and dig his way out to freedom—scoring a final Allied victory.

Questions

1. Explain how Lt. Pinsard came to be imprisoned.
2. What was his assigned job in the war?
3. Tell of his attempted escapes.
4. What was his attitude in prison? Did he intentionally work to maintain that?
5. How did his good attitude affect other prisoners?
6. Tell of his encounter with the filmmaker and what impressed him with Pinsard's attitude.
7. Why was he inspired to make a film about him?
8. Does your attitude affect those around you?
9. What can you do in your home and sphere of influence to promote joyfulness?
10. Think of an instance lately that provoked you to complain. What were the consequences of that attitude? What should you have done?

Then he said unto them, Go your way, eat the fat, and drink the sweet, and send portions unto them for whom nothing is prepared: for this day is holy unto our Lord: neither be ye sorry; for the joy of the Lord is your strength.

— Nehemiah 8:10

Kindness

Definition

Treating others as you would
like to be treated by them

Memory Verse

And be ye kind one to another, tenderhearted,
forgiving one another, even as God
for Christ's sake hath forgiven you.

Ephesians 4:32

The Refuge

Colonial America • Rhode Island • January, 1636

January, 1636. It was hard not to imagine footsteps pursuing him through the wintry woods. Shadows darted among the pines, crept along the blue snow. Roger Williams bent his dark, angular face with its prominent cheekbones and wavy, shoulder-length hair as he stumbled into a deep snowdrift. They said that this forest was evil. That Indian spirits walked here and the seductive lure of nature itself drew men deeper into rings of weak sunlight or patches of dappled shade. Bird calls, hushed now, and shifting shapes of bear and deer called man also. But men pursued him now; the Sheriff of the Massachusetts General Court laid track for him, not the spirits of Puritan legend. Shivering with sickness, he gathered his cloak around him and plunged on.

He didn't know where he was going. Only a smattering of this land had been explored by Captain John Smith between 1614 and 1616. Beyond the roots of Plymouth and Massachusetts Bay Colony lay an unknown country. The Indians must have this land or the colonists must pay for it. It was theirs by natural right. He had always believed this since he first landed on the darkly wooded shores of Boston, Massachusetts, five years before. He watched the Indians closely as he preached in the villages of Plymouth and Salem. There, he saw colonists deprive the Indians of vast tracts of land solely on the strength of company charters. He would see Baptists driven away and Quakers put to death in the colony.

When he spoke out for Indian rights and freedom for Baptists, Quakers and Dutch Jews in his tract, "A Plea for Religious Liberty," he ran foul of the Massachusetts authorities. William Bradford claimed that he fell into some strange opinions. The church failed to meet Williams' standards of separatism, while at the same time they would not allow freedom of religion.

In March 1635, the controversy over Williams' tract, which attacked both King James I and colonial charters, accelerated. Called before the General Court, Williams soon found himself in the minority and out of a job. Calling himself a Seeker, he began to meet alone in his home with his young wife Mary and a handful of followers. In October, things came to a head. Tried and convicted by the General Court, he discovered that they intended to deport him to England for trial on the grounds of sedition and heresy. They put off the arrest for two months when he fell ill in the dead of winter. Unless he stopped his attacks on the King's right to allow settlers to take land from the Indians without payment, they would issue an order of banishment. But he could not keep the truth silent.

Roger Williams escaping arrest.

Early in January, 1636, the local sheriff waded through deep snow and pounded on the Williams' door. He found the gaunt-faced preacher gone. Three days before, Williams fled southwest from Salem into the wilderness at the head of Narragansett Bay. Days passed, and a week. Then two weeks. He continued to struggle forward in the bitter cold. Starvation clawed at his stomach and pitted his cheeks. Stumbling through the drifts, he scrabbled with his hands in the ice to find roots or berries. He slept huddled in the snow.

Seven dissenting friends found their way to him in the woods. At last, he stumbled onto a band of Wampanoag Indians. Kind brown hands led him to the winter lodge of Chief Massasoit and removed his stiff outer garments. Someone gave him a bowl full

Roger Williams

of steaming beans, corn and venison. He had walked 105 miles.

Spring came. Williams bought a swathe of land from Massasoit. No sooner had he began a settlement than Plymouth Colony moved in and claimed he was within the area of their land grant. They threatened to send him back to Massachusetts Bay. Instead, he rowed across the Seekonk River into Narragansett Indian territory. There, the friendly chief sachems, Canonicus and Miantonomi, sold Williams a large tract of land called Aquidneck Island at the mouth of Narragansett Bay in appreciation of his honest dealings with them. At last, he had found a refuge from the world. He named it Providence. Later, it would become the capital of Rhode Island.

By August, 1637, they drew up a town agreement admitting a number of Ann Hutchinson's exiled free-will followers, denounced by the Court as Antinomians, or "against the law of God." The little colony flourished. Then in 1637, Puritan soldiers and their Algonquian allies attacked and burned a village of 500 Indian men, women and children, sparking the Pequot War. Terrified of retaliation, Massachusetts turned to Roger Williams for help. Respectfully, he spoke to the Narragansett chiefs. He persuaded them to join the English in crushing the Pequot uprising instead of joining the other Indian tribes. Although he spared the colony much bloodshed, the Puritans looked on his friendship with the Indians with deepening suspicion as the Narragansett quickly became the most powerful Indian nation in southern New England.

In 1643, the larger colonies tried to destroy Williams' settlement by trying to bring it under their own control. Williams fought back. With the English Civil War in full swing, he boarded a ship for England to obtain a charter for his colony. He succeeded, despite Puritan pressure, and the colony of Rhode Island became a refuge for Baptists, Quakers and Jews. Home again with Mary and his six children, he spent much time learning the Indian dialect and writing the first book on Native American languages and folklore ever published in English. In 1652, Thirty-one years before his death, he helped to pass laws forbidding the practice of slavery in Rhode Island.

Impacted by Williams' kindness in dealing with the Indians and his commitment to share the gospel, the old Indian chief Canonicus, on his deathbed, clasped Roger Williams' hands and accepted Christ as his Savior. Roger Williams demonstrated kindness by paying the Indians for the land he settled on and showing complete honesty in his dealings with them.

Roger Williams meeting with the Narragansetts.

Questions

1. What happened to put Roger Williams at odds with the authorities in Massachusetts?
2. Tell of his sickness and escape and who rescued him.
3. How did Williams finally find a refuge?
4. Why did Massachusetts turn to Williams to help during the Pequot war?
5. How was he able to avert disaster?
6. What did Williams do when larger colonies try to destroy what he had accomplished?
7. Tell how Williams is a example of kindness. What was the benefit of his kindness?

Love

Definition

Giving unselfishly in all situations

Memory Verse

Little children, let us not love in word,
neither in tongue;
but in deed and in truth.

1 John 3:18

The Flying Panther

World War II • Sens, France • August 10, 1944

The sky was clear. Not a single German *Luftwaffe* zoomed into sight on his tail or beyond the horizon. Twenty-one-year-old Captain K. Eddie Simpson smiled, his clean-shaven face calm, as he shot over the railway target in his P51 Mustang. A painted black panther, its mouth opened in a snarl and its Pegasus wings spread, soared on the side of the bomber. As the crew, consisting of Sergeant Schuenemann, Corporal Petree, and Sergeant Classens, hung tight, bombs dropped like lead balloons onto tracks looking like a child's train-set far below.

The captain had a way of inspiring men to follow him. Other squadron members of the 357th Fighter Group jumped at the chance to fly with him. His friend, Bill Overstreet, noted how Eddie Simpson brimmed over with pleasant good-humor whether at the station in Leiston, England, or in the air flying missions over France.

Simpson, in the lead as one of the 363rd Squadron leaders, slowly swung his craft to the left in an echelon turn as the last bomb fell. Suddenly, something slammed into the "Flying Panther" from the behind. First Lieutenant Donald Ferron had fatally misjudged the speed of Simpson's maneuver. The nose of his bomber plowed through the P51's metal skin as fuel burst into flames. As the two planes spiraled towards the ground, locked in a blazing death-embrace, Eddie Simpson bailed out. Farron's plane exploded instantly.

Alone in the clouds, Simpson gripped the straps of his parachute as he drifted towards the earth. Nazi-occupied territory lay just below him. Once he landed, he would have to move fast and silently to avoid capture and death. He dropped and rolled to the ground in a mass of parachute silk. Quickly gathering up the telltale evidence of a landing that would set the Nazis on his trail, he started out on foot. He had not gone far when two French Maquis freedom fighters slipped out of the woods near Orleans, south of the Loir River. They stared at his uniform. English?

Eddie Simpson and his crew

It was the first time that they had met anyone who spoke English except for a few rare British agents. Organized in the attics and cellars of Paris by Jean Moulin, a man identified only by a closely-wrapped scarf concealing his scarred throat, the French Resistance spread into the countryside. Stealing supplies from Nazi-controlled rail-yards, bombing tracks, killing *Abteilung* guards with piano wire strung across roads at neck-level and running coded messages, the Resistance carried on a desperate underground warfare while the Allies strafed the landscape from above. Led by Colonel Marc O'Neill in southeastern France, the *Maquisards* fought a guerilla war against both the Germans and the pro-Nazi Vichy government.

Now, Simpson followed the two men into the green depths of the forest. At last, they plunged through the last undergrowth and came in sight of the hidden camp. The band of 300 partisans, known as the Maquis, staged secret operations against the Germans from their base there. Even their name

Maquis resistance fighters

Captain Eddie Simpson

meant "thicket" or "bush." The Maquis told the captain that he should stay with them rather than try to break through to the Allied lines in the west. Reports had come in that American troops had reached the outskirts of Orleans. In two or three days, they might penetrate far enough into enemy territory for Simpson to link up with them. Eddie agreed to stay.

Days passed in the green-lit forest. The heavy boom of American guns came from the west. The Maquis lived on fruit and berries plucked from bushes, but they feared to hunt for game lest the Germans hear the echo of a gunshot. They also depended heavily on airdrops of weapons and explosives by the British Special Operations Expedition in France (SOE). Every day, the fighters slipped out of camp to engage in lightning attacks on German troops in the area, in an effort to keep them from organizing a counter-attack on the advancing Americans.

Eddie Simpson had stayed in camp when the freedom fighters straggled in at dawn on August 14. Silently, they laid out the nine bodies of members who had died in a firefight. Eddie took part as the Maquis dug graves deep in the woods near camp to bury their comrades. Just as they knocked in the wooden crosses, a small German patrol broke into the camp on motercycles. The partisans leaped for their guns. Under the hail of fire, the Germans swung around and rode off. But it was too late. Their position had been located. Racing back to camp, the Resistance scrambled to pack what they could carry. Leaving instantly, they planned to head north to Paris. There, they would join up with other Maquis units operating near Allied lines.

A mile deeper in the sheltered forest, the Maquis had hidden several captured German trucks. Eddie Simpson followed at a run as the partisans dashed for the vehicles. Grabbing hold of the sides, Eddie hauled himself into the last truck as the motors throbbed. Weaving along a narrow forest track, the Maquis' convoy swung onto the main road leading towards Orleans. As the trucks bumped onto the highway, a large German column with a mass of trucks and armored cars caught sight of them. The roar of motors and squeal of tires accelerated as the Nazis took off after the freedom fighters. Looking at the dust rising behind them, the Resistance knew that the entire unit would be wiped out if they did not do something immediately. They had to stop the Nazi convoy.

Maquis fighter with Sten gun

Realizing this, one of the Frenchmen shouted for the driver of Simpson's truck to slow down. As the truck ground slowly to a halt, five Resistance members and Eddie Simpson jumped out of the back of the truck. Grabbing a couple of weapons, they swung a heavy machine gun toward the advancing Germans. Then they waved the driver to try and catch up with the convoy.

Scrambling in the dust as the truck raced away, the six men quickly planted the machine gun in the middle of the Orleans road. They crouched, waiting for the German column to come within firing range. As the Nazi trucks roared towards them, the men opened fire. The first slammed to a halt in a mass of perforated metal. With the destroyed vehicle blocking the narrow road near the little village of Ouzouer-sur-Loir, the other German trucks piled up behind the dead truck. They could not squeeze around it.

Simpson and the others kept firing. But wave after wave of German troops poured out of the trucks. The road was flat and without cover. Within a few moments, Captain Eddie Simpson and the five Maquis freedom fighters lay dead in the road. The "Flying Panther" had completed his last mission. But the main body of the French Resistance had escaped. No one knows why Eddie Simpson sacrificed his life to help men he barely knew, when he could have simply waited for repatriation by the advancing American army. But he did. Eddie Simpson demonstrated true love by giving unselfishly of himself to the needs of others, sacrificing his own life that others might prevail in the war for freedom.

Questions

1. What personality did Eddie Simpson have?
2. What happened that caused Eddie to have to bail out of his plane?
3. By whom was he rescued?
4. What plan was devised to get Eddie back to the American lines?
5. What were the freedom fighters involved in doing?
6. What did Eddie and several freedom fighters do in order to turn the tide of their desperate plight?
7. How were they successful in their mission?
8. Tell how Eddie Simpson portrayed true love in choosing to sacrifice his life for the greater cause of freedom.

LOYALTY

DEFINITION

Committed to the welfare of those I serve, even to the detriment of my own comfort.

MEMORY VERSE

Most men will proclaim their own goodness; but a faithful man who can find?

PROVERBS 20:6

Greater Love

The Russian Revolution • Petrograd • December, 1917

December 20, 1917. The Cheka came at night. Between the hours of ten and dawn, black limousines roamed the silent streets, headlights sweeping the windows and catching the faces of passersby like moths in the glare. At 2:00 AM, the cook Darya Efimova sat straight up in bed. Her scarf slipped from her grey hair. What was going on? The little flat was bitterly cold. Outside, Kirochnaia Street was flooded with moonlight. The sound of knocking beat against her head. Someone was trying to break down the door.

Darya leaped out of bed. Peering through the doorway, she saw Colonel Andrei Kalpaschnikoff come out of his bedroom, thrusting his arms into the sleeves of his dressing gown. He looked tall, fair, and ghostly in the dim light. Quickly, he undid the bolts and slid back the chain. The door burst open and three semi-automatics bristled in his face. Beyond them, Darya could see 30 Red Guards in black leather jackets crowding the stairs, dirty sheepskin hats pushed back on their heads. Bayonet points flashed in the glow of a lamp swinging from a chain overhead. The Colonel stared at them, shivering slightly in his thin nightshirt.

Suddenly, a blond boy pressed his revolver against the Colonel's throat. The cold steel kissed his neck; his head jerked to one side. Darya's heart smothered. No, not the master! They couldn't kill him. The boy screamed. It was the scream of a panther.

"If you don't surrender, you are dead!"

Bewildered, the Colonel slowly raised his hands. He backed into the room, and the mob surged into the flat. And in that instant, Darya moved in a flash. I've served the family for over fifty-years. I lived with them at their country estate, cooking for them, nursing them, overseeing the servants. No one is going to hurt the master now. She slipped into the bedroom, hastily cramming bits of gold jewelry, watches and silver spoons into hiding places.

Her ear was sharp. She listened to the snatches of conversation going on in the front room above the crash of furniture as sailors jerked out drawers, overturned tables and stuffed their pockets with knick-knacks, jewelry, leather gloves, and boots.

"Are you Colonel Andrei Kalpaschnikoff of the General Staff?" demanded the commissar.

The Colonel's voice was calm. "I am Kalpaschnikoff of the American Red Cross."

"You are the chief and soul of an American Plot."

"You're mistaken."

Someone bashed a hole in the wall with a rifle butt. Plaster dust rained down.

"In the name of the Council of the Commissioners, in the name of the Soviets which represent the Russian people, I declare you under arrest," the commissar barked. "I will give you several minutes in which to dress and you will be taken to the Fortress of St. Peter and St. Paul, where you will be immediately isolated in solitary confinement."

She caught her breath. The Fortress was a big, gloomy grey edifice, surrounded by water. The Neva River streams ran underground there; damp trickled continually down the cell walls, seeping into the prisoners' aching bones. Solitary confinement meant no light. No human voice to break the silence. Scarce food. Only rats and darkness and dripping water.

She heard the Colonel protest. "But—"

"Get dressed."

Commissar Blagonravov pulled out a chair and sat down at the desk. Throwing one leg over his knee, he opened his soft fur coat lined with sealskin, pulled sheaves of paper from the

drawers and riffled through them. Darya burst into the dining room. Her cheeks blazed. She went right up to Blagonravov, who sat calmly smoking a cigarette, and shook her fist at him.

"You are a pack of robbers who are only here under the pretext of requisition to steal anything you can lay your hands on!"

Blagonravov leaped up. He seized her by the shoulders, gripping so hard that it hurt. His teeth shone wolfishly.

"Now look here, woman, if you don't shut up, I shall have you also arrested."

She jerked her chin back. "You can cut my head off if you want to," she shouted. "But I, Darya, faithful servant of the Kalpaschnikoff family, tell you that the Bolsheviks are murderers and thieves who disgrace the Russian people!"

Sudden tears ran down her cheeks. She turned towards the Colonel, holding out her hands. "Imagine what they have done! They have taken the beautiful American shoes you brought me from New York. Isn't that awful? I shall never get another pair like that."

It hurt to lose those shoes, real American shoes that cost $6.50. Not only because she had never had anything like them in her life before, but because the Colonel had given them to her. She had been so busy concealing his things that she forgot about her own.

Blagonravov glanced away from her. Then he strode to the door and bellowed to the sailors to clear out.

He returned, shrugging. "I can't help it if my men take a few things while they are doing their work. Everything has to be carefully verified in this flat. I know that a lot of weapons and documents are hidden here."

The Colonel, with his coat thrown around his shoulders, was pushed to the door. Darya tugged at the commissar's arm.

Can't he take any food or warm clothes with him?

"Not now," Blagonravov said. "We will see later, although I think he will never want anything again."

He laughed, and the sound chilled Darya.

They were going to kill him.

Behind her, the search went on. Workmen unscrewed the curtains, stripped out the lining and inspected the seams. They ripped open the covers of chairs and couches, knocked out the glass from mirrors and photograph frames, tore up the floorboards. But Darya was blind and deaf now. What was she going to do without him? How would he survive without food or blankets?

She clutched his hands, but he went away from her, down the dark, dirty staircase lined by Red Guards. In the hall below, two men lay with the muzzles of automatic guns aimed at the Colonel's chest. He would not try to run.

Darya ran to the window just as a sleek black limousine purred up to the curb. The door opened, exposing seats covered with yellow silk. She watched as they shoved her master inside, followed by Blagonravov and two guards. Four Latvians, armed with bayonets, jumped onto the running-boards as the car lurched off into the night. They passed the British Embassy on the embankment and swung towards Trinity Bridge.

Commissar Moisei Uritsky

The soldiers searched the flat for incriminating documents till six in the evening on December 21. 16 hours. Then they were gone. For weeks, Darya guarded the flat like a bloodhound. She spent hours on her knees, scrubbing the floor and worrying. What will they do to him? She must help him. But how? She filled a tub with warm water, lifted the Colonel's white Spitz puppy into it and began to soap him down. Suddenly, the telephone rang. Darya struggled up from her knees, wiping her hands on her dress. She lifted the receiver.

"Is that Darya Efimova?"

She did not recognize the voice.

"Yes, I am Darya." She spoke carefully.

"This is the headquarters of the Soviet Police. We want to talk to you."

That was enough. She began to shout.

"You are nothing but a gang of robbers and murderers! You arrested my master and you should give back the things you stole."

"You had better be careful what you say," buzzed an angry voice. "I am Uritsky, the Commissar of Justice, and if you insult me, I shall have you arrested."

Darya was too indignant to think. "I am not afraid of you! I am a poor woman, but for me you are murderers and burglars who have stolen my yellow shoes, my beautiful yellow shoes."

This was the way to make them listen. To accuse them about the shoes.

"What shoes?" Moisei Uritsky demanded in astonishment.

Her voice shrilled: "You all have no consciences, just because some fool invented some stupid stories about my good master; here in front of me, your Red Guards arrested him, raided the flat and stuck in their pockets the present he brought me from America."

"What!" Uritsky shouted.

"Yes, the beautiful yellow shoes." She sobbed.

There was silence on the other end of the line. Then the Bolshevik laughed. His tone softened. "Darya, don't be so angry and don't weep over your things."

"It isn't funny," she retorted.

"It's all right," he consoled her. "We'll find your shoes for you." However, he had called about an entirely different matter. The Cheka recently arrested a young officer on the next floor who stole money to fund the anti-Bolshevik "Direct Anarchist" society. Since Darya often cleaned his room and given him tea, they wanted to ask her some questions about him.

Go to the Cheka station? It was miles away.

"No," she said promptly. "I'm going to wash my master's dog.

I cannot run so far on foot."

Uritsky said quickly, "I wouldn't dream of keeping you long! So as not to waste time, I'll send my private car for you. It will pick you up and bring you back."

A few minutes later, a black Packard roared up and parked in front of No. 11 Kirochnaia Street. Wearing a black silk handkerchief over her head and carrying the Colonel's dog in her arms, Darya sailed down the stairs. The chauffer snapped to attention. Darya settled her skirts in the vehicle. The doors shut. People ran out of the house to look. The hall porter gaped. She was no longer a simple peasant woman. She was an important witness. As she glanced up at the windows, she could almost see her master's tall, thin figure floating like a ghost behind the glass.

Soon a grey building loomed up on Gurokhovaia Street: the dungeons of the secret police. Darya stood calmly in the waiting room, listening for her name. She did not have to wait long.

The door to Uritsky's office opened.

"Darya Efimova!"

Taking her courage in both hands, she crossed the dirty floor covered with spittle. Her shoes crunched on the shells of sunflower seeds. The door closed behind her. She was in Uritsky's den. Darya bowed deeply from the waist, her eyes searching the corner opposite the door for the holy icon. Her eyes met instead the oblique, black gaze of Vladimir Lenin. Then she looked up and saw Uritsky's flat, clean-shaven face and curving nose.

"Good morning, *Barin* (Master)." Her voice was soft, rural, the vowels drawn out in the village fashion.

Uritsky looked startled over his pince-nez. Masters and tsars, laws and police no longer existed. But he looked pleased. This was a very dignified old woman.

Her eyes searched his face. "You look like a good *barin.* You do not look wicked at all, and now that I have seen you, I really do not understand why people are not ashamed to call you an old Jew, ready to strangle everyone."

Her voice was soft and coaxing, her gaze direct. It was as if Uritsky was seeing himself for the first time. What if he did sign hundreds of death sentences every day? He was the Commissar of Justice. He had power over life and death.

He brought her a chair.

Please to sit down.

"Now that you are in a good temper," he began ingratiatingly, "I want you to be a good woman and tell me everything about the officer who lived in your house." He paused. "If you read these papers we found and tell me everything, I will help recover the stolen things and I myself will search for the yellow shoes."

Darya protested that she could not read. But she would tell what she had seen. As she finished her story, they brought the guilty officer into the room. Slowly, Darya stood up. Here was a man arrested for doing the same thing the Red Guards had done: stealing.

"It might be pardoned in a simple peasant or Bolshevik—" her voice rose scornfully—"but for an officer, it was a shame to do such things. My master would never have tried to steal! He would have preferred to die of hunger or have his hands cut off rather than touch what did not belong to him."

They were listening, now.

Her voice thickened. "My master, who has never done any harm except helping the poor people, is in prison on unjust accusations and rascals like you are running loose, committing all kinds of crime."

She didn't care what happened to her. She had turned the tables on them, made them see the truth.

"You, who are a good *barin,* ought to see the difference between such scamps and nice people like my master."

They couldn't stop her. The words poured on. Good must conquer evil. People must listen to the truth. She believed this.

An hour later, she sat in the apartment with two of Uritsky's chauffeurs wearing black leather jackets. She poured hot water from the samovar's spout, set out plates of biscuits and spooned dollops of sugary jam into their tea. All the while, she spoke gently, persuasively about her master. What a good man he was, how he worked for the Red Cross, helping wounded soldiers and distributing food to the starving peasants. They listened, their faces growing warm from the tea and from the words. It was getting dark, now. Darya leaned over to light the oil lamp before the big picture of St. Nicholas. The two men bowed deeply. At the door, they turned to look back at her. They felt sorry for the Colonel, now. He oughtn't to be in prison at all.

The next day, one of them came back. He had spoken to Uritsky and reminded him of his promise to help Darya Efimova. He came back often in the following weeks and months. Sometimes he secretly gave Darya information about the Communists.

Then suddenly, Colonel Kalpaschnikoff was released. Brought into the office of the Cheka, he stood before Uritsky. Pale and gaunt from months in prison, he could not understand the reason for this visit. Uritsky spoke to him one minute, shouted into the telephone the next.

"I told you to shoot them and not to annoy me any more about these men!"

The Colonel stood silently.

Dismissing the executions with a wave of his hand, Uritsky spun towards him.

"I shall certainly try to do something for you. I promised to do so for Comrade Efimova."

"My cook!" The Colonel was astonished.

"Yes, Darya." Uritsky smiled. "She is your best lawyer."

Colonel Kalpaschnikoff was released ten days later.

For weeks, he found it difficult to sleep in a soft bed. He was always expecting a cell door to clang, to wake up and find he was back in the Fortress. Then on August 17, 1918, a young military cadet assassinated Uritsky for the execution of his officer friends. Darya knew that her master would never be safe while he stayed in the country. The next day, the chauffer arrived with the news that Kalpaschnikoff's name was on a secret list of eighty-four people to be shot in the morning for Uritsky's murder. The plan to go to America began. Darya sent a little girl from the next flat out to buy an international train ticket. She poured the master a last cup of coffee. Then they sat down in the silent dining room to wait. An hour later the girl scrambled up the stairs, clutching the ticket. The Colonel's passport now listed him as a Communist battalion leader—not an enemy of the state.

The candle flame sputtered as Darya locked the door. "God will protect you," she whispered. "I shall continue to pray."

They went softly downstairs. Darya carried a big basket stuffed with food and clothing for the journey. She would not let him go like that again. As she distracted the ticket-seller at the bustling station, Colonel Kalpaschnikoff slipped onto the train. If he could cross the border to the Ukraine in the south, he would be safe.

Late that night, black motor cars from the Cheka roared down Kirochnaia Street and men in peaked caps surrounded No. 11. They found the flat empty, the bird flown. Darya, doddering out of bed in her shawl, obligingly showed them the house. She opened the cellar. She guided them around. Suddenly, the commissar noticed that she was smiling. Her face shone softly, contentedly through its network of wrinkles.

Where is he? If you don't tell us, we will force you to speak.

She looked at him calmly. "What can you do to me, if I persist in hiding my master?"

"Arrest you as a counter-revolutionist!" snarled the commissar.

Darya smiled quietly. "I am not afraid of you. I am a simple peasant; you have no right to do anything to me. I shall nevertheless give you the necessary information. Mr. Kalpaschnikoff is in Finland, on his way to America."

That was directly north; he had gone south. "He has gone to fetch me another pair of yellow shoes to replace the ones you stole the first time you grabbed him. It is too late, you cannot catch him anymore."

It was the last thing she could do for him. The man she had nursed, carried in her arms, sweated and cared for, was safe.

She could smile at anything.

They seized her arms and dragged her down to the car. At two o'clock that morning, the Bolsheviks shot eighty-three of the eighty-four people on their list. Only Colonel Kalpaschnikoff escaped. Darya Efimova spent a month in the same Fortress as her beloved master. In four weeks, she was transferred to an unknown place to be released. After that, she disappeared from history into the heavy snows, the meadows of birch trees, the language and color of the people she loved so devotedly.

History is not only made by people like George Washington or Napoleon. Common people, their commitment and faith comprise the backbone of history. Darya Efimova showed uncommon loyalty to those the family she served, even if it cost her her life.

Questions

1. Tell of Darya's loyalty to her master.
2. What was he accused of? By whom?
3. Tell of his capture. How did Darya try to prevent it?
4. What role did Darya play in his release from prison?
5. How did her master escape?
6. What had his job been?
7. What was Darya's fate?
8. Why was she happy amidst adverse circumstances?
9. What family/friends do you need to show loyalty to?
10. What are some specific ways you could demonstrate loyalty this week?

MEEKNESS

DEFINITION

Yielding my expectations (rights) to God
without getting angry

MEMORY VERSE

The meek will he guide in judgment:
and the meek will he teach his way.

PSALM 25:9

The Plant Doctor

Tuskegee Institute • Tuskegee, Alabama • 1896

He had always loved plants. They vibrated under his fingers like sea anemones, bursting into leaf, fruit, and flower. Pottering around in his laboratory, the tall, dark, and distinguished-looking professor felt the leaves quiver as he touched them with the same life that danced in his music or leaped onto the canvas with swift brush-strokes from his painter's pallet. Now, late at night, he hunched over a single yellow lamp. Outside, a student banged on the door.

"Are you all right, Dr. Carver?"

He glanced up, bewildered. "Yes! Yes! Please let me be."

Someday, George Washington Carver, born a slave, would produce a product that would benefit poor sharecropping farmers in the exhausted land of the post-war South.

Wearing a baggy hat and a patched sweater, Carver sauntered slowly along the country road. A white woman had called at the Institute to see if "the Tuskegee man" would help her withering peach trees. As he drew near, the woman saw a shabby, somber-faced Negro coming across the lawn.

"Do you want to earn fifty cents cutting my grass?" she called out. He remained silent. Going quietly to the mower, he began pushing it back and forth through the long grass. He crisscrossed the front lawn. He mowed the back. Then he went to the door and knocked politely.

When she opened the door, he said softly, "Now, what seems to be the trouble with your peaches, Ma'am?"

He could not remember his mother. In the shadowy nighttime of 1865, a gang of Confederate bushwhackers swooped down on

George Washington Carver

the slave cabins on the Carver farm near Diamond, Missouri. They grabbed his mother, tearing the baby from her arms and forcing her out of the cabin. Farther along the road, they threw him into a ditch and rode off. The next day, a neighbor found the baby and returned him to his owners, Moses and Sarah Carver. Raised as one of their own children, George ran about the farm, collecting rocks, digging up plants, catching frogs and examining insects. When neighbors brought him their dying plants, he took them to his little workshop in the woods and nursed them back to health. He seemed to have a magic touch when it came to the complex natural world around him. Locals called him the "plant doctor."

His mind thirsted for knowledge. But every school shut their doors to him because of his color. At age fourteen, he learned of a school for blacks in Neosho, Missouri. When he limped into town, he had no money and nowhere to go. As he ambled along the street towards the schoolhouse, a black woman called out to him from her backyard. Her name was Moriah Watkins, a childless washerwoman. From that evening, he ate and slept at her house, attending classes in the bitterly cold schoolhouse and helping Moriah's husband with odd jobs after hours.

During the next hard years, George Washington Carver finished grade school and high school, and then tried to enter college. Poor, dusty, and exhausted, the tall, handsome young man trudged on foot to Highland College, overjoyed at his letter of acceptance. When he arrived at the university's office, the president stared at him. "You didn't tell me you were Negro," he said accusingly. "Highland College does not take Negroes." But Carver did not give up. Finally, in 1890, at the age of thirty, he walked thirty miles to Simpson College in Indianola, Iowa, and was accepted. To support himself, he cooked and sold hominy and washed, ironed, and mended his classmates' laundry. He also served as a janitor, waiter, greenhouse worker, and laboratory assistant. No task was too menial, no job too dirty for him to perform gladly. Others noticed the young man's meekness, grace, and dignity. Meanwhile, he studied voraciously: music, art, botany, chemistry, geometry, zoology, and bacteriology.

In 1896, he graduated with a Master's Degree from Iowa State University. Then Booker T. Washington, struggling to keep the flame of black education alive in Tuskegee, Alabama, wrote him a letter offering Carver the chance to benefit his countrymen through research. "I cannot offer you money, position, or fame," Washington argued. "The first two you have. The last . . . you will no doubt achieve. These things I ask you to give up. I offer you, in their place, work—hard, hard work—the task of bringing a people from degradation, poverty, and waste to full manhood."

Dr. Carver studying plants

Some laboratories offered Carver over $100,000 per year (almost a million dollars today) to work for them. Booker T. Washington could only offer him a pittance of $125 per month.

Feeling that God wanted him to work for Tuskegee, Carver gave up his seat on the faculty at Iowa State University. As the Director of Agriculture at Tuskegee, he showed students that they threw away rich plant food every day. For instance, he pointed out the despised cowpea. Southerners did not even consider the cowpea as food, but rather as cattle fodder. Carver sent his students hiking through the woods to fill their buckets with leaf mold to spread on their gardens. He had discovered that cowpeas actually draw nitrogen from the air and then release it back into the soil.

Carver observed how cotton crops depleted the soil's nutrients without replenishing them. Instead of always planting cotton, he urged farmers to alternate with enriching legumes like soybeans and peanuts, as well as sweet potatoes and pecans. By promoting variable crops, he demonstrated ways to help the land recover from the destruction of the Civil War. This transition from plantations to farms run by former slaves helped the South to regain economic stability.

Years passed. Carver never married. When urged to, the professor smiled gently. "What woman would want a husband forever dropping soil specimens all over her parlor? How could I explain to a wife that I need to go out at four o'clock every morning to talk to the flowers?"

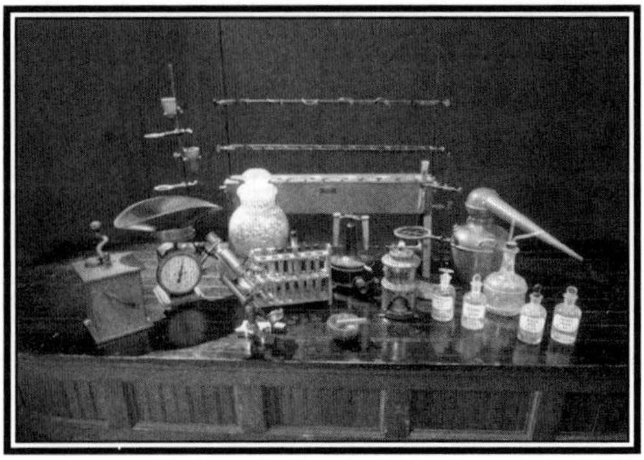

Dr. Carver's laboratory equipment

He lived in one of the Tuskegee dormitories and walked daily to work in his laboratory. The peanut grew and flourished. Working with fields and test tubes, he discovered three hundred useful products made from

Dr. Carver experimenting in his laboratory

peanuts. He made milk, cheese, soap, bleach, axle grease, adhesives, fuel, instant coffee, ink, buttermilk, mayonnaise, chili sauce, meat tenderizer, paper, linoleum, shoe polish, and pavement. As he went on testing, the possibilities seemed endless: Shaving cream, metal polish, talcum powder, synthetic rubber, and wood stain. By varying their crops and improving their diets with simple plants, Carver improved the standard of living for many rural families in the South. No longer would a farmer be dependent on a single market for his produce. Now, he could sell his peanut and soybean crops to industrialists and food manufacturers.

A devout Christian who called his laboratory "God's little workshop," Carver also taught a Bible class every Sunday afternoon. He still drew his original $125.00 a month. Under his hands, the ordinary peanut oozed milk. It turned into fine dust as a base for cosmetics. It stretched into synthetic rubber. For all of this, Carver took no credit. He refused to take out a patent on more than three inventions, saying, "God gave them to me. How can I sell them to someone else?"

George Washington Carver demonstrated meekness by performing menial tasks with humility and refusing to take the glory for his discoveries for himself.

Questions

1. What did George Washington Carver delight in studying?
2 How did he demonstrate meekness when the lady mistook him for being a servant?
3. What happened to his mother and father?
4. How did he come to live with the Carvers? Tell how he was treated by the Carvers.
5. How did Moriah Watkins prove a blessing in his life?
6. What college turned him down because of his color?
7. How did he support himself while attending Simpson College?
8. What was Booker T. Washington's offer to Carver?
9. What did Carver accomplish in his time there?
10 What was he able to make from the peanut?
11. How did he help to improve the standard of living for the Southern farmers?
12. What did he call his workshop?
13. How did Carver demonstrate meekness when praised by others?
14. How can you choose to live a life of meekness? When tempted to be angry? When tempted to take credit for yourself?

How far you go in life depends on your being tender to the young, compassionate with the aged, sympathetic with the striving and tolerant of the weak and strong. Because someday in you life you will have been all of these.

— George Washington Carver

Obedience

Definition

Doing what is expected of me cheerfully, immediately, and thoroughly

Memory Verse

Children, obey your parents in all things: for this is well pleasing unto the Lord.

Colossians 3:20

Argonne Forest

World War I • Argonne Forest, France • October 18, 1918

Chatel Chehery: October 8, 1918. This was Armageddon. The last battle between angels and demons. The stark, shredded trees burned below him with a lurid glow, stretching fearful fingers to the night sky. The flash and belch of artillery cut through the rainy mist to the steep, wooded valley beyond the hill of Montfaucon. Shells exploded around him in the dawn, tearing up the ground. Horses thrashed and whinnied in the road. The sound carried through the cold, damp air like glass ringing. Men sprawled in heaps like dead leaves, Bavarians in dark blue coats, Saxons in sky-blue tunics, Austrians in silver, British and Americans in yellow khaki and the French in smoky-blue.

It had rained all day, a drizzling, penetrating rain that soaked Corporal Alvin C. York's greatcoat, dripped from his reddish mustache and turned his tattered puttees into strips of wet cardboard. Often during these dark days, American soldiers could be heard chanting:

"We're all going calling on the Kaiser,
For we've got to teach the Kaiser to be wiser."

But the forest was worse. The cabin in the mountains of Pall Mall, Tennessee, and Gracie Williams blurred in his mind. The locals knew him at age twenty-seven as a hard-drinker and hard-fighter, as well as a deadly accurate shot at local turkey shoots. Then he met God and Gracie Williams and everything changed. He gave his life over to Christ. But when America entered World War I on the Allied side, he found that he did not believe in the war. "I was worried clean through," he said. "I didn't want to go and kill. I believed in my Bible."

Then on June 5, 1917, he registered for the draft. On his draft

Sgt. Alvin C. York

card they had printed the question: "Do you claim exemption from draft?" He wrote: "Yes. Don't want to fight."

The army denied his claim. When York received the news, he filed an appeal. Few things in the military atmosphere of 1917 were more unpopular than a conscientious objector. The other recruits viewed such men as cowards and treated them harshly. The army looked down on them, but forced them to work in non-combatant roles. While York's petition was still under review, he entered the service at Camp Gordon, Georgia. During those weeks of boot-camp, York spoke with his commanding officer, Major Buxton, who urged him seek the Bible and pray about his doubts. Finally, alone on a mountaintop, York came to the conclusion that it was his moral duty to participate in the war. From the time he went to France, he never looked back.

Russia, with the connivance of the Bolshevik Party at the Treaty of Brest-Litovsk, had dropped out of the war in March. The Germans now occupied most of Eastern Europe as well as France and Belgium. On the western front, the lines had only advanced a mile or two since 1914.

The Meuse–Argonne offensive began on the 26th of September, 1918. According to Marshal Ferdinand Foch's strangling offensive, Belgian, British, and French forces drove through Flanders to the north, pushing the Germans ahead of them. At the same time, British troops hit the center, attacking all along the

Hindenburg Line: a four-mile deep barricade of steel and concrete fortifications. Meanwhile, to the south, the French Fourth Army with General Henri Gourand and the American First Army under General John "Black Jack" Pershing would face the most difficult stretch of all. Striking between the old cathedral town of Reims and the shattered walls of Verdun, the soldiers fought along the bank of the Meuse and plunged into the Argonne Forest. In the heart of the forest, the German lines lay 12 miles deep. Trenches, bunkers, and defense wire rusting there for four years blocked their way. But the combined attack succeeded.

American soldiers in the Argonne Forest

The night before, York slept with his men in the Zona Woods. Only a few splintered trees gaped over their heads. He knew that they had not reached the real fighting yet. Since October 4, the Americans continued to throw themselves in suicide frontal assaults at the impregnable Hindenburg Line perched on the ridge at Romagne. During the afternoon of October 7, York and the other members of the American Expeditionary Force lay on their bellies in shallow holes in the roadside for hours. German airplanes with silver crosses on the wings swooped overhead with a buzz like angry hornets. Night fell as he stared at the burning woods. Somewhere in there was the Lost Battalion. 650 soldiers of the 75th Division had disappeared into the heavily-guarded No-Man's land between Bois d'Apremont and Charlevaux earlier in the fighting on October 2. No one had come back.

Before dawn on October 8, York, Sergeant Bernard Early, and sixteen men set off for the Decauville railroad. Their mission: to take out the machine guns on Hill 223 in the Chatel-Chehery sector of the Meuse-Argonne sector. The four non-commissioned officers crouched over their map, trying to decipher the unfamiliar French names. Then they set off again, crawling through the wooded terrain full of shattered stumps. Guns thundered overhead.

Suddenly, yellow gas began to creep over them. It came at them like an olive-green cloud, rolling over the ground. Yellowish-green, it grew darker where it spread along the ground, thinning out to a thin grey near the top. It made your eyes burn, gripped your stomach, tore at your lungs. Mustard gas was the most easily recognized. Chlorine gas, colorless and deadly, could kill a man before he knew it. At Ypres in 1916, they had had nothing to cover their mouths with except pieces of cloth smeared with mud. Now, grabbing his gas mask and fastening the goggles and straps, York dashed for Hill 223.

World War I gas mask

Crossing the flat, snow-covered expanse, barren of any life except for the unseen snipers, they stumbled through weedy brush towards the low hill. Soldiers fell like cut grass before the pounding machine guns. They would have to sneak around and take the gun nests from the rear.

It was after 6:00 AM. They continued crawling deep into the brush. 300 yards beyond their front lines, they stopped near the top of the hill and conferred. Some wanted to attack the Germans from the flank. But York knew that they had to spring on them from the rear. Inching forward again, they found themselves behind enemy lines. They could not see the Germans and the Germans could not see them. Sharp firing broke out in the woods as York and his men leaped across a thin stream. On the other side, twenty Germans threw up their hands.

"Kamerad!" they shouted. "Comrade!"

They had landed in the middle of the Landwehr Infantry headquarters. German helmets poked up from the bunkers like sitting ducks. They had breakfast spread out, a jumble of jams, jellies, beefsteaks, and loaves of bread. They were just tucking in when York burst into camp.

Sgt. Alvin York in the Argonne Forest

"Put 'em up!" he ordered.

They stuck their hands over their heads without muttering. Within minutes, the large German force, thinking the entire American army was behind them, surrendered. Suddenly, the German major shouted something in guttural tones. All at once, the German machine guns on the hill swung their snouts towards them. A murderous spat of gunfire burst out of the woods less than thirty yards away. All but two of York's squad toppled instantly. Sergeant Early went down with three bullets, leaving York in command. Brush whizzed past him. He had no time to dodge behind a tree. Instead, he began shooting back at the thirty gunners firing continuously at him.

American soldiers carrying M1917 rifles with bayonets

"I had no time nohow to do nothing but watch them-there German machine gunners and give them the best I had," he said. "Every time I seed a German I jes' teched him off. At first I was shooting from a prone position; that is lying down; jes' like we often shoot at the targets in the shooting matches in the mountains of Tennessee . . . But the targets here were bigger. I jes' couldn't miss a German's head or body at that distance. And I didn't. Besides, it weren't no time to miss nohow. I knowed that in order to shoot me, the Germans would have to get their heads up to see where I was lying. And I knowed that my only chance was to keep their heads down. And I done done it. I covered their positions and let fly every time I seed anything to shoot at. Every time a head come up I done knocked it down. Then they would sorter stop for a moment and then another head would come up and I would knock it down, too. I was giving them the best I had."

All the time, York kept yelling at them to come down. He did not want to kill any more men than he had to. His rifle barrel scorched his hands. He had only half a cartridge clip left in his M1917 Enfield rifle, but he flipped out his .45 Colt automatic pistol just as German Lieutenant Paul Jümer Vollmer and five soldiers vaulted out of a ditch twenty-five yards away. They charged at him with fixed bayonets. Aiming calmly, York picked off the last one first, all the way up the line. It was just like shooting turkeys back home: if you shot the last one first, the other ones didn't know and kept on going. Vollmer shot at him again and again, but he could not hit York. Then the German major scrambled up from the ground and came towards him.

"English?" he shouted.

York shook his head. "No, not English."

"What?" he demanded.

"American."

The major sighed with relief. "Good! If you won't shoot any more, I will make them give up."

Twenty German soldiers lay sprawled on the ground. York did not trust the major. He kept his automatic trained on him while the major gave a sharp little whistle. Instantly, the Germans threw down their guns and belts. But as they started back over the hill, one of them lobbed a hand-grenade at York. It burst in the air, scattering bits of shrapnel. York had to "tech him off."

Everyone held up their hands then. With only seven men left, he lined the Germans up in two rows and made them carry the American wounded out. Placing the German major at the front of the column, York kept his pistol pressed tight to his back. Suddenly, the major suggested going down a nearby gully. With a tingle in his veins, York knew that this was a trap. Instead, he nudged the German officer ahead of him. They were going back to the American front straight through the German lines. On the way, he kept collecting Germans like butterflies. Close to Chatel Chehery, the party came under heavy shell fire. York had to double-quick the prisoners through the area to make sure that he did not lose any of them. They had surrendered, and it was up to him to keep them safe.

Sgt York being congratulated after the war.

Back at headquarters, Brigadier General Lindsey greeted him: "Well, York, I hear you captured the whole German army."

York told him he had only 132.

The entire time, he had felt a deep, sweet calm. He gave the glory to God: "So you can see here in this case of mine where God helped me out. I had been living for God and working in the church some time before I come to the army. So I am a witness to the fact that God did help me out of that hard battle; for the bushes were shot up all around me and I never got a scratch. So you can see that God will be with you if you will only trust Him; and I say that He did save me."

The next morning, the 328th Regiment went in and found twenty-eight German soldiers lying behind the second line. Sergeant York's actions helped silence thirty-five machine guns and clear the way for fresh American troops to follow. Though he was only one man in one place, his actions gave a tremendous boost to morale. For his heroism, York won the Medal of Honor, the Distinguished Service Medal and the French Croix de Guerre and Legion of Honor.

Alvin C. York demonstrated obedience by carrying out orders in spite of his own feelings.

Questions

1. Why did Alvin register as a conscienctious objector?
2. What happened to change his mind about that?
3. What was the mission of Sgt. Early's men?
4. How did they manage to capture the first 20 men?
5. What happened to leave command to Alvin York?
6. How did York's experience shooting turkeys back home aid him in this campaign?
7. How many prisoners did York end up capturing?
8. Tell how he gave the glory to God.
9. How many machine guns did York end up silencing?
10. What medals did Alvin York receive?
11. Explain how York demonstrated obedience to his orders despite his own feelings.
12. Describe how his obedience affected so many others.
13. Think of how you can do a better job at demonstrating obedience in your life.

ORDERLINESS

DEFINITION

Managing my life and my belongings in order to reach maximum potential

MEMORY VERSE

Let all things be done decently and in order.

I CORINTHIANS 14:40

Confederate April

The Civil War • Appomattox Court House • April 9, 1865

During the night, the sound of horses gnawing the bark from the trees kept Colonel Charles Marshall awake. The April wind was chilly and Marshall pulled his cape over his head to muffle the noise. But nothing could shut out the sounds of hunger. After a late-night council of war, Robert E. Lee's secretary lay in the dense wood without a blanket or tent. As Lee's adjutant from 1862 to 1865, Marshall's meticulous clerical work, his careful record-keeping and drafting of hundreds of letters, dispatches, and general orders had earned him a high place of responsibility on Lee's staff.

Suddenly Marshall sat up, listening intently. It was 1:00 AM. A column of infantry was moving along the road. Had Grant's troops spotted them? Then Marshall heard hoarse voices chanting out of the dusk. It was Hood's Texas brigade straggling along in the pre-dawn darkness, their feet aching and their stomachs empty. Headquarters broke camp as Marshall buttoned on his coat, blind without the thick spectacles he wore even in sleep.

Sunday April 9th, 1865, dawned. As Marshall mounted his horse, the guns booming in the distance told him that General Gordon was trying to break out of the encirclement. But Union cavalry greeted his exhausted attack, forcing him back on Appomattox. Longstreet's division was in tatters, stragglers stretching out for miles. Yesterday, Lee received a note from General Grant, suggesting they discuss surrender. Now Lee told Marshall: "Write to General Grant." Throughout the morning, Marshall transmitted half a dozen notes between Grant and Lee. Both parties were dancing around the issue of surrender, Grant pushing for capitulation and Lee resisting. It was now almost noon. No further word had come from Grant. The officers climbed the slope overlooking Appomat-

Colonel Charles Marshall with General Robert E. Lee, signing terms of surrender ending the Civil War

tox Court House. Lee was visibly flagging, his face showing unbearable strain. An hour passed before a white flag of truce rippled towards them. Lee rose to greet the Union officers. He was ready to meet Grant. Valuing Marshall's orderly writing, Lee asked him to accompany him. Marshall was in a "dilapidated" state. His uniform was in tatters, his gauntlets nonexistent; he had to borrow a sword. Marshall's job was to find a suitable place for the generals to meet. Soon he located a two-story brick house belonging to Wilmer McLean.

A short time later, Lee entered the front room, wearing snowy gauntlets and a crisp grey uniform. Marshall stood behind a marble-topped table near the window. The wall opposite them filled with tiptoeing Union officers. Half an hour ticked by. It was now 1:30 PM. All at once, there was a loud clumping of boots in the hall. Grant had arrived. Marshall watched as the two men quietly shook hands. Then Lee got down to business. He agreed that surrender was necessary "to prevent further bloodshed." Colonel Ely Parker, Grant's Indian aide, carried a little oval table over to Grant, who hunched above it, scribbling out the terms of surrender. Marshall perched on the arm of the sofa, chatting with General Sheridan as the two generals discussed the disposition of arms, baggage and horses. They crossed out a word here, inserted a phrase there.

Glancing at the draft, Lee noticed that the surrender conditions did not allow the Confederates to keep their own animals. "That is clear."

Grant, noting the wistful tone, said hastily, "I will instruct the officers to let all the men who claim to own a horse or mule take the animals home with them to work their little farms."

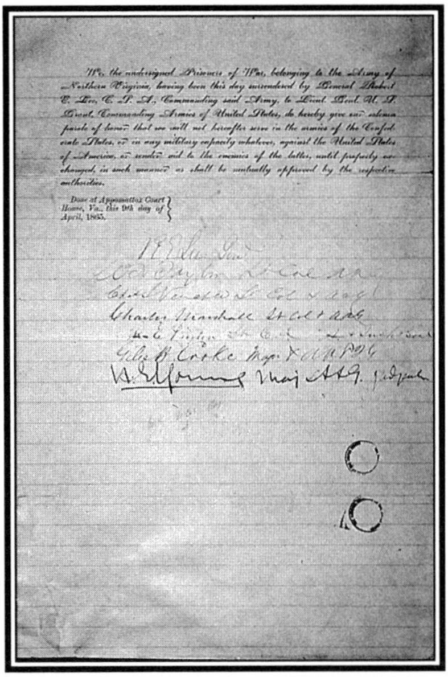

We, the undersigned Prisoners of War, belonging to the Army of Northern Virginia, having been this day surrendered by General Robert E. Lee, C. S. A., Commanding said Army, to Lieut. Genl. U. S. Grant, Commanding Armies of United States, do hereby give our solemn parole of honor that we will not hereafter serve in the armies of the Confederate States, or in any military capacity whatever, against the United States of America, or render aid to the enemies of the latter, until properly exchanged, in such manner as shall be mutually approved by the respective authorities.

Done at Appomattox Court House, Va., this 9th day of April, 1865.

Surrender of Army of Northern Virginia

Lee's face cleared. "This will have the best possible effect upon my men."

Parker went to the rear of the room and began to copy the surrender terms. But he ran out of ink. With his usual method, Marshall reached into the satchel at his side and offered Parker the boxwood inkwell he always carried with him.

Then it was Marshall's turn to draft a reply. Lee cut him short. "Don't say 'I have the honor.' Just say, 'I accept the terms.' " Sitting down, Marshall wrote in his beautiful, copperplate handwriting:

"We, the prisoners of war belonging to the Army of Northern Virginia [have] this day surrendered by General Robert E. Lee."

It was 4 PM. Beyond the window, the fifth spring of the war was beginning. Marshall had to turn his face away, because there were tears in his eyes.

Because of his orderliness, Colonel Charles Marshall was chosen to draft the important document officially ending the Civil War in Virginia. He was one of the two Confederates present at the surrender, and the only one to later write about it.

Questions

1. What quality had won Col. Marshall the position of high responsibility on Robert E. Lee's staff?
2. Why was it so important to keep careful details?
3. How did Col. Marshall's orderliness in being prepared show during the surrender?
4. Why is it important as a youth to hone your skills or orderliness in preparation for your future? (Remember David in Scripture who learned to be proficient in the use of a slingshot as a boy. How did God use that in the future?)
5. What are ways you could improve in orderliness? Your room? Your belongings? Your schoolwork? Your chores? Your ministry to others?

Teach me, O LORD, the way of thy statutes; and I shall keep it unto the end.

— *Psalm 119:33*

Patience

Definition

Waiting for God's timing with a happy heart

Memory Verse

Wherefore seeing we also are compassed about
with so great a cloud of witnesses,
let us lay aside every weight,
and the sin which doth so easily beset us,
and let us run with patience
the race that is set before us.

Hebrews 12:1

The Bridge on the River Kwai

World War II • Thailand • Malay Jungle • June, 1942

Thailand: June 1942. Warm tropical rain beat down on their heads as they trudged helplessly through the heavy silence of the Malay jungle. Birds beat overhead and rain poured ceaselessly from the thick, shiny green leaves. Soaked to the skin, they clutched their faded khaki uniforms around them like tattered shreds of dignity. Dirty bronzed fingers scooped up bits of rice and stuffed them into mouths, washed down with a gulp of onion water "hogwash" called stew.

"You are going to a health resort," the Japanese said with smiling faces.

They packed up their piano and gramophone records. The Japanese would supply them with gramophones at the resort. Piling their belongings from the Changi prison camp into metal army trucks, the weak, sick, and starving British prisoners set out joyfully on foot.

At the station, short Japanese soldiers in light-colored fatigues began pushing them into line, shouting: "All men marchee, marchee!"

"What?" Somebody asked in dismay. "We're coming for a holiday."

And then the Japanese laughter began, like birds cackling in the jungle.

The defense of Singapore had failed with the surrender of General Arthur Percival—the worst defeat in British military history. Thirty-eight-year-old Colonel Philip Toosey, his long face grim, refused evacuation to India. An officer in the Territorial Army since 1925, he chose to share the fate of his men. Now, on the border between Thailand and Burma, they arrived at the Tha

Maa Kham POW camp at Tamarkan. Sergeant Risaburo Saito met them in the muddy compound. Looking at the 2,000 British prisoners with something like pity, he listened as the commandant informed them that they would construct a bridge over the Khwae Mae Khlong (Kwai Yai). The bridge, a feat of Japanese engineering, would create a railway line from Bangkok to Rangoon. Soon Japanese troop trains would pant and whistle across the jungle river into Burma to support the Japanese army.

Colonel Philip Toosey

Toosey, listening carefully, learned that officers would be forced to labor beside their men. According to the rules of the Geneva Convention, the enemy could not use captured officers for manual labor—only supervising duties. The Japanese knew why as well as he. Forcing officers to work would break the authority structure that placed officers in charge of their soldiers. Used as slave labor, officers lost their dignity and their power to give orders. Without authority, an army ceased to exist. Both officers and men would be reduced to the position of slaves.

Work began as they headed into the miserable Thailand winter. Cold rain slid down their backs as the men slaved away without shirts. The senior Allied officer on the site, Colonel Toosey walked back and forth, supervising the labor. Patience—patience was the key. If he could keep the men working just enough to allay Japanese suspicion, keep as many men alive as possible and still sabotage the bridge, then he would have succeeded in doing something. A refusal to work amounted to instant execution. But he could do something to delay the bridge and still spare his men.

He glanced at the bridge sharply as the Japanese engineers hovered nearby. The men worked with painful slowness. They mixed the concrete sloppily and badly. He studied the steel and concrete monster arching over the slate-grey water beneath the Three Pagodas Pass. The wooden spans supported the huge structure. Suddenly, he had an idea. He gathered his officers together in a little knot and spoke quietly so that the guards would not hear.

Soon the men began overturning and digging under the wet felled trees lying on the hillsides beside the river. Fat white termites grew like mold in the humid air of the jungle. Set free in the cracks and crevices of the bridge, they began gnawing away at the wooden timbers.

In the mud below, a total of 200,000 Asian workers and 68,000 British, Australian, Dutch, and American slaves worked from the Siam and Burma sides towards the center. Lifting timbers that often broke away and crashed into the water, killing workers, stirring concrete, slapping swarms of mosquitoes, and battling jungle fever, the men worked on. Winter passed and the muggy Thailand summer began as the work edged towards completion in spite of continued British sabotage. By October 1943, 96,000 people had died, over 18,000 of them Allied troops. They called it the Death Railway.

The Colonel also worked patiently in the camp. He strode through the compound, ensuring that discipline prevailed. He battled lice, dysentery, diphtheria, and cholera in his fight to maintain some standards of cleanliness and personal hygiene. Rain gushed down the hillsides and ran continually through the huts in the lower part of camp where the men lay on hard bamboo cots. He made certain that the officers ate meals with their men, establishing deep ties of friendship, unity, and loyalty. The men became as one, a team knit together for survival. Unlike other prison camps, where the officers remained helpless in their efforts to protect their men, Toosey tried to see that his men suffered as little as possible. He complained whenever his men were physically mistreated. Each time, the commandant had him repeatedly and brutally beaten. As a skillful negotiator, he also gained favors and better treatment for the POWs.

Willing to suffer for his men, the Colonel organized at least one escape at the risk of his own life. He scraped together a month's rations for two officers. Then he managed to hide the fact of their escape for forty-eight hours—enough time for the men to make their way into the jungle and outdistance the first search parties. When the guards discovered their escape, the Colonel suffered harsh punishment at the hands of the enraged Japanese. Meanwhile, he secretly contacted Boonpong Sirivejjabhandu, a Thai merchant who risked his life to supply the starving prisoners at the southern end of the railway. With his help, Toosey smuggled in quantities of food and medicine from the outside. Mixing medicine, organizing a food supply and ensuring that work crawled on the bridge, the Colonel instilled hope in his men that they could wait and survive until rescued by Allied forces.

Finally, in October 1943, the Kwai Bridge was completed. Sometime before, the British authorities had determined that such a project would take the royal engineers five years to finish. Now, a gang of soldiers under their patient and courageous officer had built 415 kilometers of bridge and railway from scratch in just 16 months. Both the

Scene from the film "Bridge on the River Kwai" showing the bridge built by the prisoners of war

wooden bridge and the steel bridge stood for two years until blown up during a seventh Allied air raid.

Following the bridge's completion, most of the able men moved upriver to new camps. Colonel Toosey stayed behind to create a hospital for the sick at Tamarkan. The Japanese, admiring his area as the best-run prisoner-of-war camp on the Siam-Burma railway, allowed him a high level of freedom. During the last months, they shuttled him around to different camps. He and several other officers were held hostage at Nakhon Nayok when Japan surrendered in August, 1945. His weight had dropped shockingly from 157 pounds. He now weighed 105. Despite his weakened condition, he insisted on travelling 300 miles into the jungle to supervise the release of his men. During the post-war trials, Colonel Toosey met Sergeant Saito again. The colonel saved Saito's life when he defended the sympathetic guard against accusations as a war criminal. Through his contact with the British colonel, Saito later became a Christian, stating: "He showed me what a human being should be and he changed the philosophy of my life."

Colonel Philip Toosey demonstrated patience by waiting and working through his present circumstances to save the lives of his men until the situation turned for the better.

Questions

1. What had the British been trying to defend?
2. Where were the prisoners being taken? Why was their colonel still with them?
3. What project were the prisoners given?
4. What rule of the Geneva Convention were the Japanese breaking? Why?
5. What was Col. Toosey's plan to slow down work on the bridge?
6. What hardships did Col. Toosey's men endure?
7. How did Col. Toosey demonstrate patience?
8. Tell how Col. Toosey was able to help alleviate suffering of his men.
9. How did he risk his life for his men?
10. What did Col. Toosey and his men accomplish in 16 months?
11. Why did the Japanese respect Col. Toosey?
12. How much weight did Col. Toosey lose during his imprisonment?
13. What did he insist on when he heard his men were being released?
14. Tell of how Sgt. Saito came to be converted.
15. What are some ways you could demonstrate patience in your home? church? neighborhood?
16. Think of a Bible example who demonstrated great patience.

For whatsoever things were
written aforetime were written
for our learning, that we
through patience and comfort of
the scriptures might have hope.

— *Romans 15:4*

Persuasiveness

Definition

Skillfully handling truth
to lead others in a right path

Memory Verse

And when they had appointed him a day,
there came many to him into his lodging; to
whom he expounded and testified the kingdom
of God, persuading them concerning Jesus,
both out of the law of Moses, and out of the
prophets, from morning till evening.

Acts 28:23

Give Me Liberty

Pre-Revolutionary War • Richmond, Virginia • March 23, 1775

March 23, 1775. Over one hundred men with powdered hair and frock coats crowded the narrow pews of St. John's Episcopal Church in Richmond, Virginia. After Governor Lord Dunmore had forbidden the delegates to meet and discuss the "Intolerable Acts" perpetrated by the British Crown, the Second Virginia Convention found church the only suitable and safe place to gather. Glancing about him, Thirty-nine-year-old Patrick Henry could see Thomas Jefferson's flaming red hair, George Washington's strong and somber face, and the fuzzy yellow head of Richard Henry Lee. A murmur went through the room as the delegates whispered in the moments before assembly. He could feel the tenseness, the unease. Nobody was sure what to do about rising pressure in Virginia, memories of the killings in Massachusetts, known as the Boston Massacre, and the humiliation of the tea taxes. Few people wanted to make a sudden move. House delegates stood up, one after another, arguing, jabbering.

He had tried to go into business. When it failed, he took up planting, but his house burned down. Then he struck out in a new line of trade. When that, too, collapsed, he discovered his great love in the law. In 1763, he made a name for himself during the "Parson's Cause," a trial that established that the Virginia Colony, not the British Crown, would determine a minister's salary. Patrick Henry won the case. Later, he burst into the limelight when he tried to beat down the Stamp Act of 1765 with his Virginia Resolutions. He based their complaints on the rights of Englishmen to fair representation. In the middle of his speech, "Caesar had his Brutus; Charles the First his Cromwell; and George the Third—" the Speaker of the House suddenly shouted, "Treason!

Patrick Henry

Treason!" Patrick Henry calmly finished, "—May profit by their example. If this be treason, make the most of it!"

In 1774, as the separate colonies moved slowly but unalterably towards the final showdown, he joined a committee of correspondence. The Committee passed written circulars throughout the colonies and let the citizens know what was going on.

On this March day, men stood and argued. They had still reached no decision. Many things pressed on his mind today. At home, on his estate in Scotchtown, his wife Sarah, now in her mid-thirties and mother of six children, lay in the two-room basement, dying. Four years ago, she had started to look at him strangely. Soon she became unable to do simple household tasks or care for the children. When she tried to hurt herself, Patrick had to buckle her into a "Quaker shirt," a straightjacket to keep her safe. He couldn't send Sarah to an insane asylum after almost twenty years of marriage. So he built her an apartment in the basement, full of light and air, with a beautiful view of the trees and the countryside. Every day, he came to see her, bathed her, guided her arms through the sleeves of her dress and combed her hair. Sometimes he held her hands to keep her from hurting herself. Sometimes he just sat with her silently. Today, one of his slaves would take his place while he was in Richmond.

Impatience boiled up in him as the endless talks buzzed on through the afternoon like horseflies. Most of the men wavered, hoping to keep to a middle road and not offend the British. Mainly, they could not decide whether to mobilize against the encroaching British troops or not.

Suddenly, he could stand it no longer. He leaped to his feet.

"Mr. President . . ."

Words poured from his lips. "There is no retreat but in submission and slavery! Our chains are forged! Their clanking may be heard on the plains of Boston! The war is inevitable—and let it come! I repeat it, sir, let it come." He took a deep breath. "It is vain, sir, to extenuate the matter. Gentlemen may cry Peace, Peace—but there is no peace. The war is actually begun! The next gale that sweeps from the north will bring to our ears the clash of resounding arms! Our brethren are already in the field! Why stand we here idle? . . . Is life so dear, or peace so sweet, as to be purchased at the price of chains and slavery? Forbid it, Almighty God! I know not what course others may take; but as for me, give me liberty or give me death!"

They were on their feet now, shouting, "To Arms! To Arms!" Protests rose like bubbles underwater, but soon evaporated under Henry's persuasive language. Mobilization began at once, with Patrick Henry taking the lead as Colonel of the 1st Virginia Regiment. In August, he led the militia in protest when Lord Dunmore ordered the gunpowder secretly removed from the magazine during the night. In a night of torches and shouting, Dunmore surrendered the powder at the same time the British marched on Lexington. Patrick Henry's efforts,

Patrick Henry addressing the Virginia Convention

combined with those of Samuel Adams, Paul Revere, and other patriots in Massachusetts, marked the beginning of the war. Later, he served as Virginia's first and sixth post-colonial governor.

Sarah died that spring. Henry planted a lilac tree near her grave that would bloom every spring after her death. Two years later, he married Dorothea Dandridge, who gave him another eleven children. At the Virginia Convention of 1788, he voted against the ratification of the Constitution, preferring to see a Bill of Rights added first. After struggling in vain to get Virginia to endorse and fund a state religion, against Thomas Jefferson's plea for complete religious liberty, Patrick Henry spent his last years on his plantation at Red Hill. He succumbed to stomach cancer in 1799. A failure at business but a success at oratory, his "Give Me Liberty" speech touched off a spark in Virginia that flamed into a common movement for independence.

Patrick Henry used persuasive words to convince his listeners to enter the fight for liberty.

Questions

1. Why was the Second Continental Congress meeting in St. John's Episcopal Church?
2. What was pressing on Patrick Henry's mind that day?
3. How did Patrick Henry treat his ill wife?
4. What did Patrick Henry communicate in his speech?
5. How did his persuasiveness influence others to join the fight for liberty?
6. Tell in what manner Patrick Henry became involved with the militia.
7. Think of someone in Scripture who used persuasiveness to influence others for good.
8. List people who are in your sphere of influence whom you could potentially influence for good.

PRUDENCE

DEFINITION

Exercising caution in all situations;
foreseeing the consequences of my actions

MEMORY VERSE

A prudent man foreseeth the trouble
and hides himself: but the simple pass on
and are punished.

PROVERBS 22:3

War Woman Creek

The Revolutionary War • Wahatchee Creek, Georgia • 1779

Nancy Ward used to walk here. The log cabin, with its broad stone hearth, slab-rock chimney and loop-holed windows stood on the crest of a hill overlooking Wahatchee Creek. At night, owls called eerily, "huhu, uguku, uku." A panther screamed.

Nancy Morgan Hart wore her flaming red hair twisted back from a lean face pitted with smallpox. Benjamin Hart hadn't married a female relative of Daniel Boone for beauty. Her body was tough as rawhide leather, built for bearing children, carrying heavy pots, uprooting stumps. Eight years before in 1771, they moved across the South Carolina border into the fertile flatwoods land of northeastern Georgia. At forty-four, she had given birth to her ninth and last child. Only her kind of woman could last long in the wilderness of Broad River Valley.

The sound of horses' hooves splashed somewhere upstream.

She couldn't call out, didn't know if they were Tories sent by the British to burn and whip the settlers out of their homes. They lived right on the border, the neutral crossing places between the hostile Creek tribes and the friendly Cherokee.

Benjamin?

She saw the canebrake flicker, and knew he had gone, driving their horses, cows and pigs into brake so dense that the light filtered through dimly. Sharp cane shoots stabbed the feet of Tories trying to follow. The woods twisted, tripping them up, bewildering them with birdcalls, luring them deeper in. She could not read. But she knew the Indian legends, and how the forest seemed to close in around one, silent as death. And then there were the bird calls. Clear. Liquid. Sometimes you didn't know if they were bird calls at all, or an Indian whistle. She gazed down through the sunlit treetops fluttering in the breeze, to the slow-winding waters. The Indians called this place Warwoman Creek. Perhaps it was for Nancy Ward, the copper-toned, half-white Indian woman who lived in this valley before her time. When white men began trickling into this valley early in the century, she prophesied that there would be war. Blood will flow. She told the Cherokee not to fight, but to recede into the Georgia mountains, for if they fought, then they would vanish. Only a handful of the Cherokee Nation would survive. Her arms, long and strong, rhythmically beat the clothes on a rock, rinsed them and wrung them out. She had never seen a mirror—only glimpsed the thin face and fiery hair glimmering in the shallows. When she put out her fingers to touch it, the image wrinkled and went away. No, she wasn't beautiful. But she knew how to smell the wind for smoke and listen for the clomping of strangers' horses footing it up the creek bed. She stood, six feet tall, and looked back towards the cabin, less than half a mile away.

Nancy Morgan Hart

"James Thomas!"

She paused. "Keziah! Susanna! Lemuel!"

Out of 400 acres of wilderness, they had carved their own farmstead. An apple orchard spread out behind the cabin, the darker flat green leaves contrasting with the pale wine yellow color of beech and quivering alder trees. No one would take that away. At first, the war had bypassed Georgia, raging through Vermont, Pennsylvania, Virginia, and the Carolina everglades. Now, it had moved south, into the Georgia heartland. Not long ago, a band of marauding Tories had brutally murdered a friend and fellow patriot, Colonel John Dooley. Dear John. They had found his body later . . . If I find them, I'll never let them go.

The horsemen were just behind her. She slammed the cabin door, drew the latchstring in.

The cabin was dim and fragrant with bunches of herbs. Furry mullein. Purple boneset or jopai weed. Catmint and bergamot. Bags of suterberry bark, bloodroot, blue cohosh. She had brought babies into the world, cradling their soft, wet heads with experienced midwife's fingers. Her clay pipe lay on the mantelpiece, beneath an entire wall covered with huge deer antlers.

Glancing through the small, shuttered window, Nancy saw them. Tories. Six of them. They wore bright red coats like dark angels. White belts crisscrossed their chests.

The door was locked. But shoulders and rifle butts helped. From inside, Nancy, with her children huddled around her, saw the thick Georgia pine boards heave and split, and then give way under the strain.

It was too late to go for help. The nearest settlement was twenty-five miles to the southeast. Benjamin was deep in the canebrake. She would have to deal with the intruders alone.

As the door burst open, she was bending over the fire.

"Cook us a meal, woman," they demanded. "Or—"

Grimly, she moved outside. They watched her every move, careful to see that she didn't run for help. In full view of the cabin, she wrung the neck and plucked the feathers from an old turkey. Even if it was their last meal, she wasn't going to give them a good hen. Inside, the Tories sprawled around the great stone fireplace, stacking their guns in a corner. They crowded the table as if they owned it, as Nancy sliced cold venison, stirred up a batch of hoecakes baked in the hot ashes and set out hunks of sticky honeycomb. Cautiously, when they weren't looking, she slipped a conch shell into Susannah or Sally's hand and sent her out for water.

"When you get to the spring," she told her, "blow the conch for help."

Alone in the house with the six men, Nancy began slipping the Tories' rifles through the crumbled chinking in the log wall. She worked slowly yet deftly, careful not to let the guns thump or rattle. She knew the consequences of her actions. If she was caught, they could kill her children without blinking. But I won't let them. Just then, one of them turned around. As they sprang from the benches at her, she seized one of the rifles and cocked it.

It wasn't hard to handle a gun. She had done it all her life. Even Benjamin knew she was the better hunter.

She spoke in a strong voice:

"If you come towards me or even eat a mouthful of that food, I will blow your brains out."

Someone leapt at her, and the gun roared. Another tried to tackle her. She raised the rifle and the others sat still. Without turning her head, she sent one of the boys running for help. The cabin became very quiet. She fixed her eyes on them. They were strange eyes, slightly crossed. They had a hypnotic effect on the men. No one knew who she was looking at or who she might shoot next. Suddenly, she heard her husband's voice outside. The shouts of neighbors. She didn't take her eyes off them as they dragged the Tories outside.

Nancy Morgan Hart and the British Tories

Under questioning, the men admitted they had murdered Colonel Dooley in cold blood.

Benjamin Hart looked at his wife.

"Let us shoot them."

The neighbors agreed.

"No," Nancy said. "Hang them."

She had avenged John Dooley's death at last. Evening came on. Nancy helped the men dig deep graves. If the bodies were found, the whole family could be put to death by British troops.

She did such a good job, that no one discovered the graves until the Elberton and Eastern Railroad cut through the Wahatchee Creek property in Rabun County, Georgia, in 1913.

While the defense of her family and the avengement of Colonel Dooley's death were Nancy Morgan Hart's most famous exploits, they did not remain her only contributions to the American cause. She reputedly served as a spy for General Elijah Clarke. Once, she dressed in men's clothes and wandered into a British camp to sell eggs. When questioned, she pretended she was crazy, her thin, freckled face dense and a glazed look coming into the crossed eyes. But she emerged with vital secrets concerning British troop movements in the area. On another occasion, she lashed some logs together with grapevines and ferried across the Savannah River to gain information for the Georgia Whigs. One day, a gang of Tories stopped her on her way to the mill and demanded her pass. She shook her fist at them.

"This is my pass. Touch me if you dare!"

They shoved her from the horse, threw the heavy sacks of grain on the ground and rode off, laughing. Nancy stooped, lifted the two and a half bushels of corn onto her shoulders, and carried them the rest of the way to the mill. Meeting a redcoat on the road not far from the American post, she twisted the gun out of his hands and made him march before her to the fort. Looking out her cabin window one morning, she saw a rebel horseman, covered with lather, dash out of the woods. Behind him galloped the King's men. Nancy told him to ride straight through her cabin and out the other door.

"Hide in the swamp."

Moments later, the Tories rode up. "Have you seen a horseman pass, goodwife?"

Nancy pointed up the hill.

"I did see a horseman swing off into the woods two or three hundred yards back up the trail."

The Redcoats wheeled about and spurred their horses back

in the opposite direction. Had they dismounted and searched the cabin, they would have found muddy horse tracks stamped into the ground at the front door and going straight out the back, down the path to the swamp.

A few years after the Revolutionary War, Nancy Hart found peace. A Methodist meeting house, recently established in the neighborhood, drew her attention. From outside, she listened to the singing and preaching. The doors were locked. Nancy took out her knife, cut the drawstring and marched in. On learning about Christ's salvation, Nancy Morgan Hart became a "shouting Christian [and] fought the devil as manfully as she fought the Tories."

Numerous legends and folk songs sprang up around Nancy Morgan Hart. Until 1913, when railroad workers found the skeletons of six men from the 1700s lying in a neat row less than a mile from where her cabin stood, historians disputed her existence. Georgia Route 77 has since been named the Nancy Hart Highway. During the Civil War, the women of LaGrange raised a regiment of female volunteers named the "Nancy Harts" to defend the town from the Union Army. Hart County, on the northeast border with South Carolina, is the only county out of 159 in Georgia named for a woman. Today, it is not certain whether Warwoman Creek was named for the Indian prophet Nancy Ward, the brave white warrior woman—or both of them.

Nancy Morgan Hart exercised prudence in her dealings with the British. By acting coolly and cautiously when faced with the enemy, she weighed the possible consequences of her actions against her duty to her country and was able to protect her family at the same time.

Questions

1. What had a band of Tories done to Nancy's neighbor recently?
2. What did the Tories demand of Nancy?
3. What assignment did Nancy send her daughter to do?
4. What did Nancy do with the men's rifles?
5. When the men realized what she was doing with their rifles, what happened?
6. What crime did the men admit to committing?
7. How did Nancy and her husband take justice into their hands?
8. Tell of Nancy's accomplishments as a spy.
9. How did Nancy find the Lord?
10. Tell how Nancy exercised prudence in her dealings with the British.
11. What is prudence? How can you exercise prudence in your life?
12. Think of a time when you acted rashly instead of prudently. How might things have turned out differently if you had acted with prudence?

Punctuality

Definition

Being prompt in all commitments,
honoring the time of others

Memory Verse

Walk in wisdom toward them that are without,
redeeming the time.

Colossians 4:5

Tracks

Nome, Alaska • January–February, 1925

He lifted his head. He sniffed the air, delicately arching his tongue. He tasted snow. The sharp tang sent a shiver through his body though he wasn't cold. It tickled his fur, sifting like dry, gritty sand between the straps of the sled harness and his body. All around him the world was icebound. He strained forward, seeing nothing but the barren sweep of the Alaskan tundra stretching into the early arctic twilight. Above, behind, swirling in the air around him, he could hear Gunnar Kaasen's hoarse voice. The voice pulled him forward. Again.

January 20, 1925

A radio telegraph signal flashed across Alaska to Anchorage: *Nome calling. . . Nome calling. . . We have an outbreak of diphtheria. . . No Serum . . . Urgently need help. . . Nome calling. . . Nome calling. . .*

Diphtheria was sweeping through Nome like wildfire. Villages huddled like gnomes on the edge of the world. A child lay gasping, mucus closing over its lungs. Three Inuit children had died already. Desperate, Dr. Welch tapped out a message to Anchorage almost 1,000 miles away.

The message came back:

Fresh serum available here . . . Airplanes standing by to fly to Nome. . .

Anchorage located 300,000 units of precious antitoxin in a railway hospital—enough to save the children's lives and prevent an epidemic. But the lone aircraft in Anchorage lay in pieces for repair. Snow continued to fall heavily outside. As the temperature

dropped below zero, ice congealed on the blades, jamming the motor. The plane refused to start. The officials looked at each other. They needed dogs. Only the experienced teams of mushers who ran the Iditarod Trail could break through to Nome in time. They shipped the package by train to Nenana.

At the station, "Wild Bill" Shannon grabbed the twenty-pound package, lashed it to his sled and took off. When he started, it was 30 degrees below zero. Then it began to drop to 35 degrees. Then 40 . . . then 45. As the arctic blackness settled in, it reached 50 degrees below zero. Shannon pressed on, hearing only the whooshing of runners over the snow, the sound of the dogs' panting. Fifty-two miles later, at Tolovana, he handed the serum over to Edgar Kalland.

January 28

Kalland headed into the wilderness, passing the package to

Dan Green at Manley Hot Springs. Green sped with the serum into the darkness, averaging an incredible nine miles per hour, until he stumbled into Fish Lake. Johnny Folger managed twenty-six miles before turning it over to Sam Joseph. Fresh snow began to fall as Joseph's frozen fingers slapped the package into Titus Nikolai's hands. Nikolai took off. The windchill increased, causing whiteouts. And still the mushers pushed on. Rugged men, Indian, Eskimo, and white, huddled at the relay points to dash on with the medicine for the children at Nome.

January 30

The young, newly-wed Indian, George Nollner, sang Athabascan love songs as he disappeared into the darkness. The songs kept him warm, beating in his blood as the dogs charged ahead. During his bleak, thirty-mile stretch, two of Charlie Evans' dogs dropped dead on their feet. They had frozen solid. Evans strapped his own body to the traces and began dragging the sled. He made it to the next relay post alive. Jackscrew, a Koyukuk Indian, covered another forty miles, while Irishman Myles Gonangnan did the same.

January 31

They didn't stop for rest or food. Russian Eskimo Henry Ivanoff embarked from Shaktolik for what he knew was the most dangerous stretch of the run. Half a mile up the trail, one of his dogs veered off the road to chase a reindeer. Ivanoff jumped into the snarling pack as dogs, traces, and sled tangled with each other. Glancing up, he saw the Norwegian Leonhard Seppala, with his famous Siberian husky, Togo, racing down the trail. Seppala, one of the greatest mushers in the Alaskan territory, had started out from Nome, 150 miles away, to meet the relay. Storms buffeted them as Seppala approached the treacherous, frozen Norton Sound. It lay before him like the sea, grey and menacing, its banks rippled with ice. He didn't know what the middle was like or if they could touch it without breaking through.

Togo

Seppala gazed across the Sound. He could go around it, which would take him miles out of his way. Or he could try to cross it. Seppala chose the shortest route. Seawater crashed around them. The ice creaked and groaned, threatening to crack under them any second. Water was soaking over the sled runners as Togo, footing his way among the jagged ice floes, led them up the oth-

Balto

er side. Three hours later, the ice broke up in Norton Sound with a noise like gunshots.

February 1

The serum was now passed from Norwegian to Norwegian. Leonhard Seppala handed the package to Charlie Olsen, who gave it to Gunnar Kaasen—the man destined to make the last, hazardous dash to Nome. At Bluff, Kaasen stared into the horizon with crinkled eyes. A storm kicked up puffs of snow, sweeping it across the tundra like billowing white sand. Stooping over Seppala's team, Kaasen chose one of the dogs to lead him out of Bluff.

Balto felt the man's steady hands on the traces. White breath clouded his face. It was hard to talk and the men communicated with jerks of the head. Then the lead harness slipped over his dark head and tightened around his thick neck. One white-splashed paw lifted, tense and trembling. His ears pricked forward. The intelligent brown eyes gleamed. He was chosen.

They had never let him in front before. They kept him back, letting the big dog, Togo, toss his head in front. Today, he would face his first great test. He had never been a leader. Never had to sniff the wind or dig out a trail on his own. He could smell the storm coming. But the man didn't think it was severe.

Balto lurched into the wind. It was more than 50 degrees below zero. Gusting winds slapped their faces with snow that cut like shards of glass. Battling the gale-force wind and breaking a path through four-foot-high drifts, the man and 13 dogs forced their way to the river. He didn't know why they had to get there. He only knew that they had to get there on time. It was total whiteout. Kaasen was silent now, and Balto knew he couldn't see his hand in front of his face. He plunged on, pulled by some kind of mysterious instinct. Each step he put down struck firm. He couldn't miss. Suddenly, the sled twisted sideways, sliding into the Topkok River. He saw Kaasen falling. Balto struggled, pulling the sled up the cliff by sheer force.

When the team swooshed into the Safety Shelter, they found the next relay driver sound asleep, unprepared to finish the journey. No one had expected Kaasen and his team to live through the blizzard. Now, they would have to take the serum twice as far. Balto felt the man's eyes on him, gauging his strength. Kaasen crouched and lifted the dogs' paws, testing the soft pads for cuts and wounds. When the Norwegian rose, Balto understood the look on his face. They would go on.

Winds accelerated as they left the shelter. As they crossed the tundra, a gust of wind lifted dogs and sled into the air, hurling them into a snowdrift. The huskies landed in a tangle of harness and fur. Kaasen, struggling with the sled, suddenly went down on his knees. Balto saw the man look desperately from side to side. The serum was gone. Kaasen scrabbled frantically in the snow with his bare hands. Then his stiff fingers closed over the little package.

February 2

At 5:30 AM Kaasen and his team, staggering and frozen to the bone, drove past the silent streets and wooden house-fronts of Nome. They had made most of the run in total darkness. The families of the saved children crowded round him, thanking Kaasen with tears in their eyes. But Kaasen stooped to the stocky black dog with bright brown eyes. Balto, he said, should have his share of fame. More than twenty drivers and their teams participated in the 674-mile race to Nome that took just six days: a feat that mushers consider a world record.

Balto and Gunnar Kaasen demonstrated punctuality by driving themselves beyond the call of duty to get the serum to the children on time.

Gunnar Kaasen and Balto

Questions

1. What was the emergency situation in Nome, Alaska?
2. Why couldn't they just put the medicine on a plane or train?
3. The weather changed about the time Kaasen and Balto set out. How severe did it become?
4. What happened at Point Safety?
5. How many miles did Balto run?
6. What mishaps occurred along the way?
7. How did Gunnar and Balto demonstrate punctuality?
8. Were the citizens of Nome saved?
9. Does time matter? If you are supposed to do something by a certain time, should you take it seriously?
10. Is there something you tend to be late for? What steps can you take to remedy the situation?

Resourcefulness

Definition

Using things which others might discard
in a creative way

Memory Verse

And whatsoever ye do, do it heartily,
as to the Lord, and not unto men;
knowing that of the Lord
ye shall receive the reward of the inheritance:
for ye serve the Lord Christ.

Colossians 3:23-24

Over Enemy Lines

World War II • France • 1944

France: May, 1944. One minute he was looking at the altimeter. It flickered at 25,000 feet. The next, a burst of flak ripped into his oxygen line, cutting off the flow of air. Far below, Nazi anti-aircraft guns concealed in the mist and hedgerows thundered. The heightened compression in the cockpit squeezed the air from his lungs. Suddenly he was swimming in velvet blackness, without sight or sound. Then P-51C pilot William Overstreet opened his eyes. The brown-and-white Mustang fighter, with a star tipping its left wing and rear fuselage, was in a death-spin toward the ground. Clouds whirled and streamed past his window. With a cold emptiness in his ears, he knew that the engine was dead. He glanced at the fuel gauge, which was set to the main tank. It was empty.

He didn't know how it happened, but suddenly he came out of the spin. His hands located the switch to the auxiliary fuel tank. Straight ahead, a line of trees rushed up at him from the ground, but then the engine sputtered and roared to life. He side-slipped past the trees, coming down crabwise towards the earth before zooming up again. He glanced at his watch. The past 90 minutes were a blank in his mind. He had flown while unconscious for an hour and a half.

Gaining altitude again, he scanned the green spring fields checkering the French countryside. He had dropped out of flight formation, leaving his squadron commander frantically trying to reach him over the radio. He was alone and lost over German territory. Then his brain kicked in. Simply reversing the direction they had taken towards the mission, he cruised along until

P-51C pilot William Overstreet

he sighted the outline of the French coast. From there, he was home free. He dove off towards Leiston, England, landing at the Fourth Air Base. His gas gauge read almost empty.

Later, flight surgeons at the hospital estimated that he had dropped from 25,000 feet during that lost ninety minutes. If he had remained at the same altitude, he would have died without air in the rarified atmosphere. It had been a close call, but it would not be Bill Overstreet's last.

During his flight training at Hamilton Field while assigned to 357th Fighter Group, the twenty-one-year-old pilot from Clifton Forge, Virginia, bailed out of a plane in full death spiral just seconds before it crashed in a mass of wreckage.

Later in the war, he was on a mission escorting bombers to Southern France. Peering through his goggles, Bill spotted the ammunition train looming up at him along the track. Flames and smoke mushroomed into the sky. Shards of metal tore into the plane, shredding its underbelly. He popped open the door, tugged his cord and sailed towards the ground where two Nazis were waiting for him. Interrogated by the Gestapo, he found that they knew everything about him. They even knew about his past girlfriends, some before he even joined the military.

"What did my parents have for breakfast?" he demanded.

The Gestapo agent didn't flinch. "I'll tell you tomorrow," he said.

They tumbled him into the backseat of an ammo vehicle. He had to get out of here. If he didn't, they would take him to one of

The "Berlin Express"

those prison camps for American soldiers and pen him behind rolls of razor wire. One Nazi climbed into the truck and took the wheel. They were a little way into the countryside by now. Just then Bill spotted a pipe wrench lying under the driver's seat. Stooping, he picked it up and tapped the German on the head. Bill pushed the Nazi out of the truck, spun the wheel, and sped off in the opposite direction. He drove until he ran out of gas. On foot now, he located French Resistance partisans who helped him get back to England.

On D-Day, June 6, 1944, Lieutenant Overstreet took off on a mission at 2:00 AM. On the ground, the weather was foggy and overcast. After climbing for 20,000 feet, he rolled out on top of a crest of clouds. Moonlight flooded the sky as the planes broke out of the overcast, jutting up at odd angles from climbing so far on their instruments. Teaming up in flights of four, the pilots winged over to France, covering the beach area so that the massive troop invasion on the ground could land as planned. On the day of the Normandy invasion, Bill and his comrades flew eight missions. On June 10, he skimmed low to the ground, strafing trains, trucks, and German armored vehicles. Once they had eliminated the enemy ground forces, they were able to claim trains, boxcars, railroad shacks, trucks, lorries, and barges.

Two months later, Bill's group was flying a shuttle mission out of Russia. Their task: to escort B-17s from the 8th Air Force's

3rd Bomb Division. It was seven and a half hours across the ravaged steppes of Poland to the ancient city of Cracow. After being engaged in several dogfights and shooting down two Nazi fighters, they finally bumped gently onto an airfield in Piryatin. While the Russians refueled their fighters, the boys went shopping. Bill became excited when he saw beet alcohol for sale, something

The "Berlin Express" chasing a German fighter beneath the Eiffel Tower

scarce in war-torn Europe. As soon as he got back to his plane, he dumped all his .50 caliber ammunition and filled the now empty bays with the alcohol he'd purchased. Since the next goal was Foggia, Italy, where American troops had fought among the villages and mountains, Bill felt confident that they wouldn't see any Luftwaffe there. Everything went smoothly at first. Then over Romania, the Fighter Group ran into a pack of ME 109's. But when the Germans saw the Americans, they turned tail and sped for home. Bill was close on the tail of an ME 109. Suddenly the German pilot jumped out in a parachute. His plane was not on fire. It had not even been hit. Bill didn't know what had scared the man.

Later, at their debriefing, one of the officers asked: "Who was the closest one to him?"

Everyone grinned. It was Bill, only he didn't have a single bullet on him—his ammo bays were filled with alcohol.

On another occasion in Spring, 1944, Lieutenant Overstreet pursued a German Messerschmitt through Paris in his fighter, the "Berlin Express." The Nazi, hoping to eliminate the tough captain on his tail, flew straight for the center of the city, where heavy German anti-aircraft artillery aimed their sights at the sky. Several hit the German's engine and enemy flak thudded around Bill. In a last-ditch effort, the German pilot dove beneath the massive, fretwork legs of the Eiffel Tower.

Unhesitatingly, Bill swooped beneath the arch of the Eiffel Tower, flying dangerously close to the ground. He came out of the dive, pounding the German fighter repeatedly. The plane crashed in a blossom of flames. Bill ducked over the Seine River, flying low and on full throttle to avoid heavy flak from the German guns. He followed the course of the river out of Paris.

Asked later what the scenery was like around the Eiffel Tower, Bill replied: "I'm not sure, I was a little busy."

Understatement and modesty would be a lasting characteristic of Bill Overstreet's remarkable career.

Lieutenant William Overstreet demonstrated resourcefulness by making use of the opportunities available to him under stressful situations.

Questions

1. What was Bill Overstreet's assignment in World War II?
2. Tell of his first close call in this story.
3. How did Bill get captured by the Germans?
4. How did he escape?
5. Tell the incredible story of his flying under the Eiffel Tower and shooting down a German Messerschmidt. How did he get away?
6. Tell how Mr. Overstreet demonstrated resourcefulness (making use of opportunities others might miss while in stressful situations) in each of these situations.
7. We often get in a rut of doing things the same way all the time. Resourcefulness is doing things creatively in order to accomplish the task at hand or using things others might discard. How can you train yourself to practice resourcefulness?

I had followed this 109 from the bombers when most of the German fighters left. We had a running dogfight and I got some hits about 1500 feet, He then led me over Paris where many guns were aimed at me. As soon as he was disabled, I ducked down just over the river (smaller target for the Germans). Followed the river until I was away from Paris.

— William Overstreet

Respectfulness

Definition

Treating others with honor and esteem

Memory Verse

Let nothing be done through strife
or vainglory; but in lowliness of mind
let each esteem other better than themselves.

Philippians 2:3

Red Dawn

The War of 1812 • Baltimore, Maryland • September, 1814

Baltimore, Maryland: September 13, 1814. His friend was out there somewhere. Lights glimmered along the deck of the British ship *HMS Tonnant* moored off Baltimore Harbor. Vice Admiral Alexander Cochrane, Rear Admiral Sir George Cockburn and Major General Robert Ross dined aboard. Dark, curly-haired Francis Scott Key climbed into a boat with Colonel John Stuart Skinner, the American Prisoner Exchange Agent. Without Skinner's help, he would never have located the right ship. They drew close up under the great black hulk looming out of the water. Inside, soft candlelight flooded the dining room as a British officer ushered them in and invited them to eat.

At first, Key had opposed this war, sparked by friendly trading with Britain's enemy, France, and the kidnapping of American sailors by the British navy. But when the war crept into the Chesapeake Bay area, Key promptly joined the volunteer militia with the "flying battery"—horse-drawn artillery. He was in Georgetown when he received the message about his friend.

Dr. Beanes was somewhere nearby. But Key's sharp lawyer's brain told him to be careful. Before fleeing, the government at Annapolis had entrusted Dr. Beanes with guarding the state records in Upper Marlboro County. The British occupying Prince George's County marched softly over the fields and roads, bewitched by the beauty of the small towns and countryside. They kept their hands off property. They did not burn homes. Except for helping themselves to large quantities of livestock, the army seemed on its best behavior after torching Washington, D.C. two years before. But to make his job more risky, Dr. Beanes had

Francis Scott Key

two guests at his plantation: Admiral Cockburn and General Ross. When Dr. Beanes threw two drunken stragglers into jail, one escaped, caught up with his unit and filed a protest. Without thinking, he had placed the whole town and the records in danger of reprisals. Shortly afterwards, one of Ross' British detachments marched on plantation and arrested the doctor. But the state papers survived.

Key knew that he had to rescue his friend. The people of Marlboro had enlisted his help to rescue their beloved citizen. Now, Key formally asked Admiral Cochrane for Beanes' release. President Monroe had sent a vessel to use in the interests of the cartel. Then General Ross spoke up. After their prowling about in the dark and aboard ship, Key and Skinner now knew the strength and position of the British navy drawn up outside the strategic Fort Henry at the mouth of Baltimore. They also knew that the British meant to attack within the next few hours. Ross would let Dr. Beanes go, but the whole party must stay under brief arrest until after the battle.

Francis Scott Key watching the bombardment of Fort McHenry

Fort McHenry

Under the autumn sky, Key clambered across the gangplank to the frigate, *Surprise,* commanded by the Vice Admiral's son, Sir Thomas Cochrane. Then, like the changing of the guard, the soldiers soon clicked their heels and spun them about in the opposite direction. They were going back to their own vessel. All at once, the bombardment began. Guns pounded from gun-ports and decks nearby, causing a tremor to go through the sloop. Staring out over the black harbor, Key could see the sky lit by red streaks and flashes. Rockets shot upward, raining down showers of sparks as they landed near the fort. All night, the explosions went on, deafening their ears. But their flag still floated in the smoky glare like an eagle over a sea of blood.

Dawn broke in crimson red. The firing had suddenly stopped a little while before. A deathly silence fell over the harbor. Key's heart beat painfully like a muffled drum. He strained his eyes, trying to see through the fog if a British or American flag flew from the fort's ramparts. Then through the smoke, he saw the tattered Stars and Stripes still flying. A thrill ran through his body. They had held out. Searching his pockets, Key found a crumpled letter. Borrowing a pen, he sat down and began scribbling madly. He had to get the words out while they were white-hot.

"Oh, say, can you see by the dawn's early light what so proudly we hailed at the twilight's last gleaming?"

Once ashore, Key handed his scrawled poem to Captain Benjamin Eades of the 27th Baltimore Regiment. Eades, who had been under fire in the Battle of North Point, dashed the copy off to press. Then with a fresh sheet in his hand, he hurried towards the old tavern standing next to the Holliday Street Theatre. Today it was full of actors shouting, drinking, reciting lines. Printed on the headlines was the tune name that Key had chosen: "Anacreon in Heaven." Captain Eades began reading the verses aloud. As he finished, the crowd began calling for music. So Ferdinand Durang mounted a chair and sang it through to the last line:

"Oh, thus be it ever when free men shall stand . . ."

Within a short time, "The Star Spangled Banner" became known throughout the United States.

Francis Scott Key demonstrated respectfulness by going to the rescue and securing the release of Dr. Beanes. By doing so, he witnessed a great event in American history and solidified it forever in the minds of Americans through his words.

Questions

1. What had happened that led to Dr. Beanes' imprisonment?
2. For what reason did the British detain Dr. Beanes and Francis Scott Key after agreeing to release Dr. Beanes?
3. What did Francis Scott Key witness that night?
4. What were the British attempting to do?
5. What was Key inspired to do when he saw the flag still flying over the fort?
6. What did he use to write his song on?
7. What did he do with his song upon reaching shore? What did he title it originally?
8. Explain how Key demonstrated respectfulness to his friend Dr. Beanes.
9. How did he end up inspiring countless millions to have a respect for our country?
10. What could you do to show greater esteem for your parents? pastors?
11. In what ways could you live your life to show deeper respectfulness for Christ?
12. Specifically, what could you do to daily show a greater respectfulness for others?

Self-Control

Definition

Subjecting my own desire to
the control of the Holy Spirit

Memory Verse

He that hath no rule over his own spirit
is like a city that is broken down
and without walls.

Proverbs 25:28

Midnight Express

Honey Creek • Moingona, Iowa • July, 1881

Moingona, Iowa: July 6, 1881. Honey Creek was running high tonight. Flashes of lightning split the sky, and in the flickering white glare the neck of the Des Moines River came into sight, swollen, brown and muddy. Fifteen-year-old Kate Shelley, glancing out the window of the frame house, saw the water rising steadily towards the stable farther down the slope. Throwing a cloak over her head, she slopped through the mud towards the barn. In the warm interior, fragrant with hay and animal smells, she could hear the storm buffeting and raging outside. She had to get the animals out of here. She levered open the door, rain lashing her face, and slapped a cow's rump, sending the unwilling animal galloping out into the rain. Not penned up, the animals would seek the high ground behind the house.

Through the sheets of rain, Kate could barely make out the lonely railroad trestle bridging the gap over Honey Creek. Pa would have been out tonight—if the railroad hadn't killed him. Below her, Honey Creek continued to rise. It was no longer the lazy swimming hole that the boys jumped into on summer days. It was suddenly demonic, sucking chunks of wood or a terrified cow into its whirlpool. As it had taken Michael, her oldest brother, the summer she turned twelve.

Inside the house, she and her mother watched as the water level continued to rise. Night came on and they still sat up, waiting and listening. Suddenly, at eleven o'clock, Kate heard another sound over the roar of the rain. It was a pusher locomotive, No. 12, crossing the Des Moines River Bridge a short distance away. With four men, Ed Wood, George Olmstead, Adam Agar and

Kate Shelley

Patrick Donahue aboard, it rumbled towards the Honey Creek crossing. Despite the storm, they had to check the track conditions and make it back to Moingona that night.

Kate heard the bell ring twice, warningly. Then she heard a horrible crash and a fierce hiss of steam as the engine plunged through the bridge into Honey Creek below. Kate sat stunned for a moment. And then a terrible thought flashed into her mind.

Another train was due any minute now. The western express would soon approach the same bridge—and crash. She had to try to cross the long Des Moines River Bridge to stop the train before it reached Honey Creek. Kate grabbed one of her father's railroad lanterns. Dressed in an old coat and skirt, with a straw hat clamped on her head, she ran out into the storm.

Waving her lantern, she stumbled down the bank to the washed-out bridge. Lightning shattered the ground around her. In its glare, she saw Wood and Ager clinging to the branches of a tree. She couldn't see the other two men. Maybe they had washed downstream, swept out into the low-lying cornfield to rot with the grain. She couldn't help them. She could only help the coming express roaring towards Moingona on its way through Boone County. And it wouldn't stop unless she got there in time.

She reached the Moingona Bridge, the little catwalk winding up like the backbone of a lizard in the dark. It was dangerous to cross the high bridge even on a clear day. Tramps sometimes climbed up and walked along the rails. It was easy to catch an ankle and fall down as a train bore down on them. As Kate started across, she saw that large pieces of the flooring had been torn out, leaving black gaps between the ties. The wind nearly knocked her off her feet. Willow trees struggled to keep their heads above water, fingers desperately gripping the riverbank like Irish water spirits torn from the depths.

She grabbed for a tie and knelt there, panting. She would have to crawl on hands and knees. She set the lantern down, trying to see in a blur of lashing leaves and rain. The yellow light looked like a pinpoint in the blackness. The roar of the river filled her ears. Michael had drowned here. She didn't look down. Inch by inch, she groped her way along. The wind snatched at her clothes, trying to drag her off the trestle. Wood splinters stabbed her palms. Spikes bruised her hands and tore her skirt. The lantern went out. She felt before her in total darkness, concentrating on the next tie, her hand plunging into empty air over a torn-out span. Half-way, a tree crashed towards the bridge, threatening to snap the trestle in two. Then the tree slipped between the spans and hurtled into the river below. Every second, she expected to see the sudden glare of train lights, hear the deafening whoooo, the thunder of wheels on the tracks. The last thing she would hear.

Suddenly, she put out her hand and touched a railroad tie. Solid ground. She was across. She began running down the half-mile of track. Wild-eyed, she burst into the station and gasped out her story about the washed-out bridge and the coming express.

Someone exclaimed: "The girl is crazy!"

Then Kate Shelley fainted. As she lay on the floor in her torn coat, her wet hair falling around her Irish face, the station master recognized her. He knew that he had to stop the express. He ran out into the rain, waving a red lantern just as the midnight express bore down on the station with 200 passengers aboard. A few minutes later, Kate came to. Late that night, Kate led a rescue crew to Honey Creek Bridge, where the men from No. 12 had gone down. Afterwards, the passengers of the midnight express took up a collection of several hundred dollars for her. The State of Iowa presented Kate with a medal. She is the first woman to have a bridge named after her: one spanning the Des Moines River at the point she crossed the night of July 6–7, 1881.

Kate Shelley exhibited self-control by staying calm under difficult circumstances and focusing on one part of her task at a time until she completed it.

Kate Shelley Bridge

Questions

1. How old was Kate Shelley in this story?
2. What did Kate do to rescue the animals?
3. What natural disaster was brewing?
4. What had happened to her brother in the past?
5. What was the horrible sound Kate heard?
6. Another disaster was about to happen. What was it?
7. How did Kate risk her safety to rescue others?
8. Was the train rescued?
9. How did Kate demonstrated self-control?
10. Self-control can be demonstrated in times of crisis and also in day-to-day life. As you strive to learn self-control in little areas, God will grow you so you can respond to crisis situations with self-control. Think of the last time you demonstrated self-control when it was really hard to do.
11. Think of a situation that happens often that tempts you not to demonstrate self control. Purpose to pursue self-control in your life in little areas. What do you need most help with—eating? kindness to others? irritations? temper?

Sensitivity

Definition

The ability to put yourself in another's shoes
and trying to see life from his point of view

Memory Verse

Put on therefore, as the elect of God,
holy and beloved, bowels of mercies, kindness,
humbleness of mind, meekness, long-suffering;
forbearing one another . . .

Colossians 3:12-13a

Blue and Grey

The Civil War • Gettysburg, Pennsylvania • July, 1863

Gettysburg: July 3, 1863. When he opened his eyes, he could see smoke drifting like grey cotton wool around the shattered trees atop Cemetery Ridge. Marcus Wright, lying on his back, tried to shift onto his side. What is the matter with me? His blue coat smelled of blood and sweat. He remembered running across the field, wavering like a mist in the bright sunshine. Suddenly, his left leg went down as if it had plunged into a rabbit hole. He knew what hit him. A *Minié* ball.

It was morning when he came across this field, young, strong. Dew drops clung to the stalks of grass not yet trampled by the men swinging haversacks, rifles. The sun started to go down. A sad orange light spread across the fields, turning the dark smudge of woods into a heart of darkness. Nothing existed before this pain. Nothing would exist after. Pain and the heat on his forehead, these were the enemies he had to contend with now. The others were out of his reach.

Bitterness rose his throat. Just to move. An inch. It was torture to lie still while the bleak heights loomed above him like an overturned bowl and the trees walked upside-down over his head. He didn't know how long he lay there. Only that his leg was shattered like a glass figurine.

"Kill them. Kill them." The words beat about in his brain, multiplied by feverish pain and the vicious flies buzzing around his face. The Confederates were animals. They didn't deserve to live. His anger flared to a hundred degrees. If he could see one of them right now, he'd shoot them down like dogs. But he couldn't move. Couldn't move.

General Robert E. Lee

The sound of hooves. Voices muttering. Southern voices, a drawl. Then he saw them. They were riding under the shadows of Cemetery Ridge, grey men on grey horses. He focused on the nearest one with the soiled white gauntlets, grey slouch hat, three gold stars sewn onto the lapel. He recognized him from his war photographs.

General Robert E. Lee.

They were going by him, getting away. The blood swam to his head. Marcus lifted his hands high, staring straight into Lee's face. His lips, cracked with thirst, spread in a grimace.

"Hurrah for the Union!" he yelled.

There was silence. Then the man dismounted, came towards him. He could see his tall black jackboots heading for his face.

"He's going to kill me."

The boots stopped right by his head. He looked up into a tired face, the eyes so sad that he had to look away. This man was human. The winged hair under the slouched hat was nearly white. Marcus felt the fear draining out of him, seeping into the flowers, the grass, the earth. Why did his eyes look like that, so gentle? What was he going to do? Then General Lee reached down and firmly squeezed his hot, heavy hand.

"My son," he said quietly, "I hope you will soon be well."

Deep brown eyes stared into his. He could see the fine, tired lines around them, puffy dark pouches from sleepless nights, the skin burned brown by the sun. Looking into Lee's face, he felt the slow punishment of defeat, the death of one-third of his general officers, the winding path towards the Potomac. Slowly, the hand released his. He wanted to keep looking, to remember that face as long as he lived. Then he was gone, out of his life forever.

Hot tears welled up in his eyes. "I taunted him as he passed by. I wanted to hurt him, to make him feel the pain I was feeling. And he felt it. But not as I thought. I was an enemy, and he stopped to comfort me. He took the pain for me."

The stars came out. And the boy lay on his back in the bloody grass, tears wet on his cheeks, tears of loneliness, repentance, and love.

Instead of taking the insult personally, Robert E. Lee was able to put himself in his enemy's shoes and show sensitivity towards the wounded Union soldier.

Questions

1. What feeling did this wounded Yankee soldier have for all Confederates?
2. Bitterness is a poison that clouds the way we see reality. It wants to hurt others and get revenge. How did bitterness affect this wounded boy?
3. What changed the boy's attitude?
4. What can you tell of the character of Robert E. Lee by the way he treated the wounded boy?
5. How deeply did this encounter affect the way the boy thought?
6. When others mistreat us, the natural reaction is to mistreat them back. Explain how God can work His purposes when one person purposes to do right.
7. If this boy lived, how do you think his life was most likely changed by this encounter?
8. Think of an instance when someone mistreated you. How did you respond? What was the reaction of the person who offended you? If you reacted wrongly, how should you have acted? Can you begin to see how God blesses when one person determines to do what is right? Will you determine to be that person who seeks to do right even when treated wrongly by others?

A true man of honor feels humbled himself when he cannot help humbling others.

Do your duty in all things. You cannot do more, you should never wish to do less.

— General Robert E. Lee

Thoroughness

Definition

Bringing to completion each task I do
with excellence

Memory Verse

Better is the end of a thing
than the beginning thereof:
and the patient in spirit is better
than the proud in spirit.
Ecclesiastes 7:8

The Broom Test

Hampton Institute, Virginia • 1872

"Ma'am?"

His voice had a soft Virginia drawl. Miss Mary F. Mackie, the headmistress at Hampton Institute, glanced sharply over her desk at him.

"Just how much money do you have?"

"Fifty cents."

Hampton board was ten dollars a month, tuition another $70 per year. She pursed her lips and shook her head.

"Next!"

Sixteen-year-old Booker T. Washington's grubby brown face fell. She wouldn't take him. She actually wouldn't take him. After all those years working for Mrs. Viola Ruffner, scraping pennies together, they weren't even going to let him in. Maybe it was his clothes. He glanced at his filthy jacket, his muddy homespun jeans. He hadn't had a bath in months.

Tall black men in second-hand suits pushed past him, books tucked under their arms. Girls with cotton dresses and fuzzy black hair twisted into chignons signed in at the desk. They all trooped by him, a strong and smiling race, and disappeared into classrooms he couldn't see. He could hear them talking, laughing. So this was Hampton Institute, built in 1868 by its hero, General Samuel Chapman Armstrong. It had smooth green lawns, the large red-brick building with its steep slate roof stretching like a castle to the sky. The place he had dreamed about back in the little log cabin in Malden, West Virginia. The place he had walked over 500 miles to attend. Sleeping under wooden sidewalks, slaving on the wharves, begging rides, he trudged the last 80 miles on foot. Now he was penniless. And they wouldn't let him in.

Miss Mackie kept her face turned away from him, ignoring him. She looked hard as flint.

A Yankee woman. If only he had a chance to prove that he was worth something! Ever since he had sweated in the coal mines of West Virginia, teaching himself to read from letters stamped on the barrels, he had dreamed of this day. In Hampton classrooms students learned mysterious numbers, words that made your heart beat, lands and oceans, whole planets of knowledge. Books lined the shelves. He ached to know what was in them. To take them down and touch their pages.

The last students had gone. His legs hurt from standing so long. But he wouldn't leave.

Suddenly, Miss Mackie spoke. "The recitation room needs sweeping. Take the broom and sweep it."

This was his chance. Now he could prove to her that he was good enough to stay. Grimy floors, chalkboards covered with white dust greeted him as he entered the schoolroom. He set to work. He swept the floor three times. Then he wet a dust cloth and carefully rubbed down each bench, table, and desk. He climbed up to reach and dust the woodwork. He wiped the walls and the baseboards near the floor. He dragged every piece of furniture out of its place, cleaned under it, and pushed it back again. He opened doors and cleaned out all the closets. He even poked his dust rag into corners until the room shone. When he had dusted the whole place thoroughly, he did it a second time. And a third. After the fourth time around, he stepped back, satisfied. The President of the United States could want it no cleaner. How glad he was that that stern Yankee woman, Mrs. Ruffner, had taught him such thoroughness! Now he couldn't enter a room without picking up a scrap of paper or running his sleeve across a dusty chair. He called Miss Mackie.

She swept into the room. His heart pounded as he watched her. She knew just where to look for dust. Bending down, she swiped her clean white handkerchief across the undersides of

Booker T. Washington

the benches. She peered into closets, ran her hand over the woodwork, the tables and desks. She inspected the floor. Finally, she stood up and looked at him. Her handkerchief had not picked up one speck of dirt or a particle of dust from any surface in the room. It was absolutely clean.

When she spoke, her voice was quiet. "I guess you will do to enter this school."

He had passed his college test with flying colors. He would work hard, pay off his tuition. At last he had proved himself worthy of Hampton Institute.

Because he practiced thoroughness in his life, Booker T. Washington could perform a difficult task given to him. His thoroughness not only enabled him to enter college, but paved the way for a long life of usefulness to his fellow Americans as president of Tuskegee Institute.

Questions

1. How far had Booker T. Washington walked to get to Hampton University?
2. How had he earned the money to travel there?
3. Why did they initially turn him down?
4. Why did he want to attend school?
5. What test did Mrs. Mackie give to him? What was her purpose in doing so?
6. How did he perform the job?
7. How had he learned the skill of thoroughness which prepared him to pass this unusual test?
8. How had Booker's mastering the quality of thoroughness been used to impact the lives of many?
9. Isn't it amazing how God prepares people for future effectiveness through simple disciplines in the early years of their lives? Think of some opportunities you have right now to cultivate thoroughness in your life.

Character is power.

Character, not circumstances,
makes the man.

— Booker T. Washington

Tolerance

Definition

Giving others room to grow at different rates as God leads them

Memory Verse

But when ye sin so against the brethren, and wound their weak conscience, ye sin against Christ. Wherefore, if meat make my brother to offend, I will eat no meat while the world standeth, lest I make my brother to offend.

1 Corinthians 8:12–13

God's Army

East End, London • 1865

He staggered through a squalid labyrinth of twisting streets. Muck slid underfoot. The smell of gin stung his nostrils. Behind him, William Booth heard a yell in the darkness. A stone struck his head. Blood ran down the side of his face, clotting in his beard. Filthy dens crouched on every corner, where 290 people packed into a single acre. Behind the dim shutters, bottles crashed and small children climbed steps to reach the counter for a glass of gin. Tonight, a crowd of roughs had smashed the glass and threw fireworks through the windows of the Christian Mission warehouse where he and a group of worshippers huddled in the flickering light of naphtha-flares. All day, Booth, his wife Catherine, and a handful of Christian workers dished out soup in their "Food for the Million" kitchens, and visited the sick and few converts.

Day and night, he preached repentance from sin through faith in Jesus Christ. Tonight, as on many past nights, he stumbled through the East End lanes, pursued by a gang of drunken roughs known as the "Skeleton Army." But still he went on. Exhausted, his clothes torn and a bloody bandage wrapped around his head, Booth stumbled home.

"Go for souls and go for the worst!" he maintained.

He would never give up. He had come to London's East End as a thirty-six-year-old preacher, intent on winning the lost and poor to Christ. At a time in the nineteenth century when missionaries flooded overseas to mission fields in China, Africa, and India, Booth never even left London. "I seemed to hear a voice sounding in my ears," he said, "Where can you go and find such heathen as these, and where is there so great a need for your labors?"

At age fifteen, after attending a Methodist prayer meeting, Booth wrote in his diary: "God shall have all there is of William Booth." Born into poverty, he would work among the poor all of his life, eventually winning the title, "The Prophet of the Poor."

Booth initially held open-air meetings in haylofts, in the crowded backrooms of a pigeon shop, and in the old Quaker burial wasteland near Whitechapel. He used lively music to attract a crowd and then delivered a short message, exhorting them to come to Christ.

Converts came slowly in the East End. Over 500 other religious and social groups besides Booth's organization existed throughout the city. But the people were hard to win. Booth believed that Christian ministers should demonstrate their faith by "loosing the chains of injustice, freeing the captive and oppressed, sharing food and home, clothing the naked, and carrying out family responsibilities." Booth's wife Catherine was outspoken in her belief in the need for reform. Practical Christianity, she argued, should better society.

This belief extended to the Booths' children. Rather than shielding them from life in the East End slums, William and Catherine involved their children in feeding, clothing, and preaching to the poor from a young age. They saw hooligans throw stones at their father and aristocrats such as Lord Shaftsbury criticize their mother for speaking in public. They learned to condemn sin while loving the drunkards, unwed mothers, and homeless children caught up in it.

One day in 1868, as Booth dictated a letter to his secretary George Railton, he referred to their organization as a "volunteer army." His son Bramwell looked up and exclaimed: "Volunteer! I'm no volunteer, I'm a regular!"

Booth immediately ordered Railton to cross out the word "volunteer and substitute the word "salvation." The Salvation Army was born. Booth became its "general," longstanding members

Salvation Army General William Booth

became its "officers," and the rest of the workers held the rank of "soldier." The Army invented its own flags, uniforms, and stirring Christian songs based on popular folk tunes. He held informal services to encourage new believers with singing, instrumental accompaniments, handclapping, and sermons. When outsiders criticized him for using secular tunes to attract crowds, Booth shot back: "Secular music, do you say, belongs to the Devil? Does it? Well, if it did I would plunder him for it, for he has no right to a single note of the whole seven."

Money dribbled in slowly. Many of the volunteers were women, who worked hard alongside the men. They made such an impact in his slum ministry that Booth once exclaimed: "My best men are women!"

Booth continued under increasing hostility from the Church of England, who looked down on his radical activities. Lord Shaftsbury even denounced Booth as the "Anti-Christ." Members of the Salvation Army faced imprisonment for holding open-air meetings and endured harassment by the "Skeleton Army" for their condemnation of alcohol.

Match factory workers

William and Catherine Booth also campaigned for improving the conditions of working women at the large Bryant and May factory in the East End. In the days before labor laws protected workers or limited hours, these women earned a little over one shilling during a grueling 16-hour day. They repeatedly dipped match-heads in poisonous yellow phosphorus. Exposed to the deadly fumes, the skin on the side of their faces turned green and then black. In the final stages of "Phossy Jaw," the bone simply rotted away, causing a painful death.

The Booths tried to get the manufacturers to use harmless red phosphorus instead of the hazardous yellow, as many other countries did. But Bryant and May fought back, arguing that red phosphorus cost more. Customers would not pay such a high price for matches.

Unable to improve Bryant and May's working conditions, Booth opened his own match-factory in Old Ford, East End, in 1891. Under these healthier conditions, his workers produced six million boxes of matches per year. He also paid them four-pence per day, twice the amount that Bryant and May paid their employees. As interest in the Salvation Army's work grew, Booth escorted journalists and members of Parliament around his model factory. He also showed them the miserable sweatshops where workers toiled for masters like Bryant and May. Under the pressure of bad publicity, Bryant and May finally stopped using yellow phosphorus in 1901.

Gradually, public opinion turned in favor of the Salvation Army. William Booth finally established branches of the Army in 58 countries. During his later years, he wrote, traveled, and held "salvation meetings." Emperors, kings, and presidents received him in audience and supported his work. Upon his death, ten thousand workers and

An early Salvation Army band in the U.S.A.

William and Catherine Booth's nine children continued to carry on the work that they had begun. It still exists today.

William and Catherine Booth demonstrated genuine tolerance by loving the people they worked for in spite of abuse and persecution.

Questions

1. What type of people was William Booth preaching to?
2. What types of reception did he often get?
3. What title was he given?
4. How did Booth believe Christian ministers should demonstrate their faith?
5. How did the Booths train their children to tolerate the sinners but not their sin?
6. Tell how the Salvation Army got its name.
7. What became of Booth's children after his death?
8. Explain how the Booths demonstrated tolerance in the true sense of the word.

Truthfulness

Definition

Trustworthiness by accurately stating the facts

Memory Verse

Hear; for I will speak of excellent things;
and the opening of my lips shall be
right things. For my mouth shall speak truth;
and wickedness is an abomination to my lips.

Proverbs 8:6-7

Bird Woman

Lewis & Clark Expedition • Northwest Passage • November, 1804

November, 1804. The two strangers came to the lodge of the French trapper, Toussaint Charbonneau, at the Hidatsa village, on a cold winter day. Fires were burning in the rounded Mandan huts covered with turf and heavy buffalo skins. Seventeen-year-old Sacagawea, light and brown and quick as a bird, listened as the men spoke to her husband. Called the Corps of Discovery, the two men, who were bundled into warm jackets, needed a skilled interpreter to lead them through Dakota Territory and over the mountains to the east. They talked of discovering a Northwest Passage that would allow an overland trading route to the Pacific.

She spoke their strange names: Meriwether Lewis and William Clark.

She felt the child move within her as she listened. Growing up in the sweeping grasslands of Idaho as a Shoshone girl, kidnapped and held as a slave by the Minitaree Sioux at age 12, she had never seen the sea. Charbonneau began bargaining craftily with the two strangers. He would go, but only if Sacagawea went with them. The two men nodded. A woman gave an expedition a friendly tone. As an Indian, Sacagawea could also speak the Snake (Shoshone) language of the nations they passed through when they reached the headwaters of the Missouri River. She could barter for food and obtain horses.

A week later, Sacagawea and Charbonneau moved to Fort Mandan, which had been built by Lewis and Clark as a home base. Sacagawea spoke no English. Captain Clark carefully penned Bird Woman's name in his journal: "Sah-cah' gah-we-ah." At first, they simply called her "squaw." But as they grew to respect the young Indian woman, Clark nicknamed her Janey.

The expedition set up a three-way translation system. Sacagawea and Charbonneau made a husband-and-wife team, translating from Shoshone to French, and ultimately to English.

At 5 o'clock on the evening of February 11, 1805, Sacagawea gave birth to a baby boy. Charbonneau named him Jean Baptiste, but Clark called him "Pomp" or "Pompey." Still weak from the birth ordeal but uncomplaining, Sacagawea left Fort Mandan with the expedition, carrying Jean Baptiste in a cradleboard on her back.

The Corps of Discovery headed upriver from the Missouri as the April sun strengthened. Sacagawea, with her baby, was the only woman to accompany the 33 members of the party who headed to the Pacific Ocean. During the day, she dug up edible roots, foraged for plants and gathered wild berries as they ripened. She made medicine from herbal tinctures. Jean Baptiste, the "little dancing boy," frolicked and laughed as he sat beside his mother in the boats or bounced between her shoulders when they switched to horseback. She helped pole up the Missouri River in expeditionary boats called *pirogues.*

On May 14, the water, swollen with spring currents, was high and foaming. A wave crashed against the boat, tipping instruments, books, and papers into the raging yellow Missouri. While the men struggled to right the boat, Sacagawea swiftly rescued Lewis' and Clark's precious records, journals, and supplies from the water before they sank. But the medicine was lost.

When Sacagawea fell ill near the headwaters of the Missouri, the explorers, till now indifferent to the Indian woman, realized how much they needed her. Without her, they could not know if the information they received was correct. They could not locate Indian guides or horses.

On August 12, the expedition reached the Continental Divide at today's Lemhi Pass. It was the gateway to Shoshone country,

Sacagawea guiding the Corps of Discovery

the land Sacagawea had not seen for five years. No white man had ever entered the Shoshone lands. Making ground-breaking history, Lewis and three other men scouted ahead for 75 miles, chopping brush and branches out of the way.

Her face showed no emotion, not even when she pointed out the place at the Fork of the Three Rivers where the Sioux captured her and killed the rest of her family. Her low Indian jabber related the facts truthfully and accurately without concealing anything. As the only Indian, the only teenager, the only woman, the only mother in camp, she was an oasis: a world in herself.

On August 13, they stumbled across a band of Indians. Sacagawea went ahead to meet them. As she came closer, she recognized the blankets and feathered headgear of the Lemhi-Shoshones. Sacagawea began to dance in her moccasins, waving back to Lewis and Clark. "These are my people!"

The two groups converged. Suddenly, a familiar face swam into sight. Broken images flashed through her mind.

The Minitaree swept down on the Shoshone camp like leaves swirling before a summer storm. Tipis tilted and cooking pots rolled along the ground, spilling craggy knuckles of meat. Squaws and children scrabbled on their knees, digging their fingers into the hot ashes as enemy horses trampled them down. Lances decorated with Sioux war feathers, flew through the air. She felt her hands jerked behind her back, tied with rawhide. Her brother Cameahwait running . . .

Now, her brother's face smiled at her between the soft black braids of a Shoshone chief. Her brother and her sister's boy were all that survived the disastrous raid of 1799–1800.

All at once, a woman rushed into Sacagawea's arms. Lewis and Clark, standing off to one side, watched as the two women hugged and crooned. Her friend Otterwoman, captured at the same time by the Sioux, had escaped from the enemy camp and found her way home. For five years, Sacagawea did not know if she was alive or dead. In the end, Sacagawea chose not to stay with her birth-tribe. Raided by the Minitaree and Blackfeet tribes, the Shoshone found themselves forced back on poorer, barren land. She decided to continue the expedition to the sea.

William Clark & Meriwether Lewis

While Sacagawea translated back and forth, the Shoshone braves led out strings of horses. Without horses, Lewis and Clark could not hope to locate the Northwest Passage. Because of her presence with the group, the Shoshone also sent along a couple of Indian guides to steer them across the mountains. It would take months of trekking before they reached the west coast.

Early autumn had come. Snow fell in the upper Montana and Idaho mountains as early as July. Now, the wind whistled over the cliff faces and canyons, forcing the party to creep back to shelter. Carrying her six-month-old baby in a wooden cradleboard with a high, hooped yoke on her back, Sacagawea scrambled up the rocks beside the men. No food grew here. Slope after slope of the Rocky Mountains rose before them, never-ending, menacing. The skies turned grey and leaden with early snow flurries. Finally, the food ran out. Sacagawea and the men gnawed frozen tallow candles to survive. At last, they came down the other side of the mountains into a mild valley where Sacagawea dug and cooked camus roots for them.

November closed in on them. The expedition neared the Columbia River on the Pacific Coast. Trading with the Indians there proved profitable. Lewis and Clark found the present they wanted to take back to President Thomas Jefferson as a trophy: a thick soft robe sewn from the pelts of two sea otters. But the Indians would not take trade any of their goods for it. Finally, after fruitless bartering, Sacagawea gave up her precious blue beaded belt to seal the trade.

Four days later, they reached the Pacific Ocean. When the men came back from the headland overlooking the shimmering waters, the entire expedition, including Sacagawea and Clark's black manservant, York, cast their votes on where to build their winter quarters: Fort Clatsop.

January, 1806, brought harsh storms that washed up a whale's carcass on the beach. The men gathered tools together to scavenge the whale blubber needed for cooking fat and oil lamps. Sacagawea, who had not yet seen the ocean, demanded to see this "monstrous fish" for herself.

On the return journey, Sacagawea proved valuable as a guide. Reaching the great plain at the foot of the Rocky Mountains, Sacagawea told Clark that she recognized this place from her childhood. Clark had no idea which path to take. Remembering Shoshone hunting trails, she led the party through a road in a gap (Bozeman Pass) that wound down to the Yellowstone River without the danger and difficulty of the earlier crossing. Delighted, Clark called her his "pilot."

Crossing the Yellowstone, Sacagawea nearly drowned. The infant's clothes and mosquito netting swept away right from under her feet. She barely had time to grab her baby. Wet, cold and shivering, Sacagawea huddled with little Jean Baptiste, who now had no blankets. Clark, fearing lest her illness come back, hurried to camp for warm clothes to dry her off. After more than a year on the trail, Sacagawea and Charbonneau returned to live at Fort Mandan.

Sacagawea's life fades off after the Lewis and Clark Expedition. When she died remains a mystery. A fur dealer's journal entry places Sacagawea at Fort Manuel Lisa Trading Post at the mouth of the Bighorn River in 1811. Her own tribe, the Lemhi-Shoshone, maintain that she lived to be a very old woman and died among them in 1884. Historical documents suggest, however, that Sacagawea may have died prior to an Indian raid on Fort Manuel in 1812. A clerk at the Fort recorded that Sacagawea died of a "putrid fever" that same year. She was twenty-five years old and left a baby girl. Records show that Charbonneau and their daughter Lizette survived the Indian attack on Fort Manuel a few months later, but Sacagawea did not. Charbonneau handed over the guardianship of their son, John Baptiste, to William Clark while Sacagawea was alive.

Legend has depicted the "Bird Woman" Sacagawea as Lewis and Clark's guide. While it is not certain how large a role she played in leading the party to find the Northwest Passage, she did translate and report facts that helped insure the success of the mission. It is certain that she navigated more than 30 members of the expedition through the Rocky Mountains on the return journey. As a wife and mother, she worked to help her fellow members survive, served as a kind of ambassador to the Indian nations and walked across half a continent with a baby on her back.

Sacagawea demonstrated truthfulness by translating carefully between the white men and the Indians she spoke to and guiding the expedition accurately across the Rocky Mountains.

Questions

1. What incident in Sacagewea's childhood changed her life dramatically?
2. Why was Sacagewea so valuable on this expedition?
3. Why was her function of communicating with the Indians so dependent upon her truthfulness?
4. List some ways she protected the men from potential disaster.
5. Tell of her being reunited with her brother.
6. What special hardships did Sacagewea face on this journey?
7. How was the mission of the expedition benefited by meeting up with Sacagewea's brother and friend?
8. Just how important is truthfulness in our dealings with others? Do you make a point to speak with truthfulness in your everyday life? How does your truthfulness affect those around you? Think of some instances where you may not have been accurate in speaking with truth and make specific plans to correct this in your life.

Virtue

Definition

Maintaining moral excellence and setting godly standards

Memory Verse

And beside this, giving all diligence,
add to your faith virtue,
and to virtue knowledge.

2 Peter 1:5

The Secret

England, 1837

The London express train hurtled through the foggy, black night, the lamps shining like fuzzy orbs against the thick blanket of fog. Just then, the train shuddered to a sudden stop as the engineer caught sight of a figure, wearing a flapping black cloak, standing in the middle of the tracks. It waved its arms frantically. The wheels hissed and squealed as the engineer jammed on the brakes. He and one of his crewmen jumped down and ran towards the mysterious figure. But it had disappeared. They shouted into the night, their voices muffled by the drifting grey fog. No one answered. Puzzled, the two men fanned out across the tracks, walking further along the ties into the mist. Suddenly, they stopped short. The ground fell away beneath their feet: the bridge had washed out ahead of them. Chunks of wood and planks churned in the rushing torrent far below. Trembling, the men looked back at the train. If that strange figure had not leapt out in front of them to warn them, the crew and the passenger train carrying their dark-haired, eighteen-year-old Queen Victoria, would have plunged headlong to their deaths.

While the bridge and tracks underwent repair, the crew searched again through the countryside for the man who had flagged down the train. But no one appeared. When the news came out, no one came forward claiming to have saved the Queen's life. Then, as the crew inspected the train in preparation for its next run, they solved the mystery of that night. Taking down his lamp to clean it, the engineer found a huge dead moth squashed on the base of the lamp. He stared at it for a moment. Then he spread its wings and stuck it against the lamp's glass. Scrambling up into his cab, he turned on his light and suddenly, he was reliving that foggy, black night again. The "flag man" stood waving in his beam. Now the engineer realized what had happened. The moth had slammed into the beam only a few moments before the train would have tumbled off the edge of the washed-out bridge. In the thick fog, it looked like a ghost waving its arms.

The young Queen listened to the investigation's report. Then she said simply: "I'm sure it was no accident. It was God's way of protecting us."

She knew that God had spared her life for a purpose. It would not be the last time. While riding in an open carriage in London several years later beside her blue-eyed German husband, Prince Albert, she came face to face with death again when a young man aimed a pistol at her. Her husband knocked the gun away with his walking stick, while his manservant, John Brown, jumped on top of the man. It happened so fast that Victoria was not even frightened.

Queen Victoria and her eldest daughter

She had come to a throne and a country troubled by the excesses of her two uncles, George IV's and William IV's, self-indulgent reigns. In Ireland, the Catholic peasants starved while Protestants had taken over most of the land by law since the 17th century. Others formed anarchist societies to attack the power of the British Crown over their island. In addition, England in the 1840s had entered age of the Industrial Revolution. Men, women, and children flowed from the rural countryside into grimy and poverty-stricken factory towns, where they ate, slept, and died in overheated, dangerous conditions within the reach of the factory whistle. The discontentment rose so high that someone had attempted to kill the queen.

When Queen Victoria came to the throne in 1837, almost no one had seen her. She would soon change that. When told that her uncle, William IV, was dead, she summed up the next 63 years of her reign in one short sentence: "I will be good." During her reign, the British Empire expanded dramatically, establishing colonies in Africa and India. Social literature, missionary societies, and the Salvation Army all emerged and flourished during what became known as the "Victorian Era." This era saw England emerge not only as a world power, but as a superpower. Gradually, the standard of living rose and the hardships imposed by the Industrial Revolution eased under the generosity of wealthy philanthropists like Lord Shaftsbury. Evangelical preaching flourished under men like Charles Spurgeon. But Victoria did not see this change as due to her politics or personal example, but to the role of the Bible in English culture.

Queen Victoria presenting the Bible

When an African chief visited at the Court of St. James in London, he could not believe his eyes. He asked Queen Victoria the secret of England's greatness. Instead of taking him on a tour of the Tower of London or showing him the glittering crown jewels, Victoria picked up a Bible and handed it to the chief. "This," she said, "is the secret of England's greatness."

At another time Queen Victoria presented an Indian prince with a Bible. His response showed that he recognized that it was obeying the Bible that had made England great. The following is his response.

"Where did the English-speaking people get all their intelligence and energy and cleverness and power? It is their Bible that gives it to them. And now they bring it to us and say, 'This is what raised us. Take it and raise yourselves.' "

Queen Victoria demonstrated virtue throughout her long and honorable reign.

Questions

1. Tell of the experience which saved Victoria's life when she was eighteen years old.
2. To what did Victoria attribute the rescue?
3. Tell of another instance when her life was providentially saved.
4. What did Queen Victoria determine when she became queen?
5. How did this affect the entire country?
6. What did Queen Victoria say was the secret of England's success while speaking to the African chief?
7. What was her statement to the Indian prince?
8. How did Queen Victoria demonstrate virtue in her reign over England?

That book [The Bible] accounts for the supremacy of England.

— Queen Victoria

Wisdom

Definition

Learning to see life from God's point of view

Memory Verse

So teach us to number our days,
that we may apply our hearts unto wisdom.

Psalm 90:12

Sea Path

Pre-Civil War • Washington, D.C. • 1842

The round white dome of the United States Naval Observatory loomed up behind him. Superintendent Matthew Fontaine Maury picked up a weighted bottle and threw it into the Potomac River. The tide was going slow, and as the current caught the "drift bottle," it spun and bobbed just below the surface. Sealed inside the bottle, a wad of paper instructed the person who found a bottle washed ashore to return it. It seemed like a child's game, setting bottles adrift at sea, or the desperate voice of a castaway on a desert island. Maury tossed another. He leaned closer to watch, the foggy air rising from the swampy Potomac mud flats dampening the wispy dark hair on his broad forehead. It happened again. The wind did not touch the bottles. He watched them drift away from the shore, following the mysterious pattern of currents.

"The paths of the seas." The words from Psalm 8 stuck in his mind. As a Christian, Maury knew that the Bible was specific: if it spoke of creatures swimming along paths, it must mean that the sea had literal paths, not just figurative ones. And actual paths could be charted.

Weeks passed. He waited for a message from beyond. Then the bottles started coming back. People picked them up along the mud banks or lonely stretches of shoreline. They had dates and locations. Maury began digging through dusty, abandoned trunks and sea chests at the Naval Observatory. Shivering with excitement, he uncovered a vast collection of thousands of ships' logbooks and charts. The thick pages, stained from the years, dated back to the start of the United States Navy with the Maritime Committee of 1775. A great idea came to his mind.

He had always loved the sea: its mystery, its magnetic pull. Sailors relied on trade winds to buoy their vessels across the ocean. A contrary wind could drive a ship hundreds of miles off course to founder in low tides. A lack of wind could "becalm" ship and crew in waters as smooth as glass for days or weeks. Whalers sailed out blindly to hunt sea mammals, often for years, not realizing that whales migrated across the sea in a regular pattern. If Maury discovered these routes, mariners could trace the depths of the sea as easily as a man studies a land map. Scanning the ships' logs, he found that the old captains had often noted the way winds and currents affected a vessel. Hidden away in storage, everyone had forgotten these lessons.

Maury brought these studies to life. He made practical experiments such as the "drift bottles." His calculations told him where the currents had carried the bottles to and how long it had taken them to reach there. With a team of trained officers and men, he studied the stars and made weather forecasts. By the early 1850s, he had drawn the first accurate charts showing the bottom of the Atlantic Ocean between the United States and Europe.

Maury believed that communication was vital to exchanging new information. He pioneered the idea of laying undersea cables across the Atlantic to Europe. In the days before the telegraph, such an idea was both practical and revolutionary. One person could not encompass the wealth of human experience. By sharing with other nations, America would not only add to its own knowledge of science, but also set the United States on the road to working closely with international governments. Interested in expeditions and railways, Matthew Maury sponsored a mission to the interior of the Amazon and a railroad over the Isthmus of Panama.

Then in the spring of 1861, Maury's naval career came to an end. His home state, Virginia, seceded from the Union and the United States burst into war. 55-year-old Matthew Maury re-

Matthew Fontaine Maury

signed from his post at the United States Naval Observatory and moved home.

During the war, Maury put his genius to good use. Sent to England and France to obtain ships and supplies for the Confederacy, which was hemmed in by the Union blockade of the southern coast, Maury spoke out through speeches and articles, calling for an end to war. But his convictions did not stop Maury from developing an electric torpedo. From his work with Samuel F. B. Morse, Maury knew how to work with transatlantic cable and a current of electricity flowing through underwater wires. Exploding among Yankee ships, much like a modern contact mine, Maury's deadly invention caused so much damage to northern shipping that the Secretary of the Navy complained the electric torpedo had cost the Union more ships than all other causes put together.

When the Civil War ended, Maury began to teach physics at the Virginia Military Institute in Lexington, Virginia. Living in the same town as Confederate General Robert E. Lee, Maury served as one of the pall-bearers at Lee's funeral. After his discovery of the "paths through the seas," Maury published over 20 books and articles on how to make the seas safer for sailors. His *Physical Geography of the Sea* was the first textbook of modern oceanography. Edited from outdated diagrams, his books became the guide for all pilot charts distributed by the government to military and merchant mariners. Most importantly, Maury gave practical advice to shipmasters how to cut down on the time and expense of a voyage. By taking direct routes and avoiding costly delays, captains could now ship goods faster and to greater profit.

Today, the Virginia Military Institute contains a glass display case dedicated to the work of Matthew Maury. Inside are displayed photographs, maps, and instruments that depict how Maury plotted the paths through the seas. Beside the Matthew Maury Highway that runs through Goshen Pass, a statue of the officer and scientist stands in tribute to the "Pathfinder of the Seas."

Matthew Maury showed wisdom by using Biblical precepts and the resources he had at hand to plot the currents through the sea in order to make voyages safer for sailors and ships.

Questions

1 What verse in Scripture caused Matthew Maury to contemplate the paths of the sea?

2. Tell what practical plan he put into place to investigate this further.

3. What idea did he pioneer?

4. What did Matthew Maury do during the Civil War?

5. What did he do after the Civil War?

6. What practical advice was he able to give to shipmasters?

7. How did Maury use Biblical wisdom to benefit others?

Selected Bibliography

Andreyev, Ivan. *Russia's Catacomb Saints: Lives of the New Martyrs.*

Bashkiroff, Zenaide. *Nights Are Longest There: A Young Girl's Account of Revolution in Russia.* London: M. Spearman, 1960.

Berkin, Carol. *Revolutionary Mothers: Women in the Struggle for America's Independence.* Vintage Press, 2006.

Bruce, Philip Alexander. *Brave Deeds of Confederate Soldiers.* Harrisonburg: Sprinkle Publications, 2006.

Caldwell, Charles. *Memoirs of the Life and Campaigns of the Honorable Nathaniel Greene, Major General in the Army of the United States and Commander of the Southern Department in the War of the Revolution.* Philadelphia: Robert Desilver, printer, 1819. Reprint. Nabu Press, 2010.

Callo, Joseph. *John Paul Jones: America's First Sea Warrior.* Naval Institute Press, 2006.

Cheripko, Jan. *Caesar Rodney's Ride Eighty Miles for Freedom.* Boyd's Mill Press, 2004. (Grades 3-6).

Davis, Burke. *To Appomattox: Nine April Days, 1865.* N.Y: Rinehart & Company, 1959.

Delaplaine, Edward S. *Francis Scott Key: Life and Times.* Heritage Books, 2011.

Driggs, Laurence La Tourette. *Heroes of Aviation.* Little, Brown and Company, 1918 (Armand Pinsard).

Elliot, Elisabeth. *A Chance to Die: The Life and Legacy of Amy Carmichael.* Revell Press, 2005.

Fluckey, Eugene. *Thunder Below! The USS "Barb" Revolutionizes Submarine Warfare in World War II.* University of Illinois Press, 1997.

"The Flying Panther: Captain Edward J. Simpson." *American Aviation Society,* 2011.

Fougara, Katherine Gibson. *With Custer's Cavalry.* Iyer Press, 2007.

Franklin, Benjamin. *Benjamin Franklin's Autobiography*. W.W. Norton & Company, 1986.

Franks, Norman, and Harry Dempsey. *Nieuport Aces of World War I. Osprey Aircraft of the Aces*, No. 33. Osprey Publishing, 2000 (Armand Pinsard).

Gaustad, Edwin S. *Liberty of Conscience: Roger Williams in America*. Judson Press, 1999.

______________ *Roger Williams*. New York: Oxford University Press, 2005.

Gilmer, George R. *Sketches of Some of the First Settlers of Upper Georgia, of the Cherokees, and the Author.* New York 1855, 1926, p. 90 (Reprinted in 1965 by Genealogical Publishing Co., Baltimore, and 1989 by Heritage Papers, Danielsville, Georgia).

Goodyear, Robert C. *The Real Pennsylvania Dutch American, "Molly Pitcher": A Documented History*. Author House, 2012 (Suggested reading).

Grack-Koestler, Rachel A. *Molly Pitcher: Heroine of the War for Independence*. Chelsea House Publications, 2005.

Green, Roger. *The Life and Ministry of William Booth: Founder of the Salvation Army*. Abingdon Press, 2006.

Hattersley, Roy. *Blood and Fire: The Story of William and Catherine Booth and the Salvation Army*. New York: Doubleday, 2000.

Hearn, Chester G. *Tracks in the Sea: Matthew Fontaine Maury and the Mapping of the Oceans*. International Marine Press, 2003.

Hembree, Charles R. *From Pearl Harbor to the Pulpit: The Dramatic Story of Captain Fuchida and Jacob DeShazer*. Akron: Ohio, Rex Humbard World Wide Ministry, 1975.

Hocker, Edward W. *The Fighting Parson of the American Revolution: A Biography of General Peter Muhlenberg, Lutheran Clergyman, Military Chieftain and Political Leader*. Philadelphia, PA: Edward W. Hocker, 1936.

Holt, Rackham Vincent. *George Washington Carver: An American Biography*. New York: Doubleday, 1963.

Hull, Michael D. *Peter Francisco: American Revolutionary War Hero. Military History Magazine*, July-August, 2006.

Kackley, Paul. "The Dead Yank Hero of Orleans Forest." *Stars and Stripes*, 25 Nov. 1959.

Kalpaschnikoff, Andrei. *A Prisoner of Trotsky's*. New York: Doubleday Page, 1920.

Kidd, Thomas S. *Patrick Henry: First Among Patriots*. Basic Books, 2011.

Knight, Lucien. *Georgia's Landmarks, Memorials, and Legends*. Penguin Publishing, 2006 (Nancy Morgan Hart).

Lewis, Meriwether. *Original Journals of the Lewis and Clark Expedition, 1804-1806*. New York: Arno Press, 1969.

Littauer, V. S. *Russian Hussar*. London: J. A. Allen, 1965.

Marks, Lara. "Sacagawea as an Evolving Symbol of American Indian Women." Dec. 16, 1998.

Marshall, Charles. *An Aide-de-Camp of Lee*. Kessinger Publishing, 2007.

Muhlenberg, Henry A. *The Life of Major-General Peter Muhlenberg, of the Revolutionary Army*. Philadelphia: Carey and Hart, 1849.

Perry, John. *Sergeant York: His Life, Legend and Legacy: The Remarkable Untold Story of Sergeant Alvin C. York*. Barnes and Noble Books, 1997.

Phelps, M. William. *Nathan Hale: The Life and Death of America's First Spy*. Thomas Dunne Books, 2008.

Polsky, Michael. *The New Martyrs of Russia*. Montreal, Brotherhood St Job Pochaev, 2002.

Salisbury, Gay and Laney Salisbury. *The Cruelest Miles: The Heroic Story of Dogs and Men in a Race Against an Epidemic*. New York: W. W. Norton & Company, 2005.

Snow, William P. *Lee and His Generals*. New York: The Fairfax Press, 1982.

Ramage, James A. *Grey Ghost: The Life of Colonel John Singleton Mosby*. University of Kentucky Press, 2009.

Rappleye, Charles. *Robert Morris: Financier of the American Revolution*. New York: Simon & Schuster, 2010.

San Souci, Robert D. *Kate Shelley: Bound for Legend*. Dial Books for

Young Readers, 1995. Scott, Jane. *A Gentleman as Well as a Whig: Caesar Rodney and the American Revolution* University of Delaware Press, 2000.

Scott, John Thomas. "Nancy Hart: 'Too Good Not to Tell Again.' "*Georgia Women: Their Lives and Times*, vol.1. Chirhart, Ann Short, and Betty Wood, Ed. Athens: University of Georgia Press, 2009.

Silcox-Jarrett, Diane. *Heroines of the American Revolution: America's Founding Mothers.* Scholastic, Inc., 2000 (Lydia Darraugh).

Skeyhill, Tom. *Sergeant York and the Great War.* The Vision Forum, Inc., 1998.

Strachey, Lytton. *Queen Victoria: An Eminent Illustrated Biography.* New York: Black Dog & Leventhal Publishers, 1998.

Summers, Julie. *The Colonel of Tamarkan: Philip Toosey and the Bridge on the River Kwai.* London: Simon & Schuster, 2005.

Thomas, Evan. *John Paul Jones: Sailor, Hero, Father of the American Navy.* New York: Simon & Schuster, 2003.

Vaughan, David J. *Give Me Liberty: The Christian Patriotism of Patrick Henry* (Leaders in Action). Cumberland House Publishing, 2002.

Walker, Gary C. *Civil War Tales: Volume II.* A & W Enterprise, 1994.

Washington, Booker T. *Up from Slavery.* New York: Dover Publications, 1995.

Waters-Power, Alma. *Virginia Giant: The Story of Peter Francisco.* New York: E.P. Dutton, 1957.

Wellman, Sam. *George Washington Carver: Inventor and Naturalist.* Barbour Publishing, 1998.

Wetterer, Margaret K. *Kate Shelley and the Midnight Express.* Scholastic, 1990.

Williams, Roger. *A Plea for Religious Liberty* in: *The Bloudy Tenant of Persecution.* Providence, Rhode Island: Narragansett Club, Vol. III, 1867.

Wrangel, Peter N. *Always with Honor.* New York: Robert Speller and Sons, 1957.

Websites

"Bill Overstreet." http://www.cebudanderson.com/billoverstreet.htm

"Bill Overstreet, 363rd FS." http://www.cebudanderson.com/overstreet.htm

"Bill Overstreet: Barnstormers." http://www.barnstormers.com/eFLYER/2009/061-eFLYER-FA02-Legends-Overstreet.html

Winstead, Jane. "Horatio G. Spafford: The Story Behind the Hymn 'It is Well with My Soul.' " http://voices.yahoo.com/horatio-g-spafford-story-behind-hymn-is-1620793.html?cat=38

Photo credits

Alertness

Peter Francisco: Public Domain. Society of the Descendants of Peter Francisco: www.peterfrancisco.org/photos/

Attentiveness

Lydia Darragh: Public Domain. Library of Congress: [Lydia (Barrington) Darragh, 1728?-1789, bust portrait, facing left] Digital ID: (digital file from b&w film copy neg.) cph 3b01548 http://hdl.loc.gov/loc.pnp/cph.3b01548

Availability

Molly Pitcher: Mary Ludwig Hays McCauley AKA "Molly Pitcher" Painting by C.Y. Turner: globalgenealogy.com/globalgazette/gazsh/gazsh-0059.htm

Boldness

Col John Mosby: Public Domain. Library of Congress: digital ID cwpbh.03240

Gen. Edwin Stoughton: Public Domain. U.S. Military images Photo courtesy of Mass Commander of MOLLUS

Compassion

Aleksandr Ustinovich, 1994 • "A Road": http://01varvara.wordpress.com/2010/06/14/aleksandr-ustinovich-a-road-1994/aleksandr-ustinovich-a-road-1994/

Contentment

Horatio and Anna Spafford: Public Domain. Wikimedia Commons: This work has been released into the public domain by its author, Live or die.

Shipwreck: Library of Congress: Library of Congress, Prints and Photographs Division: LC-DIG-ppmsca-07650, Currier & Ives

American Colony: Wikipedia.com: Public Domain because it is taken from the American Colony Archive

Courage

Colonel Aleksandr Groten

Officer with phone: An officer in a trench on the Eastern Front communicates via a field telephone, Bisecky Collection, Prague, 2009, Source, www.praguepost.com.jpg

Army in trenches: Public Domain. The Russian army in the trenches near Sarikamish. United Kingdom Government photograph. Public domain.jpg

Decisiveness

John Paul Jones: U.S. Senate paintings John Paul Jones by George Bagby Matthews, http://www.senate.gov/artandhistory/art/common/image/Painting_31_00012.htm

Deference

Lieutenant Adrian Marks: Public Domain. Clinton County Historical Society, http://srv1.geetel.net/~cchsm/lt__cmdr__adrian_marks.htm

USS Indianapolis: public domain; http://www.secondworldwar.org.uk/indianapolis.html

PBY-5 Catalina: http://www.zenithpresstheblog.com/2010/04/military-snapshots-pby-5-catalinas.html. Photo courtesy of U.S. Navy, from *Leave No Man Behind: The Saga of Combat Search and Rescue* by George Galdorisi and Tom Phillips.

Dependability

Cecil Breeden

landing on Omaha Beach: Public Domain. http://en.wikipedia.org/wiki/File:1944_NormandyLST.jpg, photograph by Robert F. Sargent.

medic treating wounded: Public Domain. http://www.usmessageboard.com/education/120085-today-is-the-66th-anniversary-of-d-day-june-6th-1944-a.html

Diligence

Benjamin Franklin: Public domain. U.S. History images: http://ushistoryimages.com/benjamin-franklin-life.shtm

Discernment

Eugene Fluckey: Public Domain. http://www.history.navy.mil/photos/pers-us/uspers-f/e-flucky.htm. Photo #: NH 103534

USS Barb: http://www.history.navy.mil/photos/sh-usn/usnsh-b/ss220.htm. Photo #: 19-N-83952

USS Barb crew: http://www.history.navy.mil/photos/sh-usn/usnsh-b/ss220.htm. Photo #: NH 103570

Discretion

Nathanael Greene: Public Domain. http://en.wikipedia.org/wiki/File:Greene_portrait.jpg. Original portrait painted from life in 1783 by Charles Wilson Peale

Battle of Cowan's Ford: No author information. http://en.wikipedia.org/wiki/File:Cowansford.jpg
General Nathanael Greene Crossing the River Dan: http://etc.usf.edu/clipart/55900/55956/55956_greene_dan.htm
Endurance
Metropolitan Joseph Petrovykh: Public Domain. http://www.hermitage-journal.org/2011/09/metropolitan-joseph-of-petrograd-and.html
Enthusiasm
Pastor John Muhlenberg: http://explorepahistory.com/displayimage.php?imgId=1-2-28C Courtesy of the Lutheran Theological Seminary at Gettysburg, Photography by Sara Mummert
Muhlenberg portrait: Public Domain. http://www.ok-safe.com/Black-Regiment-Pastors.htm
Flexibility
Caesar Rodney: Illustration by Linda J. Linder in For You They Signed by Marilyn Boyer, 2009
Forgiveness
Jacob DeShazer: all photos: Public Domain. http://en.wikipedia.org/wiki/File:DeShazer.jpg official USAF photo. http://www.pellfamily.com/sermons/DeShazer3.jpg
Doolittle Raider taking off from USS Hornet: http://www.history.navy.mil/photos/images/g40000/g41196.jpg
Doolittle POW/Chinese: http://ww2db.com/image.php?image_id=6494 National Archives and Records Administration
Doolittle raiders in China: http://ww2db.com/images/battle_doolittle22.jpg National Archives and Records Administration
POW photo DeShazer: Photo by USAF
Mitsuo Fuchida: Public Domain. http://en.wikipedia.org/wiki/File:MitsuoFuchida.jpg
Fuchida and DeShazer: Public Domain. http://www.gerhardy.id.au/images/fuchida&deshazer.gif
Generosity
Robert Morris: Public Domain. painting by Gilbert Stuart, Philadelphia, 1795
Gentleness
President Abraham Lincoln: Public Domain. Library of Congress, http://lcweb2.loc.gov/master/pnp/ppmsca/19300/19305u.tif
Old Naval Hospital: http://www.architectural-metal.com/the-old-naval-hospital-in-washington/
Gratefulness
Amy Carmichael: Public Domain. http://en.wikipedia.org/wiki/Amy_Carmichael
temple: Public Domain. http://www.oldbookillustrations.com/gallery/monuments/ellora-kailasa-temple.jpg
Honesty
Nathan Hale: all images: Public Domain. http://ushistoryimages.com/nathan-hale.shtm
Honor
Gen. Pyotr Wrangel: all images: Fair Use. (Image taken from http://www.trio.ru/antika/belarmy/vrangel.htm (historic photo of a famous individual, reduced in size))
Gen. Wrangel praying: Public Domain. http://en.wikipedia.org/wiki/File:Wrangel.jpg
White Army exodus from Crimea: http://zolotoivek.tumblr.com/post/12860602362/russian-exodus-from-crimea-1920
Hospitality
Kate Gibson:
Fort Abraham Lincoln: National Park Service, http://www.nps.gov/history/history/online_books/soldier/sitec12.htm (Minnesota Historical Society).
George Armstrong Custer with his Officers & Their Families: Photograph by Orlando Scott Goff Taken at Fort Abraham Lincoln, Dakota Territory, http://freepages.genealogy.rootsweb.ancestry.com/~guinevere60/goff/bio/osgoffbio.htm
Indian child: Public Domain. Library of Congress, LC-USZC4-8846.
Humility
Nate Saint: with George: http://jonblomberg.blogspot.com/2010_05_01_archive.html. 007294-HQ-DG,ND1-Personnel-NateSaint.jpg
with wife: http://www.maf.org/nate_saint
Initiative
Col. John Hunt Morgan: Public Domain. http://en.wikipedia.org/wiki/File:Gen._John_Morgan_%28cropped%29.jpg

Gen. Edward McCook: Public Domain. http://en.wikipedia.org/wiki/File:Edward_M._McCook_-_Brady-Handy.jpg
Morgan's Men: Public Domain. Hunt-Morgan House Deposit photographs, 1860-1949, housed at the University of Kentucky Special Collections and Digital Programs.
telegraph: Public Domain. http://www.history.army.mil/books/30-17/S_1.htm
Joyfulness
Armand Pinsard: Public Domain. http://www.firstworldwar.com/bio/pinsard.htm
Kindness
Roger Williams: Public Domain. http://ed101.bu.edu/StudentDoc/current/ED101sp09/denimj/rogerwilliams.html
Roger Williams and Narragansetts: Public Domain. New York Public Library: http://digitalgallery.nypl.org/nypldigital/id?806876
Williams escaping: Public Domain. http://ushistoryimages.com/roger-williams.shtm
Love
Capt. Eddie Simpson: Public Domain. http://www.cebudanderson.com/simpson.htm
French resistance fighter: http://ww2total.com/WW2/Weapons/Infantry/Firearms/British/Sten-Gun/images/French-resistance-fighter-with-Sten-px800.jpg
French resistance marching in mountains: http://festungenthirdreich.devhub.com/blog/587799-partisan-warfare/#comments
Loyalty
Commissar Moisei Uritsky: Public Domain. http://www.nasledie-rus.ru/img/660000/661307.jpg
Meekness
George Washington Carver: Public Domain. Library of Congress
Carver laboratory: Public Domain. US Department of Agriculture
Equipment: Public Domain. wikimedia.org/wikipedia/en/f/ff/George_Washington_Carver-laboratory_equipment.jpeg
Obedience
Sgt. Alvin C. York: Argonne Forest: The_National_Archives,_Series,_Signal_Corps_Photographs_of_American_Military_Activity,_1754-1954_Record_Group_111;_National_Archives.
soldiers w/ rifles: http://olive-drab.com/od_other_firearms_rifle_m1917enfield.php
soldiers in Argonne: http://homepage.mac.com/oldtownman/ar/ww1/images2/CAN16217a.jpg
Sgt. York in the Argonne: Public Domain. Sergeant Alvin C. York, 328th Infantry... Argonne Forest, near Cornay, France., 02/07/1919" (ARC Identifier: 530787); Series: Signal Corps Photographs of American Military Activity, 1754 - 1954; , Records of the Office of the Chief Signal Officer, 1860 - 1982; Record Group 111; National Archives.
Sgt York being congratulated: http://www.old-picture.com/american-legacy/011/Sergeant-Alvin-York-C.htm
Orderliness
Charles Marshall: Surrender at Appomattox Court House: http://www.historyofwar.org/Pictures/pictures_appomattox.html
Surrender document: Public Domain. National Archives and Records Administration, http://www.wildwestweb.net/cwdocs/surrender.html
Patience
Col. Philip Toosey: copyright The Toosey family Collection http://en.wikipedia.org/wiki/File:Philip_Toosey_1942.JPG
Bridge on the River Kwai photo: http://www.dailymail.co.uk/news/article-2038221/Antiques-Roadshow-Sketches-British-PoWs-held-Japanese-camp-revealed.html
Persuasiveness
Patrick Henry: Public Domain. http://en.wikipedia.org/wiki/File:Patrick_henry.JPG
speech: http://en.wikipedia.org/wiki/File:Patrick_Henry_Rothermel.jpg
Prudence
Nancy Morgan Hart: Public Domain. http://simpsonhistory.com/notes/benjaminhart
British soldiers: Public Domain. http://en.wikipedia.org/wiki/File:Nancy_Hart.jpg
Punctuality
Gunnar Kaasen: Public Domain. http://en.wikipedia.org/wiki/File:Gunnar_Kaasen_with_Balto.jpg
Togo: Public Domain. http://merriemarie.livejournal.com/212859.html
Balto: Public Domain. http://perrofeliz.net/perros/la-carrera-del-suero-a-nome-y-sus-protagonistas/

Resourcefulness
William Overstreet, Berlin Express: Public Domain. http://www.cebudanderson.com/overstreet.htm
Berlin Express/Eiffel Tower: http://www.davidmaloney.com/ebuilder/mar10/overstreet.htm
Respectfulness
Francis Scott Key: Public Domain
Fort McHenry: http://members.tripod.com/~vet6_2/nationalanthem/natlanthem.html
Key on ship: http://the-english-spot.blogspot.com/2009_09_01_archive.html
Self-Control
Kate Shelley: Public Domain. Kate Shelley bridge: http://www.uprr.com/newsinfo/media_kit/regional/northern/
Kate Shelley-teen: Public Domain. http://billworld92683.tripod.com/ksg/
Sensitivity
Robert E. Lee: Public Domain. http://en.wikipedia.org/wiki/File:General_R._E._Lee_and_Traveler.jpg
Thoroughness
Booker T. Washington: Public Domain. http://en.wikipedia.org/wiki/File:Booker_T_Washington_retouched_flattened-crop.jpg
Tolerance
William Booth: Public Domain. http://salvos.org.au/hurstville/our-history/where-we-began/
"Salvation Army": Public Domain. http://baptistlandmarks.org/page93.html
Match factory: Public Domain. http://www.spartacus.schoolnet.co.uk/TUmatch2.jpg
Truthfulness
Sacagawea: Public Domain. http://www.sacagaweafacts.net/
Lewis and Clark: Public Domain. http://www.ohs.org/education/focus/lewis_and_clark_oregon.cfm
Virtue
Queen Victoria: Public Domain. presenting Bible: http://all-history.org/New%20Folder/341/10.jpg 'The Secret of England's Greatness' by Thomas Jones Barker
Queen Victoria with eldest daughter: Public Domain. http://en.wikipedia.org/wiki/File:Queen_Victoria_the_Princess_Royal_Victoria_c1844-5.png
Wisdom
Matthew Fontaine Maury: Public Domain. http://en.wikipedia.org/wiki/File:Matthew_Fontaine_Maury2.jpg

About the Authors

Marilyn Boyer is the mother of fourteen children, all home schooled from kindergarten through high school. Her passion to train up her children in the character of Christ led her to create Character Concepts Curriculum, a character curriculum for kids of all ages to equip parents in raising children of integrity!

Her many character resources, as well as books on homeschooling and Christian parenting, are available at www.CharacterConceptsCurriculum.com.

Grace Tumas is a writer and historian specializing in nineteenth and twentieth century American and European history. She is currently completing her B.S. in History with a minor in International Relations from Liberty University. She is a member of Phi Alpha Theta, the Civil War Trust, and the Association for Slavic, East European, and Eurasian Studies (ASEEES). Her research articles include "Die on Your Own Soil, Boys! But Don't Give Up Your Guns": Ricketts' Battery, First Pennsylvania Light Artillery, and the Night Defense at Cemetery Hill, July 2, 1863," and "The Secret Civil War: Officers' Underground Organizations in the Anti-Bolshevik Movement, 1917-1919." Her other interests focus on Christian homemaking skills, teaching piano, and experimenting with Russian cuisine. She lives in Bedford, Virginia.

Resources Available from The Learning Parent

Character Concepts Curriculum

CHARACTER CONCEPTS CURRICULUM
LEVEL 3 • AGES 7–10

Portraits of Integrity is a wonderful resource for family time reading. But it is also excellent as a part of *Character Concepts Curriculum Level 3,* in which it is combined with:

Kids of Character Bible Study: This is a practical study for children of the 45 character qualites Marilyn Boyer taught her own children, learning what God`s Word has to say about each one and how to apply it to their lives. An added feature contained in this study is "Ifs," a game the Boyers often played to help children learn to make wise decisions before they are even placed in a position of temptation. The adult Boyer kids have said this helped them many times to choose the right thing from having played a game which prepared them for choosing to do right based on insights gained from God`s Word.

Kids of Character Flashcards: In response to your request, here is a set of flashcards derived from Marilyn`s handout, *Character Qualities for Kids.* This set includes 45 character qualities for your child to learn. The definition is provided as children have no basis for learning honesty or sensitivity if they don`t know what it means. Also provided is a Scripture verse for each, as it is ultimately God`s Word that changes our lives and our behavior. Instructions for use are provided as well. Recommended for children ages 6-12, although whatever we learn, we usually do with the entire family! If you do this study with multiple children, you may want to get addtional study books for each to have their own to write in.

Resources Available from The Learning Parent

Character Concepts Curriculum

CHARACTER CONCEPTS CURRICULUM
LEVEL 1 • AGES 4–6

CHARACTER CONCEPTS FOR PRESCHOOLERS

- 36 weeks of character lessons from the Bible, history, and everyday life
- Teaches 12 character qualities
- Practical application projects
- Bible Memory, Bible doctrine, nature projects, crafts, family fun trips, and more!
- Organized, easy-to-implement, fun to use!

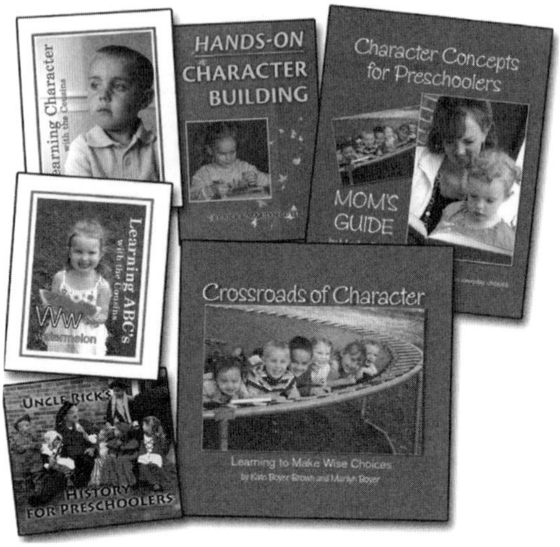

CHARACTER CONCEPTS CURRICULUM
LEVEL 2 • AGES 6–9

CHARACTER TRAILS

- 36 weeks of character lessons from the Bible, history, and everyday life
- Teaches 12 character qualities
- Practical, hands-on projects make learning come alive
- Application questions kids can relate to and prepare for
- Fun, easy way to really learn character
- Exciting stories about heroes from history

All resources available at www.characterconceptscurriculum.com

Resources Available from The Learning Parent

Character Concepts Curriculum

PROVERBS PEOPLE

CHARACTER CONCEPTS CURRICULUM
LEVEL 4 • AGES 7–12

- Study the different types of people you will meet in life and how to wisely deal with them.
- Insight into your own life (ex. diligent/slothful) from the Book of Wisdom!
- Includes example stories and fun quizzes as well as coloring pages!

CHARACTER CONCEPTS CURRICULUM
LEVEL 5 • AGES 8–13

GROWING IN WISDOM

- Study 32 types of negative behavior and their consequences.
- Learn how to make an intentional decision to choose positive, godly character.
- Every negative character quality is just a positive one misused. This study guides your child in learning to make wise decisions based on God's Word.

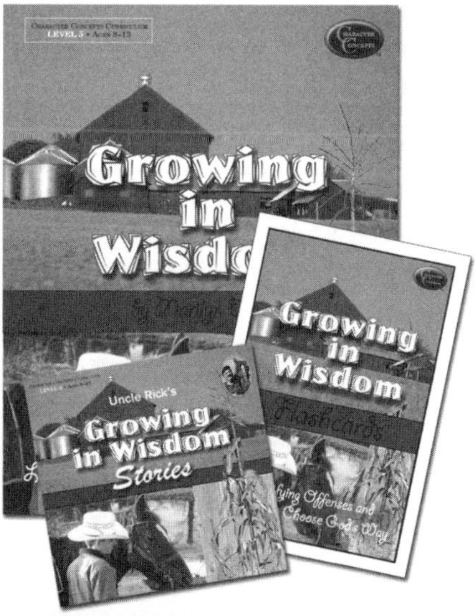

All resources available at www.characterconceptscurriculum.com